Baby Ava

First published in 2012 by
Liberties Press
7 Rathfarnham Road | Terenure | Dublin 6W
Tel: +353 (1) 405 5701
www.libertiespress.com | info@libertiespress.com

Trade enquiries to Gill & Macmillan Distribution
Hume Avenue | Park West | Dublin 12
T: +353 (1) 500 9534 | F: +353 (1) 500 9595 | E: sales@gillmacmillan.ie

Distributed in the UK by
Turnaround Publisher Services
Unit 3 | Olympia Trading Estate | Coburg Road | London N22 6TZ
T: +44 (0) 20 8829 3000 | E: orders@turnaround-uk.com

ISBN: 978-1-907593-50-5
2 4 6 8 10 9 7 5 3 1
A CIP record for this title is available from the British Library.

Cover design by Sin É Design
Internal design by Liberties Press
Printed by Scandbook

Baby Ava

An Irish Surrogacy Story

Caroline and Niall O'Flaherty

With Antoinette Walker

Ava, this book is dedicated to you from your Mom and Dad so that when you are old enough to read it, you will understand just how precious you are. We love you so much. You have filled our lives with so much joy and happiness.

Love Mom and Dad x.

Contents

Acknowledgments

With special thanks to Dr Patel, Dr Hitesh and their team, and to dear Nita to whom we will always be grateful.

We are deeply appreciative of both our families for all their help and support in this great venture.

We extend our gratitude to Antoinette Walker for her professionalism and patience and for bringing the story of Ava to fruition, and to our legal team, Deborah Kearney and Nuala Jackson, for the wonderful work and long hours that finally brought Ava home to Ireland.

Chapter I

I was meant for motherhood

From a very young age, cradling a Crolly doll in my arms, I dreamed of being a mother one day. Perhaps all little girls dream of motherhood, but I could not stop, even when the odds were stacked against me. In the face of cervical cancer, radical surgery, failures of infertility treatment and adoption, I clung to the belief that one day I would hold a babbling babe in my arms. One that I could call my own. And the long litany of disappointment, pain and despair would fade and become a thing of the past. After many fruitless years, the one glimmer of hope was surrogacy. It appeared on the horizon one day and grew as bright and warm as the country that made our dream possible: India. The baby we so wholeheartedly desired would become a reality.

If yearbooks had been all the rage when I was at school, like in American movies, I would have been labelled the 'Girl Most Likely to Be a Mother', not due to the hazards of sex but out of sheer yearning. From primary school in Palmerstown, Dublin, where I grew up, to Our Lady's School in Templeogue, most of my school friends will remember me for that. I was the one who always wanted to get married and have babies. The friends who shared my girlhood dreams became as close to me as sisters, or what I imagined to be sisters since I was an only girl. They knew me as a real girlie girl, with an insatiable appetite for dolls: Crolly dolls, Sindy dolls, Barbie dolls, of every shape and fabric, with cases of outfits for every occasion.

The years of waiting and wanting and exploring options are long and hard. You spend a lot of time reflecting on every aspect of having a child. You know that biological urge is no selfish whim but part of a much bigger picture. Because you were reared in a loving and secure family, you wish for what your parents had and grandparents before them. You wish for what seems the most natural thing in the world. You see traditions and customs handed on from your parents and want to see yourself continuing in that long line.

Both my husband, Niall and I are Dubliners born and bred, like our parents and grandparents before us. You imagine telling your children about their heritage; my parents' families growing up and working on Francis Street in The Liberties and Niall's highly skilled in damp-proofing. In my mind, I would tell my children that I was named after my paternal grandmother, Caroline, who holds a special place in my heart. Both of us knew the trauma and pressure of having children in very different ways and at very different times. By the time she died in childbirth at the age of thirty-five in 1948 she had given birth to ten children. Coming out of Mass one Sunday morning, years before, the fire and brimstone of the priest still ringing in her ears, she had told her friend tearfully how she did not want any more children. Yet contraception was out of the question; she was at the mercy of clerics, outsiders controlling her fertility. It was interference, a kind of exploitation really. It ended in heartbreak for her family. At the same age that she was laid in a cold grave, I was still childless. I had to go halfway around the world before I could call myself a mother.

You spend years hoping that you'll be as good a parent as your own. To have the brilliant, open relationship with your father and mother that I have, to be able to talk to them and confide in them about anything. To all get along so well, apart from the odd disagreement. And of course as an only daughter being daddy's girl is always something special. You recognise your parent's wonderful qualities; an intelligent, hard-working father, now retired from business life, who only sees the good in people; a mother who takes such good care of us all, taking pride in our home and being more than a mother but a companion and best friend. I too hoped to give my children memories to cherish: Christmas trips to Santa Claus, family outings, and a few summer holidays in America that I was lucky to have.

You wonder too what hobbies and pastimes your child would take up. Would they be fanatical about gymnastics and dancing like I was, or more like my brother Philip, three years older, who played quietly and calmly with his toy cars for hours on end and later took up judo. Would you hold your breath as they recited poems at the Feis, echoing the verses in your head to the very end? Or watch them on stage at the Gaiety and Olympia in tap dancing shows with the Freda Bannon Stage School, which had filled my youth with vivid dreams of being another Shirley Temple.

Or would their pastimes be a source of family pride? Both my father and grandfather played the accordion, and my brother and I too followed in that tradition. Fridays were accordion practice nights, around the corner from Francis Street where my parents were reared. Mingled with the music were history lessons in which we learned much about Old Dublin, its traditions and characters. A neighbour of ours was our teacher whose patience we sorely tested each night. At times he got so cross with our renditions of 'More and More and More' or 'Make Me an Island' – Joe Dolan favourites – that he would bang his baton furiously on the chair he was standing on. His fury ensured we practised hard every day at home. Sunday afternoons were our performance days, courtesy of Dublin Corporation in the 1980s. From St Stephen's Green and St Anne's Park, Raheny to Howth and Sandymount, we belted out many a marching song, the Triumphal March being memorable, along with the Scottish Waltz selection. On windy days, perched on the park bandstand, rocks were placed on our music stands to secure music sheets or songbooks from the force of the gale. Being in the younger class, I was sometimes forced to smile and pretend I was playing if the tune was unfamiliar to me. In contrast my brother, being older and more accomplished, was ten times better.

You wonder too what family traits your children would inherit. Would they be quiet and studious like my brother? Or more fun-loving and outgoing like me? A real case of chalk and cheese. Would they be calm and composed in the face of pressure like my husband, Niall or get anxious like me? What jobs would they have in life? What direction would they go? Would they take after me and be dying to leave school, eager to be part of the working world? Or spend years at university like Philip, poring over economic books and computers?

The late 1980s in Dublin were thrilling for your average teenager and I got caught up in that excitement. Xtra-vision had set up a shop in Palmerstown and with their flamboyant jeeps flying all around Dublin, I wished to be part of it, meeting people and feeling independent. Video rental was something new to Ireland but before long I was working part-time for Xtra-vision while completing a computer course amongst others at Dorset College. Moving on to Intel, the multinational computer chip company, I enjoyed working in production and the great camaraderie among the staff.

And later when I worked as a medical secretary, I felt at home in that world, interested in people and their health. Or would the children be more like Niall and work in building and facilities maintenance with his ingenious way of solving problems? Would they have his grasp of law, which came as a revelation to us when faced with the legal challenges of getting our daughter's passport? There was also his natural bent for computers, his analytical mind, seeing things in black and white.

One thing for sure, his trait of entrepreneurship was something to tell the children. I would have many a story to keep them entertained for hours. He was a bubbling fountain of ideas, a mixture of Del Boy and Bill Gates. An entrepreneur from boyhood, it was honed from Sunday trips to the open-air market in Jonesborough on the Border with his parents. Whenever he saw a FOR LET sign, his mind too went into overdrive, thinking of a suitable start-up business.

Yes, the years spent waiting to have children were peppered with imagining and wondering and rehearsing would-be conversations. But whatever the would-be children would do in life, I just hoped they would be happy and know their parents loved them, even more so for all the hurdles that had to be overcome in bringing them into the world.

Our story began one fateful day in April 1998. It was unseasonably cold outside as I waited nervously in the rooms of the Master of the Coombe and listened to what he had to say. It was no springtime for me. It was to get a whole lot chillier by the time he had spoken, his words delivered calmly but with an unmistakeable sadness in his eyes.

'Caroline, you have cervical cancer.'

Chapter 2

Cervical cancer

In 1998, at the age of twenty-seven, my life was moving along nicely; I was enjoying my job at Intel, had no shortage of friends and acquaintances and a busy social life. By then, I had moved away from home and was sharing an apartment in Tallaght with a good friend called Lisa. I was back to the single life again, after a relationship lasting a number of years had ended amicably. No, there was little time to dwell on illness and disease. I didn't smoke and other than having a smear test some five years before, I didn't give my health a second thought.

In hindsight my symptoms were vague. There was no big bang warning signs at first. A gradual tiredness crept over me, making me feel weaker and weaker, until I reached a stage of pure exhaustion. Absolute and utter exhaustion. It all happened within the space of a few weeks. If I climbed the stairs, by the time I reached the top, I had to pause, weak as an old woman. That type of tiredness was foreign to me; I was the kind of person usually buzzing with energy. Never in my wildest dreams did I consider it could be cancer.

To be honest, I felt a bit silly going to the GP at first. It seemed so lame to say you're feeling very tired, especially in the absence of other symptoms. It was reinforced all the more when the doctor made light of it and told me there was absolutely nothing wrong. Though relieved to hear his words, my mind wasn't entirely at ease. And still the fatigue continued. Then shortly afterwards, I was in bed one night and had a massive vaginal bleed. That shocked and shook me to the core like a horror movie. I had never experienced anything like it before and was convinced that something was radically wrong. The sight of the soiled bedclothes, the white cotton sheets nearly destroyed, more than anything forced me to seek medical attention. However, the next doctor I saw, a man at a local hospital, after hearing my story and examining me, was rather vague in his diagnosis.

'You know, this can happen. It's nothing to worry about,' he began, sitting back in his chair. 'You can go home, there's nothing wrong.'

His response puzzled me. I was really taken aback.

'What?' I said, my voice croaking in disbelief.

At that, he proceeded to say it could be this, it could be that, maybe it's hormones, maybe it had something to do with taking the Pill in the past. Nothing but a string of maybes and perhapses.

'I've seen this happen to loads of young girls of your age. It's nothing to worry about.'

And so I was sent off home again. Needless to say, it wasn't very reassuring. It just didn't make sense. My friend Lisa had accompanied me to the hospital and we returned to the apartment in stunned silence. I still didn't feel right. I didn't want to let it go, dismiss it from my mind like the doctor had recommended. The niggling doubts continued and with nothing but my gut instinct to rely on, I persisted. The same week I visited a local doctor, a GP based in Tallaght. She was sympathetic and without hesitation advised me to go to the Coombe for a second opinion. In fact, she quietly insisted.

And so I found myself on Cork Street in the heart of The Liberties, trying to cross the busy road and battling against the elements. We seemed to be stuck in an eternal winter that year with days on end of biting cold, sleety showers. I pulled my coat ever tighter across my chest and headed for the hospital entrance. Until I developed symptoms, I had never been to the Coombe before, never once had a reason to go there. Though I had been born in the Rotunda Hospital myself, generations of my father's family had entered the world in the Coombe, that is, before the premises were sited in Dolphin's Barn. The old Coombe Lying-In Hospital, not far away was where my grandmother Caroline had given birth many times before. The only trace of it that remained was its magnificent portico, preserved for posterity, which we used to pass on our way to accordion practice in my youth. I wondered did my grandmother feel as nervous as I did when she darkened its doorway one last time. It was Friday and, as I made my way to the outpatients, the hospital was bustling with numerous clinics. A steady stream of women, some with bellies bulging at various stages of pregnancy, waddled past me along its narrow corridors. Or else the teeny cries of newborns coming and going from the baby clinic filled the air.

This time a young Chinese doctor examined me. In her quiet and serious manner, she listened carefully to what I had to say and examined me thoroughly. Lying on the couch with my eyes firmly planted on the ceiling, suffering the indignity of the procedure, I hoped whatever the problem was that it could be easily fixed. The examination was suddenly interrupted when another doctor happened to pass through the room in search of some item or other. From her demeanour I could tell she was a senior doctor, and more so when the Chinese doctor asked for her opinion, which she gladly obliged. This was my first introduction to Dr Noreen Gleeson. She adroitly took over the examination, making me feel that I was in good hands. Her voice was reassuring as she told me she would need to take a closer look at my cervix and do some special tests. At last I felt I was being taken seriously. The tests were duly arranged for early the following week.

In hindsight, Dr Gleeson had spotted some abnormalities during the physical examination. The next week passed by in a haze except for the two tests she carried out: first a colposcopy and then a cone biopsy where she took a tissue sample from my cervix. Again these were words I had never heard of before let alone could pronounce. For the colposcopy she used a bright light and what looked like a large microscope to see my cervix really close up. The test didn't last long, maybe fifteen minutes, and luckily didn't hurt. But with her eyes glued to the eyepiece, I felt like a specimen under a microscope. I have no recollection of the cone biopsy as it was done under anaesthetic one morning. However, Dr Gleeson explained it was like taking a tiny piece off the top of your thumb, except it was my cervix. Later that day, she returned to the day ward and told me she had removed extra tissue. She obviously knew it didn't look good.

Back home that evening, I rang my sister-in-law Bina, who lives in Hampshire in the UK with my brother. A trained pharmacist, Bina could be relied upon to give straight facts about medical problems.

'Okay, it could be CIN1, CIN2 or CIN3 or precancerous,' she answered. 'But I'm sure it wouldn't even be that bad.'

CIN was a kind of precancerous thing – cervical intraepithelial neoplasia – to varying degrees.

'What!'

'I mean there are plenty things that can be done.'

Both Bina and my brother Philip were invaluable for giving advice. Indeed they are always very matter of fact. With degrees in business and economics, Philip works as a cancer network manager in the UK. Though not a doctor, he is still very scientific in his approach to things, which is exactly what I wanted. He kept telling me not to worry as I would have the best specialists.

By Friday that week, I had been speedily called in for an appointment with the Master of the Coombe. It was time to receive the verdict. April had never felt so cold, as I dressed myself warmly that morning, slipping into jeans, a new blue gingham shirt and a soft, cosy baby blue fleece that I loved. The early morning frost cleared but was replaced by more sleet. My mother, growing more alarmed, had come along for moral support. At the appointed time, the Master at the time, Dr Michael Turner, ushered us into a room. There would be no more examining, just talking. He sat us down and we waited anxiously to hear what he had to say. And then the words that nobody ever wants to hear arrived.

'Caroline, you have cancer.'

He looked at me with such sadness, explaining there were abnormal cells in the lining of my cervix and I would need surgery urgently. My body started to shake against a backdrop of my mother's loud sobs.

'Look, I have a daughter, I have children myself,' he continued, 'and this is not an easy thing to tell anyone.'

Then a sinking feeling arose in my chest. I could feel myself panicking.

'Is this it? Am I actually going to die?'

Beside me, my mother's wails grew louder.

'You really need to speak to Dr Gleeson before we go in and do the surgery,' he explained, conscious there was no straight answer to that question. 'We don't know exactly the extent of what's going on.'

Even today his face sticks in my mind. Amid the crying and the shaking, I remember thinking that this man actually looks upset for me. I was sure I saw tears in his eyes. So much I forgot later with the passage of time but never once his face.

'Will I ever have a child?' I whispered, the question popping out of nowhere.

'We'll have to wait until the surgery to see,' he replied gently. 'We should know how aggressive the cancer is by then.'

After that, there was precious little else I retained. All he could do was reassure us as best he could.

'Dr Noreen Gleeson is the best surgeon here to deal with the cancer. We'll get her to see you on Monday.'

Cancer is not something you give much thought to at the age of twenty-seven. There was no family history of cancer to put me on high alert. And certainly not cervical cancer. I hadn't a clue about cervical cancer or what it meant. I wasn't even sure if I had come across the word cervix in biology class before. I suppose most women are vague about where their cervix is and what exactly it does. I was no different. Although, then again, I knew that smear tests were something to do with checking the neck of the womb. I suppose we knew the layman's term but not the medical one. Cervical cancer wasn't even heard of in my day. Anything to do with women's nether regions was off limits. Maybe it was down to embarrassment and seen as a private and delicate matter that shouldn't be discussed in public. There were no celebrities then to put it on the map like Jade Goody in 2009. I suppose we have come a long way since then. Now with screening services and public awareness, young women are more clued in and knowledgeable. In my day, we were unbelievably in the dark.

***

Everything had happened at such lightning speed. Within the space of a week my world had completely changed. When you leave a doctor's appointment with this terrible, frightening news, your life is suddenly turned upside down – not only for yourself but also your family. Once the shock started to wear off, I tried to get into the right frame of mind. I told myself that I would get through it and would fight and be strong for myself and my family. My family, such a great source of pride and luck to me, have always been amazing. They brought me up to speak openly about everything. I knew they would all be there for me no matter what. But the situation left them feeling powerless too. My father's words always come back to me.

'If I was a millionaire or a billionaire, I still could not help you.'

From that moment on, I knew just how true the saying 'your health is your wealth' is. If you do not have your health, you have nothing in life!

Within hours of returning home that Friday, every family member had been on the phone, as well as my extended family: aunts, uncles, and cousins from everywhere. They were just unbelievably supportive. But in the background the question of whether I could have children or not loomed large. My mother, in particular, was worried.

'Oh God . . . if you can't have children!'

I understood her fears but my focus had now turned to survival. Everything else paled into insignificance.

'Look, I need to live. I don't care what they have to do.'

Putting aside all thoughts of children, I turned into a machine. And all the cogs whistled survival, survival, survival. I knew I would be no good to any child if my physical health was not right. My dad recognised that too and encouraged my positive attitude.

'Just do what you have to do.'

The most wonderful support came too from Deirdre, my next-door neighbour from Palmerstown, who was also a nurse. That night she was a godsend, offering such practical advice and really understanding the fears and anxieties I was experiencing. Truly, she was a rock of sense.

An arrangement was made for me to meet Dr Gleeson again on the following Monday. This time both my parents accompanied me, adamant I would not face the challenge alone. But I scarcely remember any of it. Each time I stepped inside the Coombe doorway, everything went by in a blur. I had the most wonderful doctor in Noreen Gleeson. She was warm and approachable and tried to reassure me that things would be okay. That said, I understood that until my surgery, no one could really tell the outcome of my condition.

'At the end of the day, my life is in your hands,' I told Dr Gleeson. 'You just do what you have to do to make me okay.'

The type of surgery required was experimental. Even the name of the operation was a mouthful – a radical trachelectomy. I had never heard of it before, which wasn't surprising since I was only the second person that Dr Gleeson had performed it on in Ireland. She explained it was a new procedure to try to save the womb, for which she had received extensive training in America. Previous treatments for cervical cancer had tended to be rather brutal, whipping out the womb perhaps too hastily in some cases. Now at least there was some hope I would be able to have a child. Even so, there were no guarantees; Dr Gleeson would not know until she opened me up what tissues and organs needed to be removed. So when I consented to the surgery, it was really an open consent. I had no idea what exactly would be taken, what would be spared, what would be salvaged. Within days I was whisked into surgery with little time to think, let alone talk to the other girl who had had the same surgery.

'Will I be able to have a baby?'

These were my first words when I came around after the general anaesthetic. Even though I had put it out of my mind before the surgery, it crept to the fore again, especially when my defences were down. It was something I just couldn't suppress or deny, no matter how hard I tried. I was now at the start of a long and rough road to recovery. During the surgery my cervix was removed along with the top few centimetres of my vagina and the tissue around my cervix. The lymph glands and nodes on either side of my groin were also removed in another operation done at the same time called a lymphadenectomy. Thankfully, my womb was left in place but closed off with a large permanent stitch, except for a small opening to allow for menstruation. If I were to get pregnant in the future, the baby would be delivered by Caesarean section.

Not ever having had an operation before, I was not sure what to expect. In hindsight, I didn't think it was going to be as severe as it was. Back then there wasn't the luxury of keyhole surgery; I was basically cut open from front to back in my nether region. Afterwards there were drips, drains and catheters of every size and length coming out of me in all directions. I was also plugged with a vaginal dressing. By far the worst were the tubes draining blood from the lymphadenectomy site. They were a nightmare, which I later learnt to my cost.

For days I lay in my hospital bed and couldn't move, almost oblivious to what was going on around me. I was on morphine for the pain, which knocked me out and so I didn't move. For the first week, I couldn't take even a sup of water. Nothing was allowed to pass my lips. I was constantly vomiting from the morphine and had a bowl in permanent residence at my side. To moisten my mouth, I was given citrus swabs, which had the reverse effect. Even the smell of the citrus sent waves of nausea through me. My body was bloated after the surgery and felt as heavy as lead.

The trauma of the surgery was made bearable by my family's incredible support. The love and care lavished on me by my mother helped make me feel safe and secure like in my childhood. My brother and sister-in-law arrived over from England and gave me tremendous support too. Bina was full of pearls of wisdom. I remember she would say 'What's meant for you won't pass you by'. By way of explanation she would tell me that this is just a path in life, there will be an end to it. Everything happens for a reason. Although at the time, I was saying why is this bloody thing happening? I think her attitude came from her culture, from being a Hindu; it gives its people great strength in the face of adversity. Her own family were fantastic to me as well. Being close to her parents, they too knew of my plight. At that time, her mother was visiting relatives in Kenya and she brought a small group of people to the top of a small mountain and they prayed for me. I was incredibly touched. All these small little things, these acts of kindness and thoughtfulness, just made me wonder at the sacredness of life.

Many years later I learnt just how distressing my family found the hospital visits. My illness had come as a major shock to them. As bad as it was for me, I felt it worse for my family. I was lying there, looking at them, knowing they were upset. You just feel rather powerless. I was trying to get through the cancer but there was nothing I could do to end their living nightmare. My father would promptly leave work every day and come straight to the hospital and spend as much time with me as visiting hours permitted. He became such a regular that the nurses would joke 'here's your Dad in again'. I think he felt better watching what was going on directly from the inside rather than wondering like crazy at home. He followed my progress diligently, and empathised with me each time I was sick or in pain. As indeed did my mother. The day before I was to be mobilised, the nurses confided that it would be especially tough for me to get out of bed. As a result, he made a special effort to get in quick and early to the ward.

Their words rang true. It was terribly painful that morning. Much later in the day I was returning from the bathroom to the ward and had paused at the end of the passageway. The pain was intense and I clutched onto the wall for support and slowly inched myself onto a nearby chair. A nurse had pointed my father in my direction and he walked cautiously up the long corridor towards me. I glanced up at the sound of footsteps approaching. The look in his eyes was of such loving tenderness and compassion, the kind that passes between father and daughter at special moments. No words were needed. So pitiful did I look that he felt he would have to teach me to walk all over again.

I had developed a complication with one of the drains but it would be days before it was confirmed by a scan. In the meantime the pain to be endured was so horrible that moving around became an ordeal each time. The nurses would urge me to straighten up to make walking easier but it was the one thing I could not do. I was miserable and frustrated that no one would believe me at first. The pain became so unbearable, almost like having a heart attack, that I moaned for two days solid. All I could say was that there was something wrong. Finally I was sent for a scan. It revealed that one of the drains had dislodged and the tubing was wrapped around some tissue or other. Removing the drain proved horrendous. It just had to be pulled out, without sedation.

'Hold your breath now. Deep breath.'

Needless to say, I was relieved when it was all over and could put things in perspective. The incident with the drain was a small price to pay for surviving the cancer.

My recovery continued but was slow, having to spend three long weeks in the hospital. About two weeks after the surgery, the registrar on Dr Gleeson's team, Dr Edgar Mocanu, arrived in and told us he would be back in an hour to give us the results of the biopsies taken during surgery. In all the commotion with the drain and lulled from the effects of the painkillers, I had overlooked my prognosis. Until then, I had forgotten how serious it was. At least my parents were with me that day and could share my anxiety and the suspense. Of course everything started to race through my mind. What if they hadn't got all the cancer, what if it was in my lymph nodes, what if I needed chemotherapy or radiotherapy, how would I cope with all that? Was I going to die?

The hour seemed the longest in history, as if waiting to be sentenced to death. It was a bizarre time and my body didn't feel like mine – more like I had been run over by a bus and was undergoing an out-of-body experience. I shrank into the bed like a corpse.

'I think she's going to die in the bed,' my mother said, her anguished tone audible.

I just wasn't expecting the news. For the hour we waited, Dr Mocanu's face was imprinted in my mind. And all I could think was 'Oh God'. But I needn't have worried. True to his word, he returned on the hour and with the biggest smile on his face.

'You are one lucky person, Caroline. I don't know who's been praying for you.'

We laughed knowingly. It was Bina's mother up a mountain invoking the power of God. But I did feel lucky, lucky that I had met Dr Gleeson and the GP in Tallaght. My diagnosis was early stage cancer, spreading fast into the deeper layers of my cervix. Only for it being caught at the time it could have spread to my lymph glands and I dread to think where else.

The news was definitely something to celebrate. It certainly gave a boost to my recovery. A week later, I was discharged from hospital, admittedly a little earlier than normal because I really wanted to go home. I decided to go back to the apartment I shared with Lisa in Tallaght, though my parents were a little disappointed. They would have preferred if I had gone home with them to recuperate but I was anxious to get things back to normal as quickly as possible. There was only one problem. I came home with the urinary catheter still in, as the muscles in my bladder had not yet regained control. It would take another three weeks before they did. It also meant I had to measure my urinary output during that time to make sure my bladder and kidneys were working! Little did I think that my friend Lisa would turn into my nursemaid, but I am eternally grateful she did. She took charge and before long was helping to wash and bathe me. Her kindness and goodness were truly overwhelming. My mother had also nearly taken up residence in the apartment and helped as much as possible too. Every day she came to visit and made sure I had plenty of nourishing food to eat and was warm and comfortable. Deirdre too with all her nursing skills was just fantastic.

Though I was a little incapacitated and totally bloated, it was a relief to be at home, in my own bed with familiar sights and sounds. Being girlie girls and clean freaks, Lisa and I had gone to great efforts to make the apartment cosy and a home after we first moved in. With our stylish lamps from IKEA and surrounded by photos of nights outs, holiday snaps and ornaments, it was as good as a tonic. What I loved most was our black lamp that spun around like disco lights as colourful as a kaleidoscope. It had pride of place beside one of the three sittingroom windows overlooking the street. Niall used to say he always knew if we were at home because the light would be on and he could see it from the street.

Even so, I had underestimated just how hard it would be to climb the stairs properly to my apartment. As a result I stayed indoors for the first four to five weeks. It took weeks before I could go for short walks in the neighbourhood. After I left hospital I also developed lymphoedema in my right leg. This kind of swelling happens after the lymph glands in your groin are removed and perhaps the trouble with the drain didn't help matters either. The condition was news to me, as I had not heard about it in the hospital. Luckily, after some time I got in contact with a physiotherapist in Tallaght, who had experience in manual lymph drainage, the treatment required to manage it.

Holed up in the apartment, I passed the time watching TV and videos, reading and listening to music. But without my friends and parents I would have gone crazy. I enjoyed hearing about what my friends were up to and what was going on in their lives. I always had a good laugh with Lisa. She was such a reservoir of strength and it was always pleasant to be in her company. My father always used to say if he had two daughters, Lisa would be the second. She really did become part of our family and they appreciated everything she did for me.

It took five months before I was fit to return to work. Much of that time was spent thinking and coming to terms with what I had gone through. The question of whether I would be able to have a baby or not was never far off. I wondered what the other Irish girl who had the radical trachelectomy had thought too. Had she been able to have a child? What had her recovery been like? Had she had any long-term problems? Before being discharged from hospital, Dr Gleeson had suggested it might be worth speaking to her, as she was around my age. In fact, she thought it might even do the two of us some good.

When I took the girl's telephone number from Dr Gleeson, admittedly I was a bit reluctant. At the time I wanted to put the surgery behind me. To move on and forget. I didn't want to be going to any mad counselling sessions, as I saw it. I didn't want to be asked how I was feeling and what were my fears. I didn't want anyone to tell me how I should cope. But after a few weeks at home, I had a change of heart. Summoning up the courage, I went to the phone box outside the apartment and rang the girl.

As soon as I began talking to her, her voice sounded familiar. She asked me where I was living.

'I'm actually renting an apartment up here in Tallaght,' I replied, wracking my brain to remember where I had heard her voice before.

'I'm in Tallaght as well,' she answered, incredulous.

'Oh right,' I said, 'you sound familiar.'

'No, YOU sound familiar.'

And would you believe it we actually knew each other, or rather had previously met socially on a number of occasions. After the initial phone call we met up a couple of times to exchange surgery stories. For her, it was still unbelievable that she was the first person in Ireland to undergo the surgery, while I was shocked to realise we were two girls of the same age and so young for cancer to have struck. Behind it all, we wondered how it could have happened.

Amid all the pain and distress during my recovery, there was one beacon of light on the horizon. It was an unexpected outcome that I scarcely could have imagined possible. Before the cancer, I palled around with a group of friends, many of whom worked for Intel. Niall was part of that group. I had first met him a year or so before I had got sick, when he worked for an external company that supplied parts to Intel. Years later I learnt that Niall, on those daily trips to the company, would make it his business to walk near where I worked hoping to get my attention. But of course I was oblivious to all this at the time. Maybe the fact that he was a little younger than me made me fail to notice him. Later we all socialised as part of a big group and I enjoyed his company, whether it was drinks after work or house parties. After I was discharged from hospital, Niall was one of the first to visit me in the apartment. Mostly he would call around during the day, seeing that he then worked the night-time shift. Chatting and joking, soon we became closer and our friendship deepened. I began to look forward to seeing him each day and excited when the buzzer on the door finally sounded. Before long, I had fallen in love with him.

When my strength to get out and about returned, he finally plucked up the courage to ask me out. Our first date was a trip to the cinema to watch some light-hearted film and our second was to Dublin Zoo. It might be a cliché that the zoo is a favourite haunt of couples, but it was one of the best dates I ever had. It was a joy to be out in the warm summer air strolling around, listening to the cries of monkeys and screeches of baboons and watching penguins waddling in the blue-tiled pool. Life felt like it was getting back to normal and even a simple thing like a trip to the zoo was an exotic adventure. Romance in the air just made it all the more special. I suppose I learnt too that if someone is there for you during your darkest hours, they get to know you pretty well. They see you at your worst but are still prepared to stick by you, through thick and thin, and wait for happier times. There was no pretence or playing games: we could just be ourselves. On the way home from the zoo, we stopped by my parent's house in Palmerstown. It was a sign that our relationship was becoming serious. My parents took to Niall almost immediately and within a year we were engaged.

It had all happened so fast but we felt sure of ourselves. We were only going out for four months when we took a drive one Sunday afternoon and ended up in Citywest. The building boom in Ireland was starting to take off and houses were sprouting up west of Tallaght towards Saggart. There were fine views of the Dublin Mountains and the sense of open space and fresh air was exhilarating, almost like you were in the countryside. However, our relationship, even in its infancy, was reaching a crossroads. Niall was interested in going to Australia and hoped that I would come with him and we could build a life together Down Under. Moving to Australia was an exciting prospect for me too, but my hospital appointments and check-ups prevented it. It was too soon after my recovery. I knew I would have to be followed up by the Coombe for at least ten years. That's what stopped me. So that Sunday afternoon, driving around Citywest, we decided to have a gander at the newly built houses. It was a momentous decision. As soon as we laid eyes on one house in particular, it felt so right. Before we knew it, we had applied for a mortgage and got it. We saved hard and thanks to our families, who helped out, we were able to buy a home. I hoped before long that the patter of tiny feet would echo through the house and we would be a family for real.

Chapter 3

Attending the HARI Unit

Now that my illness was well behind me, I settled down and threw my energies into building a life with Niall and making our house a home. I also got into the rhythm of going for regular outpatient appointments with Dr Gleeson at the Coombe. At first these were every three months, then weaned down to every six months for several years and then yearly. Life started to feel normal again and Niall and I eventually married in September 2002.

Only once during my check-ups did I get a serious jolt. It happened after a routine smear test.

'Mmm, I don't know if I like the feel of that,' said Dr Gleeson, after examining me.

'Oh, don't tell me that,' I pleaded.

She glanced at me and, knowing that I was such a terrible worrier, patted my arm.

'Okay, come into the day ward tomorrow at seven.'

I needed no encouragement to be there bright and early the next morning, ready and willing. Niall accompanied me to the day surgical unit and I think he was worse than me, dreading hospitals and sickness of any kind. A typical man. But I knew I was in good hands with Dr Gleeson, who was thorough and left no stone unturned when it came to my care. An examination under anaesthetic was performed and revealed scar tissue, which thankfully was easily remedied. I was discharged later that day and within days I was back to my old self.

My journey to be a mother truly began about a year after my cervical surgery. The time seemed right to start trying for a baby now that my internal wounds were well healed. Besides, I was curious to see if the surgery had worked, though at the same time I knew I was likely to face problems. My menstrual cycle was never normal after my surgery, in fact, there were times when I feared the worst after very heavy bleeding. At one point, I was almost certain the cancer had come back. Luckily, Dr Gleeson put my mind at ease. She was always very attentive and supportive. Later we postponed trying for a baby due to an underactive thyroid, but I began again in earnest around 2001.

Over the years, getting pregnant just never happened. If I did a pregnancy test once, I did it a million times. Yet there were no moments of intense joy standing in the bathroom seeing a craved-for blue line or strip. Because my cycle was irregular, I was doing tests willy nilly, buying ovulation kits or pregnancy tests to beat the band. But all without success. Each time I had myself convinced it would be positive. Eventually, I abandoned doing pregnancy tests altogether because they were only upsetting me more and seemed pointless. I never did find out if I could carry my baby to full term either. The infertility was something that Dr Gleeson was conscious of too, year after year, appointment after appointment.

'No baby yet?' she would ask each time I was ushered into her outpatients clinic.

In reply, I would shake my head and purse my lips. Those words became so familiar to me.

'When I see you next time, it'll be in the baby clinic,' she would cheerfully say at the end of each visit, pushing me just a little.

And six months later I would duly traipse in with nothing to report.

'I'm not seeing you in the baby clinic!' she would exclaim in jest.

I would just shrug my shoulders.

'Well, I'm not being left with many choices. Can anyone else help me now?'

The disappointment on my face and frustration in my voice was becoming harder to hide. After three years of trying for a baby I was getting nowhere. Towards the end, Dr Gleeson had put me on a course of Clomid to stimulate the follicles in my ovaries but other than regulating my periods nothing had happened and later I was taken off it. In June 2004, she arranged for me to have a laparoscopy to investigate the infertility. It turned out that one of my fallopian tubes was blocked at the time, though it had not necessarily always been blocked.

The time had come to refer me on to fertility experts at the Human Assisted Reproduction Ireland Unit, otherwise known as the HARI Unit. In one way, my mind was moving in that direction anyway. Over the years my GP recognised the pain I was feeling, the longing for a baby that came to nothing. The blighted hope. The hurt that never went away. She could empathise with me and help me to consider other options.

'Don't wake up when you're fortysomething, Caroline, and say why didn't I try IVF,' she advised me one day.

The HARI Unit was situated on the grounds of the Rotunda Hospital, where I had been born. Maybe that connection was a sign in itself, I thought. With some luck, it might make my dream a reality. Around September 2004, Niall and I first entered the unit, its low building dwarfed by the tall buildings and townhouses on Parnell Square, one of the biggest Georgian squares in Dublin. The vast Rotunda Hospital complex, bordered by wrought-iron railings, was the oldest maternity hospital in Ireland but looked more like a parliament with its impressive ornate buildings and social rooms of a bygone age. The unit was located to the rear in a two-storey red-bricked modern building. Stepping over its threshold, I was armed with a string of questions as long as a ladder. I would have to be as dogged and persistent as ever until I got answers. The experience of being a patient had also empowered me, no longer willing to blindly accept what was being said: 'Right, yes, yes, yes. I'll do that. I'll do that.'

Inside, along one corridor colour photographs of babies and toddlers decorated the wall like prizes; success stories I presumed. I held my breath as I too dared to dream. We were guided to a small waiting room upstairs where a number of other couples sat in silence. The silence in fact was overwhelming. No one spoke or even gave a knowing nod. It was particularly hard for me because I was born to natter. So much so that when we later left the building Niall slagged me off.

'I bet you were just dying to talk in there.'

Dr Gleeson had referred me to Professor Robert Harrison, the father of IVF in Ireland, but he had retired in the meantime. As we sat waiting, I wondered who would see us instead. And then all of a sudden a doctor put a firm hand on the back of my shoulder.

'Well, come on in. I know who this is,' he said, smiling at me.

It was Dr Edgar Mocanu, whom I had met in the Coombe six years before. He had just taken over from Professor Harrison. It was such a pleasant surprise to see him, though I was a bit shocked at first. I had been bracing myself to explain my medical history in great detail to an unfamiliar face. It came as such a relief that he knew it already having been on the surgical team in the Coombe.

'Of course, I know your medical history,' he exclaimed. 'I was there during the operation.'

Sitting back in his chair, he recalled that the surgery had been exciting because it was a new procedure and experimental at the time. Seeing him made me relax and so it was easy to put my questions to him. From the outset I had one burning question.

'Dr Mocanu, I want to know if I go down this road, am I going to be okay?'

He listened attentively before speaking.

'Well, you should be okay. You're not really any different to anyone else.'

Though I hadn't got a cast iron guarantee from him straightaway, I still accepted his answer. One of the first things we were asked to do was attend an open meeting on infertility and in vitro fertilisation (IVF) taking place several weeks later. When it finally came round, Niall and I drove into town that evening all happy and positive. But by the time we reached Parnell Square all the on-street parking spaces and car parks close to the hospital were full. We drove around for ages, seeing nothing but pregnant mothers huddled together smoking at the entrance. No spaces anywhere. We couldn't understand it. Had there been a baby boom in the hospital?

Immediately, the stress kicked in because I did not want to be late. In my mind I was thinking how awful it would look when we straggled into the room late while everyone else was on time. I imagined about ten couples or so in the room and disturbing them in the process. Well, how wrong was I! Finally, we found the venue, a hall in an old building at the back of the premises, remarkably cold in early winter. As I stepped inside it took my breath away. It was like going into a town hall for a Christmas party or to the cinema. Little did I know that hundreds of people would be in attendance from all over the country. Accents from Cork to Donegal and from all areas of Dublin city could be heard. The stage at the top of the hall appeared so far away, given the throngs in front of us. We could have been at a concert, though minus the music. On a large screen in big letters, the words 'It could be you' beamed back at us. It was unreal. Niall and I just stared at each other in amazement. I remember thinking 'holy cow, the whole world must be having the same problems as us'. And what chance had we got? I couldn't believe how big a problem infertility was. Years later I heard all sorts of statistics, like one in six couples could be affected.

As the meeting began I was still mesmerised; I could scarcely remember who conducted it and what was said and discussed. Funnily enough, the risks of IVF did stick in my mind, especially ovarian hyperstimulation syndrome. The meeting had been overwhelming and I left feeling rather deflated. Our problems seemed like a tiny drop in the vast ocean of infertility.

We attended the unit for about six months, on and off. At our next visit with Dr Mocanu, he explained in detail the fertility tests needed and what was involved in the processes of intrauterine insemination (IUI) and in vitro fertilisation (IVF). He anticipated that IUI might be suitable for us. Pretty soon, I learnt that infertility was a complicated business. There were so many things to check and monitor and even our lifestyle had to be taken into account. For Niall it was more straightforward; all that was required from him was semen analysis. I had to laugh, guys always seem to get the easy end of the stick. Luckily, it posed no problems and he duly supplied the samples, all of which turned out to be normal. For me, it was a different story and a full fertility profile had to be completed. I had bloods taken to check hormone levels and to ensure I was ovulating. Previous tests had revealed that I had very mild polycystic ovaries and would need to have follicle tracking for each menstrual cycle.

There was so much else to consider. Ways to improve conception, such as frequency of sexual intercourse, were also briefly discussed by Dr Mocanu. Once we got over the embarrassment of that, our general well-being was scrutinised, such as weight and basal metabolic index (BMI). Fortunately, Niall and I were neither overweight nor underweight, and my BMI was just right for my height and weight. We lived a fairly normal healthy lifestyle and didn't overindulge in alcohol so these issues were never in question. But it certainly got me thinking how these things could affect ovulation. Over the years Dr Gleeson had made sure I was well vaccinated so rubella was never a problem. At no point was I actually advised to take folic acid but I had started taking it myself over the years anyway, aware of the dangers of spina bifida in babies if levels were low in my body. My vitamin B_{12} levels had been monitored by Dr Gleeson too and were continued by the HARI Unit. A viral screen was carried out on both Niall and myself to ensure we were free from HIV and hepatitis B and C, which we were. So at least we got a clean bill of health from that perspective.

The question of stress and infertility has long been linked together. As I saw it, it is natural that when someone has fertility issues they will have a lot of stress in their lives. It comes with the territory. I was aware of this and over the years would always release any tension I had by taking exercise. Having pets and exercising them was always a great de-stressor for me.

I started off with the follicle tracking scans. These scans were perhaps the most challenging part of the process for me. In contrast to the majority of women who attend the unit, this is probably the most straightforward part and least demanding. The follicle tracking would trace my natural menstrual cycle, find out if I was ovulating and, if so, pinpoint the exact time when the follicle ruptures and releases the egg. As a result, I could time when exactly to have sex and so increase my chance of fertilisation or have IUI, which was more likely to succeed. The scan could also monitor the lining of my womb during my cycle and see if it would accept a fertilised egg. If the main follicle or follicles matured and grew to a size of about 16mm, it was usually ready for ovulation. At that point I could be given injectable gonadotropins to stimulate my ovary to release the egg.

In my case, the scanning was done over the course of about three months. The tracking involved a series of vaginal ultrasound scans from day 9 to day 20 of my cycle. Usually I would attend for three consecutive days and then have a break for a day or so, while they monitored the growth of the follicles. Unfortunately for me the follicles never reached the desired size on those occasions. The nurses would say to me they're coming along nicely and then the next day they would be gone.

Having the scans meant a quick visit to the unit each time. For the first one, Dr Mocanu was present and I felt confident because he knew my condition and explained to the nurse performing the scan what my surgery had entailed. Fairly soon I earned a reputation as 'the girl that had the cervical cancer'. It became the norm to be seen by a different nurse each time, so my medical history had to be explained time and time again by me before they would perform the scan. Admittedly, it could be quite frustrating and unsettling at times.

On the days when I did attend and the staff actually knew about my situation, it was a dream to be there. Things went so smoothly and left me wishing it could be like this all the time. The final straw came on Easter Monday in 2005 when my next scheduled follicle tracking fell due. Naturally, it being a bank holiday there was a skeleton crew at work. As usual, I settled down on the couch while the nurse inserted the probe and began scanning.

'I don't like what I see here,' she announced after a while.

Almost immediately I could feel my heart thumping in my chest and I struggled to take a breath.

'What do you mean?'

'There's some kind of cyst or something there.'

I gulped, unable to reply.

'Come back in a few days when Dr Mocanu is here and he can take a look.'

The news stunned me. I cried leaving the clinic and for two whole days until I returned to the unit. I felt sick to the pit of my stomach and could barely eat during those days. So it was with a heavy heart that I lay nervously on the couch, as the same nurse inserted the probe again and began scanning. Soon after, she was joined by Dr Mocanu.

'The cyst has disappeared,' he informed me after observing the screen. 'That happens sometimes, Caroline. It's nothing to worry about.'

Once Dr Mocanu had left the room, my eyes welled up with tears and before I knew it, I was sobbing with relief.

'What's wrong?' the nurse asked concernedly.

It was some moments before I could compose myself well enough to explain.

'When you tell someone who has had cancer – and who then worries over the tiniest thing – that you see a cyst or something,' I began, 'it's like giving them a death sentence.'

'Oh, I'm so sorry, I didn't realise your situation.'

The fear that Dr Mocanu would not always be around for any emergencies, especially when the IVF treatment proper began, undermined my confidence. Other doctors would naturally be there yet without his breadth of knowledge and experience. But I knew it was unrealistic and unreasonable to expect him to be there all the time. That was not how I wanted it.

Finally, the follicle tracking came to an end and Dr Mocanu suggested that IVF would be the best option for me. At this stage he was in regular correspondence with Dr Gleeson, whose clinic I was now attending at intervals of six months. Niall and I had to sign consent forms for the treatment to go ahead, but the nagging doubts were still skirting my mind. The more I researched IVF and the more questions I plied Dr Mocanu with, the more uneasy I became about the risk of ovarian hyperstimulation syndrome (OHSS). Part of my anxiety lay in the fact that a cousin of mine had attended the HARI Unit for many years but without success. The period had been particularly stressful for her and her husband as she had developed OHSS and had been extremely ill.

When I conveyed my concerns to Dr Mocanu, he assured me that there were new protocols in place and at the first sign of OHSS the treatment would be stopped for that cycle. Other times, I quizzed other doctors on the team about the condition.

'But what happens if I get it?' I persisted.

'Okay, we can't say that you're not going to get it.'

'And if I did?'

'Well, if it happens, you'll have to come in and we'll drain the fluids off.'

At the mention of the word drains, I shrank. The memory of having my lymph nodes removed and the hullabaloo with the drains afterwards had been hard to erase from my brain. The pain flashed before me.

'Oh no, don't talk to me about drains!'

Then I started to create all sorts of scenarios in my head.

'What if it happened that I came in during the weekend for it to be drained, and somebody else is here and Dr Mocanu is not? And the person who is here doesn't know anything about my situation.'

I think the doctors must have scratched their heads in despair at that stage. There was no comeback for them. Maybe they thought I was overly anxious and always thinking the worst. But the experience of cancer had made me that way. When I think of it now, I laugh. Oh, the luxury of hindsight. The doctors were just unfortunate to be pressing all the wrong buttons with me. Drains! That was a right red rag to me. Poor Dr Mocanu got twenty questions from me each time.

'When I'm taking the fertility drugs, all those hormones, what is it going to do to my cells? Would it activate the cells, I mean, cause cancer?'

'Caroline, it's probably not going to happen,' he replied. 'Chances are it's very unlikely.'

The fact that there was even a tiny risk was too much for me. Nobody was going to say it was or was not going to happen for certain. It wasn't enough for me. As time passed, I just didn't feel confident enough. My head was stuffed with these thoughts and buzzed like a beehive.

Given that there was so much anxiety attached to our decision, it was just as well that counselling was a necessary part of the procedure. We attended a number of sessions over the course of six months. In hindsight, the counselling service was very good and professional, although I didn't always agree with the counsellor's views.

As summer approached, it was time to make up our minds about IVF. One fine day we found ourselves again in the counsellor's office upstairs in the building; the room was small and plain and we sat around her desk facing her. On her desk a box of tissues stood at the ready. We had been given loads of consent forms to sign for IVF and I still had not signed two of them. In my hand I nervously held the consent forms, my mind full of niggling doubts. True to form, I expressed my concerns and plied her with questions again. She pulled no punches and gave us the facts in the cold light of day. In agreement, she said it would be difficult with my medical history.

'Are you prepared to lie on your back for nine months? You have a 90 percent chance of a miscarriage at any stage.'

These were sobering words indeed. My mind hadn't even stretched to that stage. I suppose the onus was on me and Niall to decide. Over the years since our engagement, Niall said it never bothered him if we had children or not. He knew only too well about my surgery so infertility came as no great revelation to him. Time and again, he would say in his relaxed, easy-going manner that it didn't bother him at all. Even at the HARI Unit, he would sit and listen to the doctors and counsellors and turn to me.

'Whatever you want, Caroline,' he would say. 'I can't advise you medically. Do it or don't do it. Whatever you decide.'

However, I got the impression that the counsellor was losing patience with us.

'Look, if you have that many questions, should you be going through with it at all?'

'But these are questions about my health,' I responded defensively.

At that point I got upset. The tears just flowed and I dabbed my eyes with a paper handkerchief.

'If you're going to get that emotional before the process even starts,' she pointed out, 'how are you actually going to deal with IVF itself?'

I said nothing.

'Maybe the process isn't for you.'

'Look, I understand that you can't guarantee anything,' I replied. 'I'm not stupid, but I really need to know if my own health is not going to be jeopardised.'

'I don't think you're really ready for this,' she finally concluded.

Her words and tone stung me. I had to admit that it was more than just a question of being ready for the treatment. I had doubts about whether it was right for me at all.

'No,' I said calmly.

I wanted to ask how could I overcome my lack of confidence. But that's not what she wished to focus on. Her words did help me in one way, however. That moment I realised I would never feel confident and be willing to take the risk. It then helped us to make up our minds rather quickly. As we walked out of the room that day, Niall said to me: 'You know what, this is just crazy.'

You can talk to all the doctors and counsellors in the world but you are really left on your own as a couple to decide. During this time Niall was very supportive, as was my family too. Niall never put pressure on me to decide one way or the other. That I was comfortable with my decision was important to him. And he wanted to make me as happy as possible. Like me, he did not want my health jeopardised in any way. No baby was worth that, as he saw it. With his dread of hospitals and sickness, he would have hated to see me unwell. As for my family, they felt it was not their business to tell me what to do, but were aware of the tremendous stress the treatment could bring. Not alone from watching my experience of it so far but also that of my cousin. I suppose the person who was straight up in his advice from the very start was my brother Philip. From working in hospitals, both he and his wife Bina were hyperaware of these treatments. They had a lot of contact with UK specialists and had sought their opinion.

'You know, I'm going to see this IVF doctor,' I mentioned to him and Bina, when I was first referred to the HARI Unit.

'Don't do it. Leave it alone.'

'But you don't understand, Philip. I'm not just going to leave it alone.'

'It's too risky.'

'I have to try something.'

'You're just a number. They will say do this, do that. They're using you as a test case.'

There was also my cousin's experience to consider. I had heard IVF stories from her, having been through it loads of time some years before, however in vain. She had a really bad time, getting OHSS, and rolling around the house in pain one night. Her advice couldn't have been any clearer.

'Please don't do it, it's horrendous.'

All during the follicle tracking sessions, I had tried to put their views out of my mind but to no avail. In the end I didn't attempt IVF because I couldn't get the reassurance we needed. My confidence was undermined by the possible risks to my own health and the staff's unfamiliarity with my medical history. Maybe others would have taken the chance, threw the dice and played Russian roulette. I know some women would do anything for a baby and would overcome every obstacle, take every risk. But it was not so easy in my case and with my medical history. The experience of cancer had scared the wits out of me and made me more cautious and anxious. Each examination saw me petrified they would find more cancer. I felt I couldn't fight it again and come out as strong a second time around.

I laugh now when I think about how petrified I was. As the years go on and the longer you are cancer free, you can feel a bit more confident about recurrence. But those few months attending the HARI Unit and the constant cancer reminders plunged me back to those agonising days in the Coombe. Fortunately, we did not leave the HARI Unit on bad terms or anything like that, I would have hated that. After all, the staff were lovely, hard-working professional people. It was more a case of 'we'll come back when we're ready'. Luckily, there had been no huge financial outlay. The cost came to about €1,000 and we were spared having to fork out €5,000 if we had gone ahead with IVF.

Though disappointed, I didn't regret my decision. Perhaps it was for the best. It was a setback admittedly but one which I knew would not stop us in our goal. It was time to pick up the pieces and start exploring other options. In my heart, I was still sure there was a baby out there for us, whom we could lavish with love one day. On this journey there was no way of knowing how many miles we would have to travel before we reached our destination.

Chapter 4

Life goes on

The longer I lived with infertility, the more I thought about it. Not being pregnant became my whole world and invaded every waking moment. Perhaps other people reach a point where they accept they will never have a baby, but not me. It was never a case of saying, it's the will of God. Though life did go on after every setback, and I got up every day and went to work, I was really only going through the motions. I walked around in a daze half the time because of the hurt and anger I felt. The sense that something was missing in my life, a void that could only be filled by a baby, never left me. A baby was the vital ingredient to put the spark back into my body, light up my eyes, and bring a spring to my step.

My world was defined by visits to doctors and check-ups, tests and drugs, and exploring new options. I measured it by hospital appointments and menstrual cycles. It was incredible how life passed by so quickly, living for the next month or appointment, almost in dread each time. The two-week wait from ovulation to hopefully fertilisation sometimes became an unbearable endurance test. Infertility consumed my life, yet I seemed to have little or no control over this world, over what was happening.

Through it all, I clung to the belief that I was meant to be a mother. It was destined for me. But as time wore on I felt increasingly that something had been denied me. I began to almost resent Mother Nature. It's so ironic that the best time for your body to have a baby is in your teens and twenties, when you might least want one, and then perhaps too late when you reach your thirties and forties, when you want one the most. Sometimes there's neither rhyme nor reason to Mother Nature. Or maybe she just doesn't care about our modern lifestyles and careers. Even assisted reproduction techniques seemed to be based on absolute luck. The feeling that time was running out for my body gave rise to intense panic. I was only in my thirties and already my body was like an old woman's. I was barren, broken, damaged, redundant, only good for the scrap yard. And nothing seemed to be able to fix me. I'd failed at being a woman. Or rather I was failing some law of the universe, the most basic one – procreation. It was a very lonely and isolating feeling. I could be in a crowd of people and still feel utterly alone, abandoned. I would pray to God for a baby but to no avail and then wonder was he punishing me for something in my past. Had I done something wrong? Said something, been unkind, unknowingly offended someone? I would reel back my life in my head, frame by frame, trying to figure out what it could be. Something in the schoolyard, at dancing classes, at work, in my neighbourhood? Nothing.

Being childless hurt like no pain I ever had. Sometimes the pain and hurt distorted how I felt about Niall. It skewed my thinking. It all boiled down to the fact that I wasn't able to give him a child. Wouldn't he be better off then without me and free to have a child with someone else? I couldn't give him what he wanted. When you love someone, you don't wish to deny them any happiness. And here I was denying him the joy of having a family. Trying to conceive had taken the romance and spontaneity out of our lives too. Instead it got all technical with timed intercourse, semen analysis, fertility drugs, endless scans and tests. Like most couples we felt that strain on our relationship. From a financial viewpoint, because we didn't go through with IVF, it wasn't a huge strain on our resources. However, I knew from friends, my cousin and other couples attending the HARI Unit that every penny could go on IVF or other assisted-reproduction methods.

You immerse yourself in infertility. And in this world you speak a different language. The world really comes alive on the internet, it becomes a community. A virtual world where information and pain is shared and everyone's story becomes real to you. A lifeline where you are not alone, battling against the forces of nature. You learn to manoeuvre your way through all the information and logistics of infertility options. Learn the parlance of IVF, adoption agencies and legal contracts. Learn the lingo on internet message boards, blogs and chatrooms. Medical jargon and acronyms. Sometimes I nearly needed a glossary to understand the terms. TTC boggled me before it dawned on me that it stood for trying to conceive; DH was for dear or darling husband; and of course the one you would love to be using: PG – pregnant.

Many people have likened infertility to bereavement. Yes, it's true, you grieve every day. You cry for a loss: for the baby you will never have. The baby that is so real to you that you can actually feel their weight in your arms. My heart too ached so badly for what I craved. But honestly I have always felt it is worse than grieving. I would tell my friends that it was literally a silent cry. For years, I used to cry myself to sleep, silently into my pillow. Granted, I had good days and bad days and dare I say almost got used to crying. So hard did I try to keep it to myself, that Niall would sleep on oblivious beside me in the bed. I didn't want to upset him and make him have to comfort me every night. Nothing could console me. During my really bad days, I would say to myself, how can this get any worse? I would tot it up in my head. Number one, I had been hit with being sick, having cancer. Number two, why could life be so cruel to some people and so blessed for others? Why could most women give birth to children without a hitch and even have broods of them? It was a sickness in the pit in my stomach that never went away, which no food or painkiller could relieve. No matter what I did, going on with my daily business, it would hit me over and over again. Neither could I stop researching different avenues nor stop thinking about it, every day, until that void was filled.

At least with a normal bereavement, you adjust or come to terms with it, or it gets somewhat easier as time passes. But with infertility there seemed to be no closure. There was no accepted period of mourning. In fact, every month I was plunged into grief when my period arrived. Empty arms and a broken heart once again. It was most definitely like experiencing a life crisis. And unless you go through it yourself, walk in my shoes as they say, it is very hard for people to understand the hurt I felt inside. It was easy for them to say 'just let it be', and though I appreciated their concern for me, their advice did not dissuade me.

On one occasion I paid a visit to my brother and his wife Bina in Hampshire and got talking to her mother one day. Though sympathetic to my plight, she felt I should move on and not let it consume me.

'Can you not just live your life and not have a child?'

'No,' I replied. 'I couldn't. I just can't.'

'Why not?'

'I will be going through life missing out on the one thing I want more than anything. I can't give up.'

Constant reminders were all over the place. Everywhere I looked there were babies of family, friends and neighbours, and of total strangers on the streets. But I knew I could not divorce myself from everyday life just because I couldn't have a baby, especially family life. Birthdays, Christmas, Easter, summer holidays, family celebrations came and went, and not least the birth of my nephews. I saw the joy in my parents' faces at these events. In my heart I hoped that one day Niall and I would add to their delight and happiness. For some reason, however, the birth of my nephews Caelan and Ethan did not make me feel 'Oh God, why is this not me?' I genuinely was over the moon for Philip and Bina. Caelan was born first in 2002 a few years after my cancer treatment and I can still remember the day he arrived. We had some advance warning because he needed to be born by Caesarean section. The day before his arrival, I had been attending the Coombe for a check-up and as usual Dr Gleeson had enquired about any baby news.

'No, no news,' I told her, 'but I'm really excited because my brother's baby is due tomorrow. It's going to be a boy.'

'Have you bought all blue?'

'Oh yeah, I've loads of blue stuff.'

'I wouldn't advise that,' she smiled, shaking her head.

'No, she's had a scan. It's definitely going to be a boy.'

'Oh, you're alright so.'

We laughed. The next day my father and I couldn't get over to England quick enough; we nearly broke our necks in our haste to get there. As soon as we heard that Bina had gone to theatre that morning, we immediately booked a Ryanair flight. It was a mad dash to the airport and as we buckled up on the plane, nervously excited, the significance of the occasion struck my father. For him, it was the most important flight he was ever on, going to meet his first grandchild. That situation would never present itself again. It was the dawn of something special for him: a new generation. At home my mother felt it too but, being more pragmatic, delayed arriving over until Bina and Caelan were out of hospital when she could be of more assistance. She would follow a few days later after our return and stay on for several weeks. Five minutes after our plane touched down in Gatwick, Caelan was born. Our joy was intense to say the least, when we later got to cradle him in our arms and witness the first of a new generation. It was repeated all over again four years later at the birth of his brother Ethan. The bonds that began that first day grew stronger with every passing year and I loved my nephews to pieces, especially being godmother to Caelan and Niall godfather to Ethan. Though the Irish Sea divided us it did not deter us from visiting Caelan and Ethan for all their birthdays and every Halloween. I followed the milestones in their lives – teething, talking, crawling, walking, first days at school – with such delight and diligence they could have been my own children.

Seeing how much happiness the children brought Bina and Philip and my parents, I longed for the same. Being around the children of friends and neighbours I found so much harder, however. I spent years watching friends have children and of course I was happy for them yet it hurt deeply. I would ponder why it came so naturally and quickly to them, whereas it was a battle-ground for me. At the news of each birth, my congratulations were genuine and heart-felt but inside I was crying. As time went on, I became aware of some friends treating me differently. This was very obvious to my friend Lisa, who remarked one day.

'People treat you like you're an alien. Like you're afflicted.'

Infertility was a total taboo, the subject that dare not speak its name. In my circle, I had about ten girlfriends and I'd always be the last to know if one of them was pregnant. 'How could we tell her?' became a common refrain. It was true that people felt sorry for me and pitied me. In fact, I was asked to be a godparent ten times over. On the one hand, I knew people were well-meaning and perhaps felt they wanted to compensate me in some way. But I was torn between trying to appreciate their views and really resenting them. I didn't mind being a godparent for family members and close friends but not to a whole host of children. It was a role I took very seriously; it was more than just being an honorary aunt. And then of course people treated me with kid gloves, speaking in hushed tones, whenever babies were around or at the mention of them. One day a neighbour of mine stopped me on the street and whispered to me.

'I don't know how I'm going to tell you this?' she began with an anguished look on her face, 'I even said it to my husband.'

'What,' I interrupted, 'you're pregnant?'

She nodded, stunned by my reply. What did she think I was going to do? Burst into tears?

'I'm delighted for you. That's great news.'

Sometimes at social gatherings the concerted effort made by friends to protect me just got too frustrating.

'Are you okay holding the baby?'

The tentative look in the mother's eyes made me feel like I was something fragile, damaged. At times, I sensed those eyes betrayed a fear that I was unhinged, maybe liable to do anything. What does she think I'm going to do, I would yell in my head, run away with the baby? Sometimes it was all too much.

'What do you think I'm going to do? Rob your baby? I'm not going to do that.'

A dumbfounded look appeared on the mother's face, lost for words. Not surprisingly, I was never asked to babysit or very rarely invited to children's birthday parties. Afterwards, I would hear about them and their mothers would whisper apologetically.

'We didn't like to ask you because you know . . . '

Perhaps it was from a sense of self-protection that I started to avoid situations or reminders of children, aside from those with my immediate family. Some were fairly harmless, like avoiding the baby section in the supermarket or steering clear of playgrounds or primary schools at break time. But then I started to isolate myself and that was worrying. It wasn't healthy. In later years, we might get invited to birthday parties for the children of Niall's friends. It was tough because I really enjoyed the company of his friends but every party ended with me returning home and lamenting 'why is that not me?' Soon I was concocting excuses not to go, every excuse under the sun, pleading illness and whatnot. I just couldn't face it any longer. I got so used to muttering afterwards, 'well, I was sick . . . '

One day in particular it hit me badly. It was Christmas time and I caught sight of an old school friend in Boots Chemist whom I hadn't seen in quite a long time. Being such a family-orientated time of the year, the shops, of course, were full of toys and presents for children. This friend would have known that I had wanted to be a mother from our earliest days in school. More than anything I wanted to go over and talk to her, poring over a cosmetic stand. As I stepped towards her a very young girl suddenly walked around the corner of a stand and ran up to her, tugging at her coat. She was about ten years old. I stopped in my tracks, unable to move forward. It was unbelievable, especially knowing how much I wanted to chat to her. The fear of what I imagined to be her first question paralysed me. *How many children have you got?* I knew I couldn't handle that question. I quickly turned on my heels and left the shop.

However, sometimes there was no escaping and I just had to take it on the chin. There was no place to hide when attending the Coombe for my regular check-ups. These outpatient appointments religiously followed on from the Baby Clinic and it was torture having to sit in the waiting room or walk along the corridors, looking at all the buggies and babies parading by. Tiny bundles wrapped up against the elements and lovingly cradled in the arms of adoring mothers. The soundtrack of baby cries and soothing mothers was like piped music on continuous play. Meanwhile, I wailed inside, 'Am I ever going to have a baby?' Over the years I bumped into pregnant women on their way to and from antenatal classes at the Coombe as well. On occasion, these were women from my old neighbourhood of Palmerstown or those met through work or school. I wouldn't know them well enough to tell them my story, but they fixed me with a kind of knowing look. *There she is, she must be pregnant.* Reports would eventually filter back to my mother, who would give me regular accounts. *Such and such saw you in the Coombe the other day, you must be pregnant.* If only.

Defeat was a word not in my vocabulary, however. Because of this I never gave up hope that one day I would have a child. When one option failed, I tried another. I tried every avenue. You name it, I researched it. Any herbal tablet that came my way I would have taken it. Maybe I wanted to hedge my bets and maximise my chances of getting pregnant. Maybe it was just a case of not giving up. And people were always forthcoming with advice on what to do or take. My sister-in-law Bina used to say eat properly, eat your greens and take herbal things – stuff you would see in a health shop. I also asked Dr Gleeson to recommend what should I eat or not eat, what should I take. Her advice was that everything was fine in small doses, everything in moderation, like vitamins and supplements. But there were all sorts of things I heard or read about: avoiding salt, eating lettuce and lots of vegetables, even taking nettles. For all the good they did me!

Complementary and alternative treatments were all genuinely considered. Though it is easy for people to frown upon these treatments, it's another matter when you crave a baby. You clutch at straws, not quite the weird and wacky but almost. You explore so many things that you wouldn't otherwise think of doing. You look into every and any sort of infertility treatments. I would never have thought of trying acupuncture until I heard it had a positive effect on fertility. And so I trekked out to Rathcoole for several weeks to attend an acupuncturist, who gave me a variety of herbs as well. But after a while I thought to myself, 'what am I doing?' I suppose I had lost faith in the therapy, even though it did have a calming effect whenever I felt stressed. And you never know how long you should persist with it, even when you didn't get pregnant.

From knowing and mixing with other infertile women over the years, I learnt a lot about various treatments in vogue. One being preached around the country at the time was NaPro technology, a type of natural procreative technology that can involve various drugs to correct infertility. Basically, you have to chart your cycle by noting changes in your cervical mucus. I had also contacted a clinic in Galway that carried it and was told there was a waiting list for months. Because of my medical history, I asked to speak to a doctor before a consultation was arranged. I didn't want to have to wait for months only to find out that the clinic could not help me. At first the secretary was reluctant to allow me to speak to the doctor beforehand, as it was not the norm.

'Can I just have two minutes of his time, please? My case is unusual.'

Eventually she relented and the doctor returned my call some time later. After hearing my medical history, he abruptly told me that kind of surgery couldn't possibly have been done. Again I insisted it had been carried out. We eventually reached an impasse. Finally, he said that he was unable to help me as he didn't know anything about the surgery. It was the brush off. Another door closed. Even so, I still tried the method for two months. In the meantime I had made contact with one NaPro adviser based in Dublin and she charted my cycle about twice a month at a cost of about €40 per session. But it was a total waste of time as my cycle was so erratic it made the method extremely difficult.

Despite not being superstitious, I still scrutinised old wives' tales for any nuggets of truth. *If two women pour from the same pot one of them will have a baby within a year. / Sit down in a chair right after a pregnant woman sits in it.*

/ *If you accidently drop a spoon it means you'll get pregnant.* / *It is bad luck to knit for a future child without actually being pregnant.* And then of course there were the modern myths. *Men should wear boxer shorts instead of briefs.* / *After sex, lie on your back and lift your bottom into the air for 20 minutes to increase the chance of sperm fertilising the egg.* So we gave them a chance, what had we to lose? We were constantly thinking of things, even religion. Though I personally didn't visit places of pilgrimage like Knock or Lourdes, loads of people brought me back medals and holy water. In fact, it was almost like a campaign. Friends of my parents would be constantly praying for me, making novenas and saying rosaries, in Padre Pio groups, or praying to Saint Gerard Majella, the patron saint of motherhood, or others associated with infertility and hopeless cases like Saint Anne and Saint Rita.

The support of Niall, my family and close friends made the years bearable. Where there is love, there is hope. Nothing is more true than that. And so I found ways to keep positive and hopeful. One of the main ways was never to take anything for granted. And, in the process, I found an inner strength I didn't know I had. Maybe it was a mixture too of stubbornness and not wishing to give up. There was also a certain solidarity among my close female friends, some of whom had experienced the pain of infertility and upheaval of treatment too. They were my constant companions, talking and sharing everything, and are still my good friends to this day. Women perhaps more than men feel the pain of infertility acutely and can speak about it. My friends knew exactly the heartache of not being able to give their husbands a child, almost willing them to go off with someone else to make it happen. We were like a team, struggling in a league, and only by bonding and supporting each other could we come through victorious, despite being relegated or confined to the subs bench at times. They just simply understood what I was going through.

One of the best coping strategies for Niall and me were our dogs. The dogs became our babies, our lovable rogues. We could nurture and protect them, become attached to them, and they to us, and watch them grow. Niall would even talk to them like they were babies, petting and holding them. First there was one dog, then two, and before we knew it, three. That's what happened. It was funny because on the surrogacy online forum we later accessed, so many people had pictures of their pets, great big families of cats and dogs. Perhaps it was a pattern but the dogs certainly made us feel good. They became an outlet for us, got us out walking and exercising, clearing our heads and at times diverting my mind away from being childless. Tiny came first in 1999 from a rescue centre. She's a mixed breed terrier that was hauled out of a bin. With her thick coat she looked like a black fox but with a grey patch under her chin. A year later Ruby arrived, a pure-bred Cavalier King Charles spaniel. It was at that point that Niall and I started to attend dog shows and would spend hours on end grooming Ruby's sandy-coloured coat. To our amazement, she did well at the shows, winning several prizes. The dog shows were a whole world in themselves, with all their protocols and regulations. Even Tiny came as a spectator, much to the disdain of the purists.

'What is that black mongrel dog doing here?' a steward would exclaim.

'Wherever Ruby goes, Tiny goes!'

The spaniel and terrier were the best of pals. There was no separating them.

'What breed is he?' someone would ask disparagingly.

'He's the Tallaght Special!'

Two or three years later we got Sophie, another Cavalier King Charles. She was a right quality dog and could boast the best of pedigree from Lamonts in Ballymena, County Antrim. They rule: the king of breeders known all over the world. The plan was to put Sophie into shows as well but she proved too erratic and excitable on the day, and dare I say it, too spoiled by us. For Niall, the dogs were the answer to everything. His defence against infertility. Sometimes on nights out, people would ask him how many children he had, you know, everyday small talk:

'Three. Three girls,' he would promptly reply.

And of course there would be an inevitable chorus of approval.

'Do you want to see a picture of them?'

And from his mobile phone he would present the latest picture of Tiny, Ruby and Sophie up to whatever mischief. That was his answer. Many years before, we had attended a wedding where later in the evening a heavily inebriated guy had asked me the dreaded question. Of course, I couldn't lie.

'What do you mean you don't have children?' he slurred.

For ages he banged on and on about it, oblivious to the attempts of his partner to shut him up. Finally, I escaped his clutches. I think men and women are different in how they handle infertility. In one way, men do hurt, but still seem capable of wrapping it up well in humour. For me it was harder to wear a mask.

I suppose it was inevitable to have low periods in all those years trying to conceive. It was the rollercoaster effect: one minute sky high with the expectation of motherhood and then sunk low when a period arrives or some other setback. Outwardly I did try to put on a brave face and keep my infertility worries to myself. As my friend Mary once said, people think you just go on every day and you're not thinking about it. And you put it off. I would be all on a high if, for example, I got a letter from the adoption agency and then down again if it came to nothing. Emotions were always up and down. I really have my family and friends to thank for keeping me sane during that period and especially the dogs. Mentioning adoption, now that's another story.

Chapter 5

Adoption option

Adoption was something that had always crossed my mind, even when recovering from cervical cancer. Deep down, I felt I might have to explore it at some stage. But I suppose I saw it as a last resort. After the IVF setback, I questioned why I should put myself at risk when there were so many children in dire need of a good home. The fact that the child would not be biologically ours did not matter. I wouldn't think any less of the child whatsoever. Once a child was handed to me, I would consider it my own and that was it. Gradually, Niall and I both came to that conclusion, though he was sort of against it at first. He didn't want to talk about adoption at all. But then when the IVF wasn't working out, we registered our names anyway with the Health Service Executive (HSE) for intercountry adoption.

It's funny because I imagined a completely different process. There was no initial interview as such. I just phoned the office and asked for the application form, which was duly sent out. At that stage just our birth and marriage certificates were required, no detailed medical history or social circumstances. By then, I guess I was very excited. I could feel my spirits lifting and hope was most definitely in the air again. A letter soon followed issuing us with a registration number and informing us that we were on a panel and required to wait for assessment – at least twenty to twenty-two months by their reckoning. However, I did not realise it would take years before we would hear from them again. Boy, did we wait. I could ring them up every week or every year and still be told that it could be another two years or more of a wait. There were literally thousands on the list. This was partly because the catchment area for the HSE office at Dartmouth House where we registered was the highly populated counties of Dublin, Kildare and Wicklow. A good friend of mine saw sense and moved herself and her husband to County Meath and registered there.

After five long years, our number finally came up. In hindsight, I would have put my name down much earlier, but you are not supposed to be pursuing any form of fertility treatment whatsoever when you register. Later when you are assessed by social workers, if they get wind of any ongoing treatment, you are promptly taken off the list. Which is ridiculous because how can you sit there for several years and do nothing? Perhaps they thought the long wait helps couples to adapt and ready themselves for adoption, but I'm not so sure about that. I suppose we had expected to be interviewed at the very start and given an opportunity to discuss what was involved. In retrospect, if there had been a preliminary meeting, the HSE might have assessed our suitability or otherwise earlier and not wasted so much time.

Nonetheless, I was exuberant in late Spring 2009 when the letter arrived saying we must be available to attend a course of lectures over the following six months. True to form, Niall took it all in his stride and was glad for me that something was finally happening. This preparation course on inter-country adoption was compulsory, along with a home study and assessment by social workers, before a declaration of parentage could be issued by the Irish Adoption Board. This was the vital legal document that every would-be adoptive parent needed for approaching adoption agencies.

From an administrative point of view we had to be vetted medically, socially, financially, legally, you name it. Everything about our lives was scrutinised as we expected it would be. We had to submit birth and marriage certificates, certificates of earnings and financial statements, as well as sign consent forms for child protection/health board area clearance and for postplacement visits and reports. Not to mention completing Garda enquiry forms, notification forms for foreign police clearance, two referees, and of course a medical report and consent forms to obtain medical and fertility reports (in my case) from specialists. As it turned out the adoption process took so long that by the time the assessment came around many of the documents were out of date. So we had to resubmit Garda enquiry forms twice and all the other forms and certificates again. Needless to say, I knew my medical forms would be a big rigmarole. Both Dr Gleeson and my GP were very supportive of us exploring adoption, though Dr Gleeson had some reservations. Perhaps she had not completely ruled out assisted reproductive techniques for me.

'Are you sure this is the road you want to go down?' she asked as she filled in the form during one check-up.

I sighed and shrugged my shoulders.

'Well, I'm running out of choices.'

Not surprisingly, with the word cancer on my medical form, the HSE had cause for concern. Later they wrote to Dr Gleeson separately requesting more details. Maybe they wanted to check my chances of long-term survival or that I was at least ten years free from cancer. It gave rise to a slight panicky feeling on my part. I even joked with Dr Gleeson that if she said I was investigated for anything else, I'll probably be put in an even bigger pile. Unlike IVF, there were no fees involved when applying for adoption. However, we both needed full medicals at a cost of €120 each. Luckily, we could go to our own GPs and not someone nominated by the HSE.

***

The sessions were held during a weekday, usually Friday, from 9AM to 5PM, and involved six sessions over a period of six months or so. We were given the dates to commit to in advance. Having to take time off work proved difficult, especially for Niall trying to run his own business, but he moved heaven and earth to be there each week. The venue, Dartmouth House, was fairly easy to find on Kylemore Road in Ballyfermot: a long, low two-storey building in grey and white with wide windows and flanked by a row of young sycamore trees on the street. On the first day, about eight couples turned up, as well as a woman on her own going for a single adoption. The couples came from all walks of life and with a variety of infertility stories. In our early to mid-thirties, Niall and I were the youngest of the people there. Most were in their late forties while one man was much older and on his second marriage. At first, as we gathered in the room no one spoke. Absolute silence reigned. It was torturous. So being the chatterbox I am, I broke the ice and started talking.

Shortly afterwards the facilitator from the Irish Adoption Board, as it was called at the time, entered the room. From the start, she set the tone: no pleasantries, just an authoritarian, laying-down-the-law kind of manner. Attendance was compulsory and pretty soon we learnt there was no leeway or excuses tolerated. Full commitment was required or else there would be consequences. Straightaway it felt like school, though we were grown adults. The first thing we had to do was write down some details about ourselves and pass them to the person beside us for discussion. The atmosphere was so tense you could cut it with a knife. It was not what we were expecting at all. None of us felt relaxed or comfortable enough to talk about ourselves so the discussion was rather stilted.

To our dismay we also learnt that another long wait was ahead. The assessment process could take months and months, if not a year to complete. And after that if we were lucky to be approved by the placement committee and get a declaration of parentage from the Irish Adoption Board, it was up to us to contact the various adoption agencies, which would take more time, if not years. I could sense all the couples were taken aback at those timeframes. And the excitement we had felt on entering the building was soon replaced by crestfallen faces.

Much as we tried to appreciate the preparation course and keep an open mind, it was a nightmare for Niall and me. On the positive side, it did provide us with a lot of information on the adoption process, on how to choose a country and what we might face as adoptive parents. It opened our eyes in many ways. We got to think deeply about how to protect and nurture a child as would-be adoptive parents by having a care plan in place. All these positives, however, were overshadowed by the teaching methods and attitude of the staff.

There was no let-up in the school-like format of the sessions. Week after week, we were given buckets of reading material and paperwork to digest, articles from magazines and newspapers on adoption stories and the like. We were on constant media watch. The course also involved workshops and homework, having been issued with workbooks to record our thoughts and reflections on various topics and activities, as well as feedback from the sessions. These had to be handed up at the end of the course so the social workers could assess our suitability as would-be adoptive parents. We ended up writing on absolutely everything, from bonding to loss and countless other topics. Gosh, we nearly wrote a book on the stuff. I had no problem with all this, except our views were always challenged by standard textbook answers. It soon became apparent that there was little or no room for our own personal opinions. It was like doing the Leaving Cert all over again yet there were only 'right' answers, no room for interpretation. Niall and I spent weeks and weeks labouring over these assignments. If you left a question blank or wrote 'I don't know', it was unacceptable. For example, we were asked what things are taboo in the country we are thinking of adopting from. There was just no leeway.

Perhaps other couples had less scruples and just gave the course organisers the answers they wanted to hear, shielding their real views. If being less than truthful got you a declaration of parentage, what was the harm? But Niall and I struggled with this. We wanted to be honest but at the same time ran the risk of failing the course. If we were totally honest, our views would make us stand out as being different and perhaps not model parents. I was bewildered by some questions: 'What have you done in your life that has prepared you for adoption?' It just sounded absurd to me. Finally, deciding to be pragmatic and not rock the boat, we toned down our comments. Sometimes we had to make up an answer just to fit the question. And always we had to provide examples.

So that meant we kept repeating ourselves, but we especially made sure all our answers matched the original material. By the end of the course, Niall had completed the workbook and writing assignments but was far from happy when he handed them in.

'I've done it the way you've wanted me to do it,' he told the facilitator, 'but it's not the way I would have done it.'

In hindsight, surely there must have been a better way than that.

One of the tasks in the workshops was to compile family trees and ecomaps – a map of the connection between you, your family and your community. Admittedly, these tasks did help us look at our own personal history, especially relationships within the family, to better equip us for being adoptive parents. But sometimes when we were exploring the bonds of attachment, we felt the staff were hanging on to some old-fashioned and outdated views.

My most abiding memory, in this regard, is the black and white video of a boy called John. The purpose of the video was to make us reflect on attachment and bonding issues and how they could be seriously affected when a child, who already enjoyed a secure relationship with his parents, was separated from them. So it was with some anticipation that we watched it – finally we would learn who this John character was. As it turned out we found the experience rather disturbing. No one wants to see a young child so distressed after being wrenched from his parents.

***

To be honest, the preparation course was difficult for Niall as he had a lot of work commitments. In fact, the course coincided with the construction of the Luas Citywest extension, for which he was contracted to do maintenance work. It was a hectic period as there was intense pressure to complete the project on time, given previous overruns on other sections of the Luas. He was practically working day and night and had already been late for one of the sessions. His lateness and struggling to keep awake that day had not gone unnoticed. He was sternly warned not to miss any session.

The night before the third session, Niall was called in to work because there had been an accident underground. Twelve hours later the problem had not been rectified and he was up to his knees in water. Early the next morning he rang me. By now I was panicking, wondering where he was, as I was ready to drive to the course. However, there was no way he could down tools and leave mid-job.

'Niall, we'll be thrown off the course if we're late or don't show up.'

'Honestly, I'm not going to make it,' he said, the tiredness evident in his voice. 'Go on your own, Caroline, and explain the situation. It's better if you go.'

And so with great trepidation I attended the course. Making my way into the building, my heart was pounding worse than being summonsed to a head-master's office. Before the session began, I approached the facilitator to explain the situation.

'Where's Niall?' she demanded loudly, catching sight of me on my own. There was no mistaking her extreme annoyance.

'He's had to work. He's going to try and come later,' I explained.

'You just sit there for a moment,' she said crossly, pointing to a chair in the reception area. 'I have to go to my supervisor now and check if we're going to let you proceed with the course at all.'

My worst fears were materialising. I was left sitting at reception in full view of the other couples, many of whom had overheard the conversation. One couple, seeing that I was getting upset, sympathised with me.

'This course is unreal,' they said, shaking their heads in disbelief.

'She caught me on the right day,' I wailed. 'I just can't put up with all this anymore.'

The couple nodded. In fact, most couples were thinking the same thing but afraid to say so. Most had grown sick and tired of the attitude of the staff. As the couples trouped into the room, I was left alone, wondering what was in store for Niall and me. Before long, the facilitator reappeared.

'You can come into the room for now,' she began, 'but I'm speaking to my supervisor at the break, so I don't know if you'll be allowed here in the afternoon.'

Before I could speak in my defence, she raised her hand dismissively.

'We'll probably have to put you back to the end of the prep course list.'

I gasped. That day, sitting in the room with the other couples, my mind was a blur; I was barely able to concentrate or even listen to the facilitator. Everything went in one ear and out the next. At lunch break, I rang Niall, still struggling to fix the pumps at work, and got upset once more.

'Oh Niall, what are we going to do?'

During lunchtime the facilitator came over to speak to me. She had discussed it with her supervisor but they had not decided whether we should proceed with the course or not. But one thing had been decided. Niall and I needed to be there the following morning, when our case would be adjudicated upon. As instructed, we turned up the next day to plead our case. The facilitator was joined by the course manager, who was equally unforgiving and unapproachable. We felt like the accused in a criminal trial waiting to be sentenced to prison.

'Right, I want to speak to you first, Niall,' the course manager began. 'Explain where you were yesterday.'

'Well, I was called in, there had been an accident,' replied Niall. 'I had to fix this pump and that pump . . .'

As Niall went on to describe the emergency situation, he was cut dead.

'I'm not interested in that, Niall,' she interrupted. 'Let's put it this way. Your job came before the course.'

'Look, what do you want me to say,' he pleaded. 'You're saying I have to go out and earn a living. Well, I work for myself. So I would've lost the contract on the Luas if I didn't go out and do the job.'

'That job came first,' insisted the manager, considering Niall's behaviour to be totally unacceptable. 'So if you had a baby in the house and your job called you out and if Caroline had to go out, are you going to leave the baby in the cot on its own? Is that what you're telling us?'

'Well, I'm hardly going to do that now,' Niall answered. 'I'd have to . . .'

'You'd have to make provisions, Niall,' she answered quickly. 'There you go. You should've made provisions and been here yesterday.'

Niall sighed in exasperation. I could feel the anger rising within me and struggled to stay calm. What they were saying was totally ridiculous. They seemed to have no concept of the demands of work in the real world. There was no give, no leeway at all. After much deliberation, our punishment was decided on: probation. We were put on probation for the rest of the course and left wondering if the home visits with the social worker and their assessments would go ahead. If not, we might not get a declaration of parentage. We also had to do the particular session that Niall had missed, but on our own.

As I left the building, I was still angry and, to be honest, did not feel like returning. The manner in which we had been spoken to had been unpleasant and upsetting. My emotions were all topsy turvey. It was very hard on Niall, forcing him along to everything, seeing that I was the one who was mainly pursing adoption. But I knew we had to persist, I was no quitter. My yearning for a child had not abated one little bit. I just hoped it would all work out for the best in the end. Later as I confided in a friend, who had applied for adoption at the same time as us, she roared with laughter. The idea of probation was the most bizarre thing she had heard in a long time.

The course was indeed proving to be very challenging. Of course we understood the need to be fully informed when adopting a child and not naïve and unprepared, but shock tactics seemed to be deployed at every hand's turn. Were they really trying to turn us off? Were they separating the wheat from the chaff, the men from the boys? During the course, some couples were told out straight to lose weight, others their medical condition was not acceptable, while others again that their financial situation was not good enough. Because of my illness I was questioned at length about my medical condition and how I had coped with it. Both Niall and I were asked to do a loss graph and explain a time when we felt sadness and hurt and to rate this grief. With the graphs, you draw a timeline from the year you were born and then record your own losses and how you dealt with them over the years. It took me weeks to work on the graph and look at it from every angle. And then I was requested to do it again because I had not taken the cancer sufficiently into account. On the other hand, Niall refused to do a loss graph.

'Well, thankfully, I didn't experience any loss in my life,' he explained to the facilitator.

Suffice to say, this didn't go down too well.

'But you have got a loss,' the facilitator insisted.

'No, I don't,' Niall repeated.

'But you do.'

This argument went on and on. Finally, Niall was forced to back down and supply a graph as it was a course requirement, but very little direction was given to him.

During the course, much time was given over to the type of child we wanted to adopt. However, with so few Irish adoptions taking place, the reality was that we would have to look overseas. Like every parent, we wished for a healthy child. Even though health was our preference, we were aware that problems could arise if not initially then as the child got older. Certainly the fact that many of these children might need special medical help and support was driven home during the course. We had to think very carefully about the country that we planned to adopt from because of different health risks associated with different countries. If the child was coming from a Romanian or Russian orphanage, for example, chances were they would have some health issues. But aside from that, the child's nationality, race and colour were not an issue whatsoever for Niall and me. We considered the topic from every aspect. In one exercise, there were fifty questions to answer about the country and culture you were considering adopting from – everything from its politicians and national pastimes to attitudes to gambling and social taboos. This helped us to focus on valuing the child's original nationality and culture, and the effect of them living in Ireland.

Soon afterwards we were asked for our country preference, but to be honest at that stage we were only starting to look into the matter. We actually hadn't decided on any one country in particular. At first we suggested America, seeing that it was English-speaking and a popular place.

'Well, we were looking at America.'

'Oh, that won't be happening,' the facilitator snapped, 'because in America you won't get back home to Ireland. You won't get in with a child. There are too many backhanders going on. We wouldn't recommend going there.'

That shut us up so she probed further.

'Why wouldn't you go to Russia?'

'Well, if you want my honest answer, I personally don't want to go to Russia,' I said. 'My GP has seen Russian babies here with severe medical problems.'

It was true. I had nothing against Russian children, but from discussions with my GP, the issue of them often having significant health problems was brought to my attention.

'Why wouldn't you take a child with medical problems?'

This issue harked back to a form we had to fill in asking would you take a child with medical problems. We had been given a list of diseases and illnesses to focus our minds. It started off mild with conditions like hard of hearing and then moved on to HIV, full blown AIDS, physical handicaps, all those sorts of things. A very nice woman, who had adopted a sick child from Ethiopia, was also brought in to talk to us. She relayed a horrific story of how her child had nearly died on the plane coming home and afterwards had spent three months receiving medical attention in an Irish hospital. This story and others we heard had a powerful effect on us.

'I'm being honest,' I told the facilitator. 'It's not that I want the perfect child but I don't want to set myself up when I personally know I couldn't cope with a child that has HIV.'

'Why is that?'

I said nothing. Sometimes there were just no answers.

'Would you not consider India, Mexico or Vietnam?'

We hesitated, not sure how to respond. As it subsequently turned out some of those countries ended up being closed to adoption because of fraudulent adoptions taking place there and concerns for the welfare of children. Many parents after receiving their declaration of parentage in Ireland had applied there in good faith, but it was too late.

Other times it felt like they were deliberately trying to trip us up, challenge us. I can understand them trying to get us out of our comfort zone, but it was done not in a supportive way but very provocatively. Yes, deciding on which country was hard going. We obviously got a black mark for suggesting America.

There was a lot of emphasis too on telling the child about adoption from an early age. Too much really, I thought. They advised you to tell your child all about the country they came from and also to celebrate birthdays and adoption days. We fully understood that a child needs to be aware of his or her background and culture from an early age, but the staff were putting too much pressure on the child's past and not enough on their future.

Like many on the course, including about three people who were actual adoptees, Niall did not agree with this view and thought it ludicrous. He was trying to put himself in the shoes of someone who had been adopted, especially those encountered in his own childhood. All that constant harping on about being adopted, he felt, would not be beneficial to the child. It just reinforced that they were different, when all they wanted was to be like everyone else.

Later we got the views of friends and acquaintances who had themselves been adopted. Granted they were all Irish, but they found the message negative and a bit horrifying, especially drumming the word adoption into the child every day. Perhaps it's now part of modern thinking or research to tell the child early on but how comfortable are parents with that constant reinforcement in practice?

Again, because of the oppressive atmosphere, I felt you could not be too vocal and critical in your views, especially in front of the facilitator and other speakers. Otherwise, you might be thrown off the course.

Finally the preparation course and our probation came to an end and the next phase began – the home study and assessment by the social worker. This lady came to visit our house about three times over a period of six to eight months in order to do a report. The three visits were very helpful in the main. Though the process was difficult and intrusive, looking all around our home and asking about financial details again, work plans, childcare plans and so on, it was made easier by the fact that she was a lovely young woman. Her manner was helpful and she informed us exactly what was involved. One of her tasks was to interview the referees whose names we had supplied to the adoption board. The first referee, Mary, I had known for many years, having worked together at Meteor Mobile, and she was a good friend. Another referee, Deirdre, was a nurse and friend who lived next door. These two referees were contacted by the board but only one couple, Mary and her husband John, were interviewed by the social worker in their home. It was a fairly intensive affair, lasting three hours and the couple were plied with detailed questions about us. It must have felt like a Garda interrogation.

Unlike the course leaders, the social worker was not judgemental without knowing us personally. In fact, she was far more in tune with the adoption process and we could be really honest with her. Her visits gave us an opportunity to vent our frustrations and pent-up emotions about the writing assignments and workbooks. We felt like we were being shoehorned into neat little boxes. And if we didn't fit in a box, they didn't know what to do with us. It probably meant we weren't suitable to be adoptive parents by their standards.

The social worker admitted that the course leaders did not know what to make of Niall. He was so black and white, he couldn't fit in a box. To me, Niall is just a totally honest person who has no time for bullshit. I suppose I felt there was no such thing as perfect parents, so there had to be some flexibility if we didn't fit into tidy little boxes. Life was not perfect.

It sounded like the social worker had heard it all before and, not surprisingly she left the adoption service shortly afterwards. She nodded her head in agreement and kept repeating 'I know' at our grievances. She admitted that it was literally a case of ticking the right boxes; personal views were something not taken on board. She even confided that the preparation course could do with some updating.

'Of course we would like to give you a child,' she said sympathetically. 'I would tomorrow if I could. But it's just ticking boxes.'

At that time, it was decided that the course participants had to supply all their documents a second time – birth and marriage certificates, Garda Clearance, medical assessments, financial statements. It meant paying €120 again for my medical history. Even though nothing had changed and we would be supplying duplicates, they told us they wanted them nonetheless. Being self-employed, it had taken Niall a very long time to provide his financial details in the first place. They certainly were not something he could easily run up overnight.

After we had sent in all the documents, I had some unexpected bad news. My job as a receptionist in Citywest came to an end. So it was with a heart and a half that I relayed the news to the course leaders.

'This changes everything now,' they said. 'You have lost an income. We'll need all financial reports sent in again because now we don't know if you'll be able to financially support a child.'

I groaned internally.

'How will you cope because now you have lost an income?'

I couldn't believe it because we weren't actually in the process of adopting someone. All we were looking for was a declaration of parentage. I knew that I would find a job soon again, as I had never once been out of work since leaving school. But there were other things that had not met their approval.

'There's still a lot of things we're not that happy with here,' the course manager said. 'We're still not sure if you and Niall have coped with loss very well. We don't feel you opened up enough and we're afraid that if you can't speak about it, how can you speak to a child about it?'

As far as they were concerned, we required a lot more work. A few weeks later we were called in again for a meeting. There were still ongoing issues with us deciding on a country for adoption; they weren't happy that we had picked America. Weeks before I had started emailing a few adoption agencies in America, just to get a feel for things and find out what the process was like. But obviously they would only deal with us if we got our declaration of parentage from Ireland first.

'I also need you to come back with financial statements,' the course manager said.

'I'm starting a new job,' I quickly informed her.

'Maybe . . .'

At hearing the word 'maybe' I knew she was going to suggest something that would bring more and more hurdles.

'Listen, let's postpone this for six months,' I added swiftly.

'What?' said Niall, surprised. He had no idea I was going to say that. But I knew by his face that he wasn't unhappy at the decision either.

'You know, let's postpone the whole thing for six months,' I repeated.

'Well, I wasn't actually going to say that,' said the course manager.

'But I'm saying it now,' I said. 'Financially, maybe we're not ready.'

She had threatened us with that argument for so long, it was my defence now.

'Okay, so that's definitely what you want to do?'

'Well,' I said, 'it's what we both want to do.'

Our case never got as far as the placement committee – no one adjudicated our case and deemed whether we were worthy of a declaration of parentage or not. I could not take any more as I felt our dignity and self-respect were being eroded at every opportunity. The constant prodding and poking at us had taken its toll.

Our experience of the adoption process was disappointing. I still felt that we would have made good parents but the system seemed stacked against us or else we were unlucky in our choice of HSE office. We knew it wasn't just our fault. Other couples on the course, whom we met away from Dartmouth House, all had similar views about the course. It put huge pressure on their relationships too. In fact, there was only one person from our group who eventually got the declaration of parentage. Most couples had dropped out because of the way the course was conducted and one nearly split up; the process had been so traumatic and had caused such severe tension at home that the husband did not want to go through it anymore.

The story of our baby, Ava began just a few weeks after we abandoned the adoption course. Little did we think that a TG4 documentary would change our lives forever. It truly was a turning point and probably gave us the very best value ever for our TV licence.

Chapter 6

'Yes, we can help.'
Dr Patel's fertility clinic

I can still remember the night so clearly. It was a frosty, foggy one on 18 February 2010 and I had just arrived home from visiting my friend Sharon, having chatted beside a lovely cosy open fire. It was near 11 o'clock and Niall had gone to bed. I switched on the television in the bedroom for what I thought would be a quick telly fix before going to sleep. As I flicked through the channels, with the sound down low so as not to disturb Niall, a TG4 documentary in Irish called *Páistí Ginte san Ind* caught my attention. Before long I was utterly engrossed in the programme. It featured an Indian doctor called Dr Nayna Patel, who was the medical director of Akanksha Infertility Clinic in Anand in the province of Gujarat, in northern India. Since surrogacy was declared legal by the Indian government in 2003, the clinic had offered surrogacy services as a way of giving babies to infertile couples and was now internationally recognised. Everything about the clinic seemed positive and professional, while the surrogate women were well cared for and treated with respect.

I remember lying in bed as the programme went on and suddenly this feeling overcame me – here I was in Ireland watching a programme about surrogacy in India and I knew in my heart and soul that this was for me, that I was going to contact Dr Patel. In a strange kind of way, I felt closer to reaching our dream of having a child than the previous day. It was like a bridge had opened up before us, after spending years stranded on one side we could now safely cross to the other side.

That very night I emailed Dr Patel and told her about my fight with cancer and how I longed so much for a child. To my surprise, my friend Sharon had coincidentally watched the programme as well and rang me the next day, thinking this could be a golden opportunity. A few days later I received an email from Dr Patel saying 'Yes, we can help'. Those words stood out like a beacon the minute I opened the email. For the first time in my life there was someone who could genuinely help us. However, she did draw our attention to the legal end of things. We would have to find out the legal position of surrogacy in Ireland and the implications of bringing a surrogate baby into the country. Later I learnt that only one other Irish couple had attended Dr Patel's clinic but for reasons of patient confidentiality we could not contact them.

Until I saw the documentary about Dr Patel, it hadn't dawned on me and Niall that surrogacy could be a real possibility for us. Naturally, we were no strangers to surrogacy. I had heard of the word before but, I suppose like many people, I had fears about surrogacy; certainly the media had depicted it as the exploitation of women, the rent-a-womb scandal. During the adoption course, it had come up in conversation among the couples when chitchatting. But the only country mentioned at that stage was America and there were huge costs involved there. One couple had stated US$250,000. My immediate thought was who on earth can afford that. Niall had read about one Irish couple who did go to America for a surrogate baby. They financed it by getting a loan from a financial institution for a house extension, or rather that was cited on the paperwork.

The previous year when we had been emailing US adoption agencies, they had asked had we considered surrogacy. When I enquired about the cost, again it was phenomenal money. We received prices from US$100,000 in Boston and almost US$300,000 in Florida. One agency told me I could come in and they would show me profiles. *You can pick the colour of the hair and of the eyes.* I balked a bit at that. It was like making a doll. Nonetheless when reading the email, I felt so desperate.

'Okay, but I wouldn't be entering into all that,' I found myself replying.

And I left it at that. Then one day out of the blue I got an email from an American woman living in Florida that I had emailed the previous year about adoption. *Just thought I'd drop you a quick email. I remember your email where you told me you had been sick. There's a little boy going to be born in March. I thought I'd give you first refusal.*

I could feel the shockwaves surging through me. It was like she was selling a parcel. In the little boy's case, the intended parents had got divorced or separated and wouldn't be in a position to accept the surrogate baby. The boy would be put up for adoption in March after his birth. *But if you would like to have it, can you forward US$70,000.* The sense that they were 'selling' the baby grew stronger. My mind was racing, everything turned upside down. On the one hand I was saying, 'Oh my God I could have this baby' but on the other, I was rather horrified. Straightaway, I rang my dad for advice.

'Oh my God, what will I do?' I pleaded.

'Caroline, if it was genuine, I would sell my house . . . you know, if I thought it would make you happy,' he said. 'But read that email again, someone is actually flogging that child.'

He was right of course. And then you turn your attention to the child and think about his plight. God help the little boy, where will he end up? But the transaction seemed so easy, all for a down payment of US$70,000. As simple as buying a car. It would be comical if it wasn't so serious.

After seeing Dr Patel on television, I was in the right frame of mind for surrogacy. I was ready for it. I was giving it serious consideration. I suppose I was aware that surrogacy was sort of permitted in Ireland, but the scenario was that the surrogate mother was the legal mother and her husband the legal father and that no money was allowed to exchange hands. In that case Niall and I would then have to adopt the child. I presumed we would need a declaration of parentage for that to happen and we certainly did not have that.

***

As soon as Dr Patel had accepted our case, over the following months, I researched every aspect of surrogacy in India. I tried to get as much information as possible online. I looked up many different Indian clinics and read through mountains of pros and cons on different practices. Given the lack of legislation on surrogacy in Ireland, we really tried to do our homework in terms of what Irish couples had experienced. Initially, when I went on the internet there was practically zilch information on surrogacy from an Irish perspective. Websites like *www.rollercoaster.ie* were useful for infertility issues, even for stuff on adoption, but no good in the way of providing information on surrogacy at the time. I was in touch with so many women. When I got responses, I rang the people recommended in emails, blogs or chatrooms. But there was no joy, nobody had any information on surrogacy. Much later I received emails from other women who had started to look into surrogacy in 2009 and they forwarded on relevant emails, especially those sent to the Passport Office. So we knew what kind of responses to expect from it. Some women were considering Ukraine and Eastern European countries but India was becoming more and more popular.

Dr Patel never mentioned any specific cases of surrogacy at the clinic. When chatting to her over emails, however, she did send me a list of references from people who had attended the clinic. Obviously, she tried to connect people near enough geographically. The nearest couples to me were in the UK. I emailed two different ones, enquiring about their experience of Dr Patel's clinic. Both were very frank and straightforward. They had no complaints about the clinic but their biggest problem was getting back home due to bureaucracy. Surrogacy in the UK is legal, though not commercial surrogacy and there are very stringent guidelines attached to it. Like in Ireland, the surrogate mother is recognised as the legal mother. One girl told me it took them a long time to process their application; they were stranded in Anand for up to three months while the British High Commission in Delhi dealt with their paperwork.

The global support forum on Dr Patel's website soon became my lifeline. I was on it morning, noon and night. It helped because I could speak to people from all over the world who were going or had gone on the same journey as us. By April 2010, I was also in touch with another big clinic in India called Surrogacy India. I figured it made sense to research as many clinics as possible just to put things into perspective. Whenever I needed information, I posted a number of comments on the Surrogacy India website. On their forums and blogs, you could read about surrogate mothers, IVF, donors, the surrogacy process, everything possibly related to the different types of surrogacy.

I had my doubts about some organisations that offered surrogacy services in India. There was nothing but bad reports about one in particular. From one intended mother I learnt that the organisation offers you a kind of 'package'. They tell you not to worry, as they will have someone to meet you at the airport and bring you to your hotel, etc.. You think this sounds great because you are going over to a country where nobody knows you and vice versa. Even I was wondering why Dr Patel did not provide this service. However, this particular woman's surrogacy was not successful in the end. She told me that it all appeared impressive at first and there were flowers and all sorts of niceties in her room but that the doctors literally scanned their website every day and looked at the comments posted. If you were posting lovely complimentary messages every day, then you would get the best of everything, the four-star treatment. But if you stayed a bit dormant online, you seemed to be treated differently. Amazing really, it was almost like you were expected to publicise the clinic and, if not, it could affect your care. A sale tactic in the commercial world of surrogacy! The same organisation kept emailing me if I had not posted a comment in a while. They would send a message asking have you not made your decision yet, whereas I could never imagine Dr Patel doing that. She never forced us to come to a decision or put pressure on us in any way.

There is no doubt that some Indian surrogacy organisations will apply extreme pressure, once you have registered with them, to accept their services.

I always remember Niall's vivid description of the sales pitch process.

'Say you're on holidays in the Canary Islands, for example. You come out of a restaurant and you don't know where to go, so you turn left. Then you walk past a gang of idiots trying to give you concessions into a nightclub; you say no but you walk back past them two minutes later and they try it again. They keep going back and forth and harassing you.'

From another forum, I learnt that one woman in particular was not happy with Dr Patel's set-up. She had paid Dr Patel a visit at her clinic in Anand, Gujarat and did not approve of the hygiene there. Her main gripe was that the examination couch did not have disposable sheets but blankets. I didn't see this as a problem – there was a time when the same could be said of Irish hospitals and not in the distant past either. Even so, Dr Patel stood out from all the other clinics for a number of reasons. First, I felt I was in safe hands given my medical history. She sets out strict criteria for the intended or commissioning parents and the surrogate mother, whereas other clinics will accept almost any couple or single person as an intended parent(s). In particular, she only helps couples that have a medical need for surrogacy treatments. Neither designer babies nor sex determination are permitted. Indeed, in India it is illegal to tell parents the sex of the child for fear of female infanticide.

Following the embryo transfer, the surrogate mother stays in Dr Patel's clinic for a period of fifteen days; this is to ensure the well-being of the surrogate mother and also to monitor the development of the embryo. The health and well-being of the surrogate mother are paramount at all stages. Another factor that stood out for us is that the surrogate mothers live under Dr Patel's care for the duration of their pregnancy. On the sixteenth day, provided both surrogate and embryo are in a healthy state, the surrogate mother is moved to the surrogate house. The surrogate house is operated by the clinic and the surrogate mother remains in the house until she gives birth. During her stay at the house she can learn new skills and be educated if she wishes. For Niall, the surrogate house was also a leading factor in our decision, as the surrogate could have 24/7 medical attention if required, regular health checks and monitoring, and a balanced healthy diet. In fact, everything needed for the development of a strong and healthy baby.

Niall had done a fair bit of research on surrogate mothers. In fact, it annoyed him when people talked about all surrogate mothers being exploited in India. If anything, their health was protected in India, judging by what happened in Dr Patel's clinic. In America and elsewhere there was no way of ensuring that the surrogate mother would lead a healthy lifestyle. She could drink or smoke or take drugs unchecked for nine months if she desired. There was no way of knowing what exactly was going on. Niall used to say they could be bungee jumping for all we knew. Whereas in India, with the mothers living in the surrogate house, you're guaranteed that the surrogate's health will be monitored – and the child will be healthier. In terms of financial exploitation, I had heard that some surrogates in other clinics or agencies in India are exploited in that they may not receive the amount of money agreed in their contracts. But that doesn't happen at Dr Patel's clinic.

As time went on, Niall certainly became more and more convinced that surrogacy was the answer. From his point of view, it was a quicker process. Once you signed the agreement, it took about eleven months for surrogacy, whereas with adoption it was six to eight years from initial acceptance to the issuing of the required declarations. The eleven months allowed for one month for preparation, travel and legal affairs, nine months from the time of embryo implantation to the birth of the child and one month for domestic legal affairs and travel documents from the Irish authorities, all going well. Adoption costs were certainly more expensive if you went abroad.

Both our families listened as we went through all the pros and cons and showed us great support. None of them expressed disapproval; they knew the heartbreak and disappointment we had experienced. They were as eager and nervous as we were. Even Philip had come around and felt we were doing the right thing.

***

Meanwhile the preparations with Dr Patel were continuing apace. I had sent on my medical records from Dr Gleeson, after seeking her advice first.

Luckily, she could not have been more encouraging. In fact, both my GP and Dr Gleeson were very supportive about surrogacy in India. Knowing the trials and tribulations I had been through, they told me to 'just go'. Everything looked above board: Dr Patel was a highly qualified consultant gynaecologist and obstetrician, who had excelled at MP Shah Medical College in Jamnagar, Gujarat, and passed her MBBS and MD medical degrees with five gold medals. In 1996, she attended IVF workshops at the National University of Singapore and subsequently received extensive training for ART techniques in US, South Korean, and UK centres of excellence.

I had also written to the HARI Unit requesting them to forward on my medical details to Dr Patel, but unfortunately they never replied. This was probably understandable, as I later learnt from their receptionist that because surrogacy was not legally recognised in Ireland, the unit did not get involved in the process. However, there was no problem for Niall paying for semen analysis there. The results of blood tests done at the Coombe, mainly checking my blood count, hormone levels and a viral screen, were also sent on to Dr Patel. This included a HIV test, which was standard practice.

An opportunity to meet Dr Patel in person presented itself in June 2010 when she was coming to London for consultations. Now that the surrogacy was under serious consideration, we set about organising our finances and saving money. I didn't know how long it would take us to raise the amounts required. My father would always laugh at what he called my daughter and dad act.

'We're starting to save again,' I told him as I prepared to meet Dr Patel in London.

'There's no point saving, just do it,' he urged.

I hugged him, thinking how blessed I am to have such a great parent. I am eternally grateful to him for helping us out and so lucky he was in a position to do so.

'Conned again,' he would say, highly amused.

So I needed no encouragement to book a flight to London as quickly as possible. By this stage, Dr Patel was in possession of all my medical details and the results of all the health screenings. The consultation took place in a private house in Harrow, a large suburb in northwest London and home to a large Indian community. The Victorian red-bricked terraced house belonged to a couple who had a baby through surrogacy in Dr Patel's clinic several years before. As a token of their appreciation, they invited her to visit them yearly and 'sit' in their house. In effect, it was an open house for anyone interested in surrogacy, though admittedly it was mostly Indian couples that frequented it. It was a very informal consultation and free; no money changed hands.

I flew over at the crack of dawn and was collected by Bina at Gatwick Airport. Our appointment was for about 10 o'clock but we made it to the house earlier than that. It was a daunting prospect, arriving at the home of a total stranger, but thrilling too.

'We're going into this with an open mind,' I declared to Bina, as we pulled up outside.

She nodded. With her own background in pharmacy and her brother Kartik a paediatrician, she was much more scientific in her approach than I was. You could say I was walking on air with excitement. However, Bina was on a mission; keen to ask her questions – A, B, C – and not leave until they were answered to her satisfaction. It was almost like a good cop/bad cop routine: she sussing out the doctor and on the lookout for any loopholes or discrepancies, while I just wanted to feel I could trust Dr Patel and that everything would be alright. It was as simple as that. And with Bina's Indian background – she's a Kenyan Indian – it helped no end. Without her I would have been lost; it was just brilliant to have her there.

On the doorstep, as we rang the doorbell, I spotted a shoe rack stuffed with about thirty pairs of shoes, a typical Indian custom. Once the door opened, Bina greeted the family in Gujarati – the language native to the state of Gujarat – which eased any tension I might have experienced. The wife, who acted like a facilitator, made us feel at home immediately. Inside, the set-up was priceless; there were no half measures, as typically Indian as a

Bollywood film. A statue of Ganesh, with his distinctive elephant head, inhabited one corner and reigned over the proceedings.

Despite the early hour, the small house was packed to the rafters with Indian couples casually dressed, all just wanting to meet Dr Patel or catch a glimpse of her like a guru from the east. Couples who had successful surrogacy births at her clinic also came along with their prized babies in tow, eager to get photographed with her. Funnily enough, babies were the last thing I expected to see. The open day ran from about 9AM to 5PM. As it happened, I was the only non-Indian woman in the house but never once felt like an outsider. We were first led along a narrow hallway to the kitchen. In the kitchen and conservatory leading from it, bowls of food and jugs of fruit juices – orange, mango, all sorts loved by Indians – were laid out in the best banqueting style. In the middle of a coffee table was a little ceramic pot with a handle. An attached note requested a small donation for any food or drink consumed. I laughed and whispered to Bina that back in Ireland the pot would probably be robbed! It being a warm sunny day more couples were outside in the garden making the most of the weather.

The lady of the house was a perfect host and eager to make us comfortable and quench our thirst as the day was quite hot. While we waited our turn, there was a lively buzz of conversation. Couples were very open, recounting their experiences, whether before or after surrogacy. I got chatting to an African gentleman, sitting beside me in the conservatory, the only other non-Indian person in the house. He had come without his wife as she was unsure about the process but they were desperate to have a family. Everything about him was nervy, his voice quaked and his hands trembled.

'I'm so nervous going to meet Dr Patel,' he confided.

But at the same time he was really pleased to be there and, like us, had great hope in his heart.

Finally, it was our turn to meet Dr Patel, installed in the sitting room where we could talk in private. At first I thought 'wow, finally I'm meeting her', but quickly composed myself as we entered the room. I was expecting her to be dressed in a sari and look typically Indian, but she was not. Instead, she wore a black knee-length shift dress with pearls set magnificently against her dark sallow skin, her long, glossy black hair and her bright and expressive brown eyes. I remember thinking how beautiful and well groomed she looked, with such fine features, and put her age at around late forties. Everything about her, sitting stately on an armchair, was composed and tranquil like a Hindu goddess. Not only was she a doctor but a mother too, of a son and daughter, and had given untold happiness to so many couples.

'I'm Caroline,' I announced, extending my hand.

'Yes, yes, I have your medical records here,' she smiled and shook my hand.

In front of her was a small coffee table with some leaflets about the clinic. There was something charismatic about her; her smile was warm and relaxing as we sat down and made ourselves comfortable. Behind her a big standing fan whirred away, keeping us cool.

'So what are you hoping for?' she asked.

'Well,' I hesitated, not knowing where to begin.

Dr Patel was already familiar with my medical history but I explained again and sought answers whenever I was unsure about something in the surrogacy process at her clinic. True to her word, Bina was very straight up as we went through the questions. But Dr Patel answered every question posed without hesitation. It was even Bina who raised the question of cost and Dr Patel showed a rate card that outlined all the various prices for the different stages of treatment. I suppose the biggest revelation was the huge variation in the cost between America and India. In America it could cost from US$70,000 to US$100,000 or much more, while at Dr Patel's clinic it was around US$15,000.

'Why are you wasting time?' Dr Patel finally enquired. 'Why don't you just come?'

It was crunch time. It had taken Niall and me nearly three months to get to this stage. Deciding on surrogacy was a big decision for us and we were careful not to rush into it. Even though I was convinced in my heart it was the right decision from the moment I saw the documentary, my brain took longer and wanted to work out all the details.

'When?' I asked, suddenly getting excited.

'You can come in August.'

August, wow. I was shocked it was so soon but kind of happy too.

'What are you waiting for now?' repeated Bina, smiling at me. From her voice I knew she had approved of Dr Patel.

After that Dr Patel went through what arrangements she would make and what we could expect. After about thirty minutes, we left the house and returned to the car. Not quite believing what had happened, Bina and myself laughed in the car from sheer excitement. We had spent almost three hours in the house. Before returning to Dublin I met my darling nephews and brother at a restaurant for a quick lunch. Caelan, being extremely perceptive and clever for one so young, asked me all about the baby. Outside the restaurant, we paused to take a family photograph and all of us looked blissful on that happy, memorable sunny day. I returned to Ireland and Dr Patel emailed several times with more arrangements and profiles of surrogate mothers.

***

Now that our minds were firmly made up, Niall and I looked forward to making the trip to India in August. In a funny kind of way, it all seemed to fit into place. We were actually going to India. Ever since my brother Philip had married Bina, a Kenyan Indian, I had wanted to travel to India. My thoughts flew back to the first time I had met her. Like Philip, everyone in my family fell in love with her from the very start. She was just like my father and did not have a bad bone in her body. Her intelligence and gift for languages was impressive – aside from English, she could speak Hindi, Swahili and Gujarati.

Their marriage had involved two days of celebration, first the Catholic ceremony and then the Hindu one. After the Catholic wedding, Bina was not technically married in her culture, so Philip spent the night on his own in the hotel while she returned to the family home. Only after the Hindu wedding could they go off and celebrate their honeymoon in earnest. The Hindu wedding was absolutely spectacular, rich in ritual and style. It was stunning, so colourful and exciting, like something you see in a film. The many rituals of the wedding were fascinating to watch and all captured on my camera: the couple standing under the wedding mandap – the decorated canopy with pillars – the priest or rather Brahmin reciting the holy verses, Bina and Philip being joined together by a white cloth, feeding each other sweetmeats as a sign of their fidelity, and ending the day dancing to romantic Indian music and Bollywood songs. One of my favourite parts was the hand painting, the Mehndi, which was a sort of pre-wedding ceremony and a huge tradition in Indian culture. Bina, being the bride, naturally was first to have the elaborate designs applied to her hands and feet using a kind of special henna dye. All the girls took part, even me, and it was as much fun as a hen party. I was even quite sad when the temporary tattoo started to fade some weeks later.

My brother used to say that from the day of the wedding, I had wanted to live in India. Both the people and the culture appealed greatly to me. Bina's family and relatives always struck me as being gentle, kind-hearted people. In fact, they are like family to me now. Over the years Bina herself has been a great support to me, through everything. I could ring her and say I'm thinking of this or that and seek her advice. And she would always have a very definite opinion on something and tell me whether to do it or not. A real rock of sense. I knew I would get to India one day, but little did I think it would be under surrogacy circumstances. I suppose India was an obvious choice for surrogacy when I thought about it more.

***

As the clock ticked down to August we made preparations to fly to India. There was so much to organise from travel vaccinations and flights to packing. I hoped and prayed the surrogacy would work. Realistically we had run out of options. Being a worrier, I wondered what to do if it did not work out. I reassured myself that we could always try again. It's not as if the door was completely closed. There was just no way I wanted to go back down the adoption route. At any rate, the surrogate mothers were a hundred times healthier than me. Their bodies a hundred times better able to cope with a pregnancy than mine. Everything was stacked against me carrying a baby to full term. So if the pregnancy was unsuccessful, we could find out what went wrong and try again. Move on to the next stage, at least as I envisioned it. Obviously, there was the money aspect of it too. The costs involved staged payments. In my mind I was saying 'Oh God, we'll have to start saving again.' But at least it would not be the end for us. Surrogacy was such a broad area and we were only at the start of the journey.

I often thought about the hordes of people who had attended the open meeting at the HARI Unit that first evening we were there. I could understand why so many of them would resort to surrogacy in the end. Like Niall and me, their need to have a baby was just as pressing and IVF and adoption would not work out for all of them. With the scale of infertility worldwide, regardless of opinion, surrogacy was a solution. It could not be banned but needed to be regulated and controlled in as professional a way as possible. The time had come to see it as something positive and not all negative.

We were extremely lucky it worked for us first time around.

Chapter 7

India-bound

The day finally arrived, Saturday, 22 August 2010, when we were off to the land of tigers and Mahatma Gandhi. The only hurdle now to be overcome was my absolute fear of flying. Yes, our path to parenthood always seemed to be paved with some kind of cobblestone, twist or turn, even pothole. I didn't know how I would fare with all the different flights on our itinerary – Dublin to Heathrow, Heathrow to Mumbai and then Mumbai to Ahmedabad. However, I just kept telling myself that our journey served a true purpose and I was getting on that plane, nerves and all! It was the only way I managed to get through it. As it turned out, it took almost twenty-four hours to get to Anand, the town where Dr Patel's clinic was situated, which was about five-and-a-half hours ahead of Dublin, time-wise. Most of that Saturday was spent travelling: after leaving Dublin we had a six-hour layover in Heathrow followed by a nine-hour flight to Mumbai.

Descending into Mumbai the first thing that struck me was the slums right beside the airport. It was like landing into a scene from *Slumdog Millionaire*. There were scores of slums for miles and miles around, slanted tin-roof shacks and huts perched precariously on top of each other. The place must have been home to thousands upon thousands of slum dwellers, their only respite from the searing heat and monsoon rains. I looked at Niall in amazement. How could they tolerate the noise level? I could scarcely imagine. It was like an aeroplane landing in your kitchen every few minutes.

After a layover of about three hours, dozing in the transit lounge, we were airborne again. This time to Ahmedabad, a short sixty-minute hop away. Sunday morning had dawned by the time we landed in Ahmedabad, the largest city in the province of Gujarat. Steeped in history, Gujarat lay on the northeast coast of India and bordered Pakistan. Luckily our hotel had arranged a taxi to pick us up at the airport in advance and before we knew it we were on the open road and heading for Anand. The road was a superb dual carriageway, an express highway, that linked the city of Vadodara; it impressed Niall no end, thinking it far superior than the M50 back home. Gujarat was one of the wealthiest and most industrialised states in India, yet parts of the land we travelled through were dry and sandy, almost desert-like. You felt in no man's land except for the fantastic road you were travelling on. The jet lag was starting to set in and I dozed on and off for the ninety-minute journey. On approaching Anand, however, we perked up again and Niall started to record the early morning scenes on his camcorder.

The first thing that took me by surprise was all the cows! Anand, being the dairy capital of India, meant cows were everywhere – ambling around, resting or walking in the centre of roads, even on the busy streets. Sometimes they were literally racing after people. I knew from Bina that the cow is sacred in India and the animal could wander where it liked, but still I was amazed at their sheer number and the safety hazards they posed. Drivers had acquired the amazing knack of not knocking them down – as much out of reverence as safety I think. The tuk-tuk drivers whizzed by in their distinctive yellow and green three-wheelers, hooting their horns and skilfully negotiating their way past each cow by a hair's breadth. Even a motorbike stacked high with family members managed to skirt safely by them too. The sight took my breath away. The cows were far from the fine Friesians you would see grazing on an Irish field; these sandy-coloured creatures were big and bony and looked emaciated by our standards and some rather scary with horns like antlers.

Anand was a large bustling town, with a population of about 15,000, with long dusty streets, but not your average holiday destination. Being a city girl, all I could think of as I arrived in the town was where were the shopping centres?! There were plenty of shops and bazaars of course but not the malls and centres I was accustomed to seeing in other holiday hotspots. Even though our trip was not a holiday as such, the fact of being in a foreign country and feeling the heat of the sun on your face made it feel like we were. It was almost like a big adventure.

The taxi made its way through a very dusty street before pulling up outside the Madhubhan Hotel, located in the southern part of the town. There was security at the gates with mirrors checking for bombs and explosives beneath the cars. Since the 2008 Mumbai attacks by Islamist terrorists, security at international hotels had been stepped up. It brought home to us just how real the threat of terrorism was in the region. Because we didn't know what conditions to expect in Anand, we decided to go for an upmarket hotel for our short visit, especially as so many couples on the forum had recommended it. The hotel was set in beautiful lush grounds with swimming pools and plush cottages and it oozed luxury from every pore. The best part was the air conditioning, given the heat and humidity of the climate, although the monsoon season had begun several weeks before.

By now I was ready to collapse from exhaustion and could barely string two words together. While checking in at reception, I overheard an American woman in mid conversation. From the sound of her voice, I figured it might be Crystal, who I had been communicating with on the forum. Based in Washington DC, she worked as a facilitator for surrogacy in India, helping couples navigate the system. Some years before she had had a baby boy by surrogacy at Dr Patel's clinic – and later on during our second visit, it was followed by twins – so she was well placed to advise and inform intended parents. She had put her consulting services at our disposal if we needed someone to accompany us while in Anand. However, we had declined and decided to go it alone. It emerged in previous emails that she would be in Anand around the same time as us and was eager to meet up. Later after some hours' rest, I did meet Crystal in the foyer but our chat was brief as she was busy with a client, an American couple, surrounded by bundles of paperwork. With her iPad resting on her knees and business-like manner, Crystal was every inch the professional. Through Crystal we heard about Uday, who was basically the guy you needed to know when in India.

On our second day in Anand we got an opportunity to meet Uday, sitting in the hotel foyer. By Indian standards he was very tall and he carried himself very well. Dressed immaculately in a pressed white t-shirt and light-coloured linen trousers, the middle-aged man was rather stern looking at first but as he got to know us his face relaxed into a smile. Once he gave us his business card, it was the beginning of a great relationship with him. He had so many different roles: taxi driver, guide, interpreter, adviser, chaperone, almost personal assistant on occasion. But for him, our time in India might have been a lot rockier, especially when I returned on my own eight months later for the birth of our baby. He looked after us so well, for a modest fee, though at times it might have felt he was too attentive. Nevertheless, I could not have done it without him, coming to our hotel every day to make sure everything was in order.

***

Monday morning, sometime before 10 o'clock, we set off by taxi for the clinic, officially named the Akanksha Infertility Clinic based at Kaival Hospital. It was situated at the eastern side of Anand in a lane off Station Road, not far from the railway line. As we stood outside the salmon-coloured three-storey building in the leafy courtyard under the hot sunshine, I took a deep breath. Finally, we were actually here. I could hardly believe it. The clinic had been in existence since 1991, at first offering obstetrics and gynaecology services and then in 1998 IVF to Indian couples. It was only in 2002 when the Indian government legalised surrogacy that it was able to provide such services. Dr Patel's first surrogacy case was for an infertile Indian couple living in the UK, but it proved almost impossible to find a surrogate mother. Eventually, the woman's own mother, residing in Anand, became the surrogate in 2003 and delivered twins at the age of 43 for her daughter in January 2004 – her own grandchildren in effect. Naturally, it hit the headlines not only because it was Asia's first case of surrogacy, but the world's fifth surrogate grandmother.

Though many western people would hold the view that India was a backwater in terms of medical science, it was far from the case, as we learned. India has its fair share of ground-breaking doctors, especially in assisted reproductive techniques. It was, in fact, an Indian doctor who pioneered the birth of India's first IVF baby back in 1978. On one side of the globe, the world hailed the medical breakthrough of the birth of Louise Brown through IVF in Oldham, Lancashire on 25 July 1978. Working at the same time, Dr Subhash Mukhopadhyay pioneered the birth of Kanupriya Agarwal, alias Durga, in Calcutta just 67 days later on 3 October 1978. Unfortunately it would take several years before the Indian scientific community believed his claims.

Once inside the clinic we approached the reception desk on the ground floor. A young nurse dressed in a sari stood behind it and spoke good English and was very friendly. The hospital was buzzing with the nurses bustling by in their pale blue tunics with navy trim and navy trousers. Many people were milling around in the corridor, some Indian women were queuing for medical appointments or others waiting around in red plastic chairs. The clinic was run by a team of doctors, nurses, embryologists and technicians. And in the middle of it all was Dr Patel, meeting intended parents, surrogate mothers or donors, assisting in the delivery of babies – essentially directing operations.

First we met Dr Patel's husband, Dr Hitesh Patel, whose office at the time was just inside the entrance of the building, past a sizeable shoe rack holding dusty footwear. That was something we realised fairly quickly – the hot climate made the streets unbelievably dusty. Originally an orthopaedic specialist, Dr Hitesh had become more involved in his wife's clinic over the years and developed good organisational and counselling skills. Cricket mad, he was a warm and welcoming gentleman, with a sense of humour that could lighten the heaviest load. His office was a real chill-out room for couples to hang out. Outside the main building there was an adjoining room where couples could also sit and wait, usually during various procedures. It was Dr

Hitesh who set the scene for us and told us what was involved and organised all the paperwork. On the second floor of the building semen analysis was carried out along with IVF, ICSI, egg retrieval as well as embryo transfer. This was the high tech sterile floor. Aside from being a maternity hospital, the clinic could also accommodate surrogate mothers in later stages of pregnancy or if any complications arose.

Some hours later we got to have our medical consultation with Dr Patel. Inside her office, she sat at her desk dressed in a beautiful sari, not your traditional white coat, and looked immaculate. As soon as she spoke, I got that sense that we were in good hands again. Since our last meeting in London, my fears of IVF and other treatments had abated and I was prepared for whatever was necessary. Her office was relatively small and rather dark with little natural sunlight. And as we talked, my eyes could not help but ramble around and take in the surroundings. To the left of her large desk was shelving space interspersed with beautiful stained-glass panels of plant fronds. Aside from papers and a stack of newspaper cuttings, it was filled with objects obviously important to her: photos of babies born at Kaival from thankful parents and small statues of gods and deities from various religions. Among the figurines of Hindu gods was a Christian crucifix, a picture of Sai Baba – a guru sacred to Hindus and Muslim – and a framed photo of Mahatma Gandhi, born in Gujarat in 1869. I remember reading an article about her saying that she believed in all religions, even though she was Hindu by birth. It gave her spiritual calm and strength, she said. Indeed most Indians filled their homes with statues, even Bina and Philip. A big picture of Oprah Winfrey had pride of place on the shelf too; Dr Patel was interviewed by the world famous host in October 2007 and the show had put her clinic on the international surrogacy map. So much so, the clinic was dubbed 'the cradle of the world'. What struck me too was a large rectangular painting on the wall facing her desk, depicting six pregnant bronzed women with a white figure in the middle, a kind of angel, with arms protectively outstretched. For many couples, Dr Patel was that angel.

In one corner of the room was a desk with a computer, which held patient medical records, emails and patients accounts as I was to learn. Beyond the room was a screen with a small examination couch where ultrasound scans could be taken. But the one thing I did learn was that Dr Patel was extremely busy. Now that I could see the clinic at first hand, I could understand why most of her email responses to my queries had been of the yes-no variety with little elaboration. The more I saw, the more I wondered how she managed it. She was on the phone, scanning surrogates, organising paperwork, dealing with the embryologists – literally doing a thousand things.

Some emails and reports on the internet claimed that Dr Patel's clinic was dilapidated but I would not agree with that, not by any stretch of the imagination. Before our visit, I did fear the conditions might not be up to scratch given that I am so fussy myself. From a hygiene point of view there was nothing wrong with the hospital, apart from being a bit old and dated. Yet it was as sterile as the next hospital. Niall used to say it was like going into the old Meath Hospital rather than the Blackrock Clinic. Perhaps the décor could have done with some refreshing but from my perspective the staff were constantly cleaning the place. The hospital beds were not as state-of-the-art as those back in Ireland, but everything was clean and tidy.

Before you get there, Dr Patel has everything timed. We already knew who our surrogate mother would be as we had received a profile some weeks before we travelled. Her name was Nita and while we hadn't seen a photograph of her, we knew her details. For example, her age, height, number of children, surrogacy history, obstetric history – she never had a miscarriage and had given birth naturally, that is, a vaginal delivery. Prior to our arrival she had a check-up and was screened for any infectious diseases as was her husband. And of course both Niall and I had the same done in Ireland and forwarded the results to Dr Patel.

Before we met Nita, there was a lot of paperwork to go through. As director of the clinic, Dr Patel has ultimate responsibility for deciding whether you can have treatment or not. She does not have to refer to any ethics body as such; however, her clinic is licensed. It also conforms to all the

Indian regulations and legislation in respect of artificial reproduction technology (ART), in particular in the state of Gujarat. She is not interested in the legal end of things, like getting passports for babies, and left that up to us to sort out. And you can see why. If she was to get involved in everyone's case, their legal wrangles, it would be impossible for her to do her own job. She was there to do the medical end of things. But obviously there are some legal aspects that do have to be established at the very start. From a legal point of view, we would be considered the legal parents. In India like in some American states, the intended parents are automatically registered as the legal parents on the birth certificate.

Unlike in other countries, for example the UK, we did not have to sign a document saying what would happen if we changed our mind or if our circumstances changed or if the child was physically or mentally disabled or if we felt we weren't able to cope with the newborn. But we did have to sign a document saying who would take the child if we got separated, divorced or died. Basically, it wasn't the responsibility of the clinic or the Indian state. This had happened back in 2008 at Dr Patel's clinic when a Japanese couple had divorced shortly before the birth of their child Manji. Neither the Japanese mother nor Indian surrogate mother wanted to take custody of the child, but the Japanese father did. However, Indian law prohibited single men to adopt. Eventually, after months of legal wrangling, the case ended up in the Indian Supreme Court and it granted custody to the Japanese paternal grandmother. And the court also ruled that commercial surrogacy was legal.

In our case, we nominated my brother Philip and sister-in-law Bina to be legal guardians in the event of any mishaps. We had to sign that document in front of a lawyer in India. It also meant that we or rather Niall had to make a will to cater for any future arrangements. In addition, we did have to sign a formal surrogacy agreement. Nita had to sign a form along with her husband to relinquish any guardianship rights to the child. That was basically the surrogacy agreement. At Dr Patel's clinic, the surrogates are not biologically connected to the child at all. If couples need an egg donor then a different woman supplies the eggs. While it is possible for surrogates to be the egg donor as in traditional surrogacy, the practice does not occur at Dr Patel's clinic. From her perspective, when the surrogate is also the donor, there is a higher chance of greater bonding and the woman may want to keep the baby.

Unlike other countries, we did not have to take out insurance cover as such if anything happened to Nita during her pregnancy. However, as part of the surrogacy agreement, we did agree to pay a death benefit should anything happen to her, God forbid. If she had died, we would have had to pay €2,000 to her family, which was understandable under the circumstances.

The fees are set out in a schedule given to you by Dr Patel beforehand and the cost of the very same treatment does not vary between couples. Extra expenses could be incurred if the embryos need to go to five-day blastocysts – maybe a couple of hundred rupees – or if twins were born. But all these possible eventualities are pointed out beforehand. You pay the fees in staged payments. So if the process doesn't work at any stage, you don't continue on. I thought that was a pretty good system. It was different from other surrogacy agencies where you might have to pay a lump sum at the start. I had heard stories of some couples losing considerable sums of money with those kind of agencies and especially if the transfer of embryos or pregnancy failed and you had to repeat the process all over again. If women at Dr Patel's clinic need an egg donor it is arranged before they go to India and I heard they could pay up to US$2,500 for the service.

As it turned out we didn't run into any unforeseen or unexpected expenses because Dr Patel had carefully laid out all the costs beforehand. There was some discretion in how much money we could give Nita, however. The question of paying her reasonable expenses was discussed at some length when we met her. As she would be staying in the surrogacy house for nine months, it meant her husband would have to take time off work to care for their young son and daughter. We had to compensate him for loss of earnings. But that was all tied in with the surrogacy agreement.

Commercial surrogacy has become big business in India and obviously the clinic was making a lot of money. At one level, money was not foremost in Dr Patel's mind. In fact, it was Bina who had brought up the subject originally when we met Dr Patel in the UK. Any money she does earn pays staff and is ploughed back into the clinic, improving and upgrading the facilities all the time. With a strong sense of social responsibility, Dr Patel is interested in the welfare of the surrogates as well as their families in the long term. For this reason, she set up the Anand Surrogate Trust. It provides education to the children of the surrogates, medical care throughout the surrogates' life, activities to improve the life of their families and works of charity for their benefit. For example, one scheme supplied schoolbags and schoolbooks to children of surrogate mothers. The Trust also launched a handbook on surrogacy in March 2009, called *The Last Ray of Hope: Surrogate Mother – A Reality*, where all sale proceeds go towards the health and education costs of the families.

***

Counselling is a necessary part of the process as well. With very good people skills, Dr Hitesh handled a lot of the counselling himself. He sat us down and went through all the paperwork, explaining the process and procedures and answering our queries. It was all very clear cut. He was quite thorough and left no stone unturned, whether it was talking about the risks, the embryos or giving us Nita's medical history. I felt we could ask him anything, given his friendly and approachable manner. Several times he would ask had we any doubts or worries, and if there was anything he was not able to answer, he directed us to Dr Patel herself. I suppose the room wasn't entirely private and we were interrupted from time to time. But it never felt intrusive or anything like that because all the couples were going through the same thing. There was nothing rushed about it either; I felt comfortable because the doctors were up-to-speed with my medical history and could give us their undivided attention, unlike the HARI Unit where I felt I was on a conveyor belt and everything performed so quickly. The sense of personal attention was strong. When back in Ireland if I had an urgent question for Dr Patel, I could pick up the phone and ring her or email her. Despite her hectic schedule, she would come to the phone for a quick moment. Often I'd get through quicker to her than I would to a Dublin hospital.

Like her husband, Dr Patel did enquire was there anything we wanted to ask her. However, there was nothing pressing on my mind nor Niall's that needed to be addressed before we went ahead. Most things had been thrashed out beforehand, via all the emails and the consultation in London, and the global forum on the clinic website had been of enormous help too. If I keyed in a question online it was answered within 24 hours. The only thing that remained was to meet Nita in person. Admittedly, the care of the surrogates, of Nita, during pregnancy made me curious. But I was given the opportunity to visit the surrogate house and speak to some of the surrogate mothers. From then on, I knew we were not going to change our minds.

Chapter 8

Meeting Nita, the surrogate mother

On the third day of our visit we met Nita. For so long I had been gearing up for this moment and now that it had arrived I felt both nervous and excited. Curiosity as to what she was like increased, as well as how we would communicate since she spoke no English, and how we would get on. It was becoming the most important part of the trip. At the clinic, Dr Hitesh showed us into a private room where Nita was sitting. She was dressed in a beautiful stripped sari with gold trim, with long black thick hair and a red bindi mark on her forehead. Like many Hindu women her nose was pierced and she wore gold earrings as well as her wedding necklace. Aged twenty-eight, she looked much younger, perhaps because she was so petite. From her profile I knew she was about five foot, just a few inches shorter than I was. Accompanying her that day were her two young children, a boy and a girl, and her husband, a vegetable vendor. Like Nita, her husband was equally short with a small thin physique and was smartly dressed in a check shirt and dark trousers. The family lived in Anand, not far from the railway station.

On the forum some couples say they didn't get emotionally attached to the surrogate mother, but straightaway I did. Of the two of us, I was probably the more emotional. The minute I saw her I started crying. The tears just flowed. God only knows what she must have thought. But the tears were not out of pity or anything, for she was lovely and well groomed, but maybe it was seeing her children. All I could think was how unbelievably good she was. Observing the young boy I immediately thought of my nephew Caelan – they looked about the same age and had the same brown skin colour. But I have to admit I was taken aback to see the children in the room.

'These are her children?' I whispered to Hitesh. 'What do her children think she's doing?'

'Well, I'll ask her,' he replied.

And he did.

'My job. I'm doing my job,' Nita replied in Gujarati.

Surrogacy was just her day job. I had never considered it like that before.

'Obviously, they don't understand everything,' Nita continued. 'No, they're fine, they just know I'm going to do my job.'

'We are so thankful to you,' her husband added.

'No,' I kept saying, 'I am thankful to you.'

'We want this for you,' he continued. 'We want you to be happy.'

'Gift, gift, gift,' Nita kept saying.

At the mention of the word gift, Bina's words came back to me. She had urged me to remember that in Hindu culture there are so many fertility gods and that to do something like surrogacy, you're giving someone the gift of life. It was an act of altruism, doing good for your fellow human being. Giving birth is nature's greatest gift in your entire life.

Obviously, there's the money end of things too. It's only natural the women want to build a better life for themselves and their families and escape the cycle of poverty. Providing basic needs like food, clothing and shelter in India is a huge burden for some, not to mention funding other family finances or paying off debts. There is no provision for social housing in India and access to quality healthcare is limited, unless you have plenty of money. Nonetheless, these women were so good and generous and, as I saw it, you still have to be a certain type of person to do it. What people call 'rent-a-womb' is not all black and white – it's not a case that you go over to India and these people are queuing up saying I need the money. But because I got to know

Nita and the other surrogates, that's not the way they are, they're human beings. Most of them would say this is a wonderful gift we are giving. And I don't think they were purely motivated by money and justifying it under the guise of a Hindu gift.

The surrogate mothers are entitled to a certain amount of money every month – an allowance of about US$25 or US$50. In Nita's case, she asked would it be possible to have a little bit extra, say US$75. The fact that it was her second surrogacy and her mother would have to move into the household to share the childcare duties with her husband complicated matters.

'Now, you don't have to give anything extra,' Hitesh explained, 'it's up to you.'

'Look, she's only asked for a small amount, of course she can have it,' I said.

'We can give you 100 dollars every month,' Niall offered.

The fee for the surrogacy itself was US$8,000, which was given in instalments and a lump sum at the end. We had heard that it was the equivalent of about ten years' salary for rural Indians. Nita's husband was a street vendor who sold vegetables and earned about 1500 rupees a month (about €22), which she said was not enough for them to run their household. Her plans for the money were centred totally on her family. The money from the first surrogacy had been kept for her children's education. And we knew from Bina how much Indians value education; it was the best route out of poverty for them. Nita wanted to send her children to college, get jobs in the city and make something of themselves. The second time around she wanted a house, a brick house, and to move from her cramped flat so her children would have plenty of space and security.

Months later I learned more about Nita's situation. In a BBC documentary, she revealed through an interpreter that her in-laws used to harass her at lot. After the birth of her second child, she and her husband decided to live separately from his family. She took a job at a place where they printed wedding cards and worked there for eight years. Then she heard about surrogacy, and after further enquires, brought her husband to the clinic and they discussed it with him. Initially, he disagreed and said such things were not acceptable in their society but finally she convinced him after much persuasion.

At the end of our meeting, once everything was sorted out, it was time to say goodbye for the moment. I really hoped it would all turn out for the best. When Nita and her family finally left the room, I was kind of wondering what to do with myself. It was all new territory for us with no handbook on surrogacy to guide us.

***

My curiosity about the surrogate house began to grow and grow. Even Niall too wondered what it was like. So the next day I asked Uday to drive us to where Nita would be staying, just for a quick visit. I really needed to see what living conditions she would be under for the duration of the pregnancy, all going well with the embryo transfer. Both Niall and I were not immune to the claims that surrogate women were exploited and I half-visualised her tucked away in some field or chained to a bed in a locked room. We were really glad to have made the trip because it put our minds at rest. The surrogate house we visited was about a ten-minute drive from our hotel. It was a large building on the corner of a leafy street bordered by a head-high concrete wall and wrought-iron gate. Inside was a tiled courtyard and a garden with steps leading up to the entrance. A local tax office in a former life, the two-storey house was bright and airy and a ceiling fan whirred busily inside. Though sparsely furnished there was plenty of life in the building. To begin with, a popular Indian soap opera was on the television as we entered. In one way, it was kind of funny because surrogacy was starting to become a theme in soap operas in India, as well as in films in regional dialects and Bollywood productions. I suppose it had a rich source of conflict and emotional storylines to keep viewers hooked.

The families of some of the surrogates were visiting and they sat on the ground or on white plastic chairs chatting while the children looked on obediently. I suppose the one drawback is that the women share rooms so there was nowhere private or secluded for them in the house. Downstairs there were about three dormitories, with three beds or so to each room, while upstairs there was another two or more dormitories. Close together, the beds had brightly patterned bedspreads and there was some basic shelving in the rooms for a few private possessions. In fact, the entire house was neat and tidy, though the pastel pink walls were probably due a lick of paint.

Downstairs the kitchen was a hive of activity. All the food for the surrogates was cooked for them, everything prepared, so that they got the best of nutritious food, in particular milk and eggs. On the upper floor a door led to a large balcony with a clothesline and a view of the leafy neighbourhood. Despite its basic facilities, by Indian standards the house was luxurious – it had running water and electricity and was comfortable. All their needs were met; the surrogates didn't have to get out of bed for anything. Indeed some of the women likened it to a stay in a hotel.

There was also a mother figure in the house, a nurse they called Auntie, who oversaw the care of the women, whether taking their blood pressures or easing any morning sickness. She was a real mammy of the house and in fact had been a surrogate in the past and so could support them in various ways. Much loved, she was showered with kisses and hugs whenever she brought them tea or did them a good turn. In terms of occupying themselves the women could chat, watch television, sew, use a computer or go for a walk in the fresh air. However at the same time, they weren't free to come and go as they pleased. Unlike in their own homes, they did not have to get up at the crack of dawn – Nita used to get up at 4am for work – and could lie in with less issues to stress them. It was hard to work out how many surrogate women were in the house. I only had a quick look but it wouldn't have been more than fifteen. I had heard there were usually about fifty surrogates pregnant at any one time, at least when I was there. I later learnt that from 2004 to 2012, nearly 500 babies have been delivered through surrogacy, involving about 370 surrogate mothers.

On the way back to the hotel, after the visit, I told Uday that Nita was the name of our surrogate mother. She was familiar to him as indeed were all the surrogates. He knew just about everyone in town and I joked that he could run the entire town of Anand like a kind of mayor. He laughed. Knowing the ways of the world and well educated, nothing much escaped his attention. For one thing, he was fully aware of how Indian people viewed foreigners, especially those coming from western societies. With poverty so rampant in the country and millions trying to eke out an existence, people had to survive and get ahead in some way or other. Though many of the surrogates were literate and in possession of jobs, they did see surrogacy as an opportunity to rise above the breadline.

***

Staying in the surrogacy house was sort of mandatory so that Dr Patel could supervise the antenatal care throughout the pregnancy. Usually for most rural Indians the care provided by the state health services was inadequate at the best of times with high infant mortality rates. There was also the worry that if the surrogate mothers stayed at home, they might be working or not eating a balanced diet or not taking proper rest. We just assumed that everyone stayed there. However, we discovered that most of the women opted to stay there too for various reasons. At the house, they could take classes in English or computers, tailoring, get an education or train as a beautician. In later conversations with Nita she told me she preferred to learn how to use a sewing machine because she wanted to make clothes that she could sell, become a dressmaker in fact. I joked would she not like to learn computers and so keep in contact with me, but no it was not for her. As she saw it, sewing would be more practical and beneficial for her future.

The camaraderie among the women was evident and they enjoyed the easy-going atmosphere. You could see there was a good bond between them all. They all got on with each other like sisters. I subsequently learnt that many of them would have known each other because the women were from Anand. Naturally, it was hard for them being away from their families but they could still come and visit, though not late at night.

Dr Patel does have a strict policy about surrogate women. In fact, there are criteria for the surrogates, donors and intended parents. It's not as if a woman can walk in off the street and take a ticket and hey presto give birth nine months later. Dr Patel chooses carefully from the women who appear at her clinic requesting to be surrogates, making sure they are fit for surrogacy. Many of the women come from lower middle-class families. First of all, the would-be surrogates have to be married women. For if they were single, it would make them prostitutes or adulterers in Indian eyes, as the country is still a very traditional society by and large. Naturally, there was some suspicion in Indian society about surrogacy, with many people believing that the surrogate had to sleep with the father to get pregnant rather than it occurring in the laboratory. The second criterion is that they must have had children themselves, carried to full term and have had a natural birth, i.e. a vaginal delivery. This was important for so many reasons. Not only because their obstetrical history was established but also the first baby is probably the hardest delivery for any mother. It is also a major emotional experience, with the nine months of pregnancy being a time of bonding, of preparation for being a mother. However, with subsequent pregnancies, the mother is more likely to take it in her stride. So when it comes to surrogacy, it is natural that she would have emotional feelings towards the baby in her womb, regardless of who the genetic parents are. But she is probably better prepared to give up the baby.

That said, the surrogates try not to become attached and try to remain as emotionless as possible, from what I witnessed. Perhaps it is hardest for the first-time surrogacy. Despite this, many of the Indian women go on to be surrogate mothers a second and third time. I always felt that if it was too difficult the first time around, they would not repeat the experience. The women also needed to be young and healthy. Luckily, Nita had a good obstetric history and never suffered from postnatal depression or anything like that. Usually the surrogates are in their twenties, like Nita, or early thirties. In reality, Indian women tend to have babies way younger than western women do, often in their teens. Once you're past twenty-five, your eggs start to decrease, and then the chances just get slimmer and slimmer. The surrogate women also have to be counselled to ensure they understand the process and whether they are ready for it and want to go through with it. Nita, like the others, had been made aware of the health risks as well. For example, she might need a Caesarean section, blood transfusions or if there were any complications, a hysterectomy. Dr Patel also had to make sure that she would be capable of giving over the baby to us after the birth. These considerations were explained to Nita and her husband beforehand.

I could see that Dr Patel invested a lot of her time in the surrogacy house and visited every Saturday or whenever she was needed. It is fair to say that she is interested in the welfare of the surrogate mothers, not only medically but also emotionally. The personal bonds she develops with the women are deep and protective. In fact, I could see how much they trusted her and felt safe and secure in the surrogacy house. While the clinic is run on a commercial basis it is not strictly commercial at the same time. The human element is not overlooked and Dr Patel tries to ensure that all the parties concerned are treated fairly.

No one forces the women to become surrogates and they come of their own free will. With all the talk of exploitation in the media, Dr Patel is keen that the surrogates are empowered to some extent. She knows the women are doing it to make a better life for themselves. If anything she is rather feminist in her outlook and oversees the negotiations between the intended couple and the surrogate to ensure the women get a fair deal. She encourages the women to set up their own bank accounts so they can renovate their home or buy a house in their own name, or a shop or kiosk, a motorised rickshaw like a tuk-tuk, or a piece of land for farming or whatever. Many women end up investing in small businesses and so secure their future independence or put money aside for their daughter's eventual marriage. However, under new legislation passing through the Indian parliament at present, Dr Patel and other clinics would be banned from brokering any surrogacy transactions in the future. There is always the fear that the women could be exploited by their own husbands too, so Dr Patel helps to minimise it. In Nita's case, she wanted the bank account in her own name to enable her to buy a house. Dr Patel will not transfer the money to their bank account until everything is in order. A member of her staff has responsibility for setting up the accounts and doing the paperwork.

In Anand, you're considered very lucky to be selected for surrogacy. Ultimately, Dr Patel runs a professional clinic and is extremely particular about who will be taken on as a surrogate. The women are vetted, not only medically, but socially and psychologically. She lets them know exactly what is involved in the process so that they are fully informed; she also stresses they must part with the newborn baby under their agreed contract and will have no future duties towards the child. If she has the slightest sense that a woman will be exploited by her husband and is vulnerable, then the contract will not go ahead. Dr Patel doesn't want any unsavoury practices as she has her professional reputation to maintain. She's the kind of person that certainly will not tolerate any misbehaviour or ulterior motives.

I can't speak for the other surrogacy clinics or agencies in India, whether they have surrogate houses or look after the best interests of the women. But I believe some have apartments in local villages where the surrogate mothers can stay if they wish. I gather it is a much looser arrangement, where they can come and go as they please. With a few hundred surrogacy clinics in India, there are no standard practices; some would say it is a free for all and admittedly it needs to be regulated.

***

The question of the social stigma of surrogacy too was never far off. Sometimes I came across articles on the internet saying the surrogate houses were places where the women could hide for nine months given the shame attached to surrogacy. From my experience, I think there's less of a taboo about surrogacy from an Indian perspective, especially in Anand. I don't think the surrogate mothers see it in the same way as westerners do. They can justify it as giving the gift of life, the most precious gift you can give in Indian culture. With a largely uneducated and laid-back population, Niall wondered would many people actually be aware of surrogacy taking place or even care. But I had my doubts; as a commercial enterprise I'm sure news of it had spread like wildfire.

Perhaps it is different in other parts of India, but in Anand, the mothers of many of the surrogates knew what was going on, even though the surrogates might deny it publicly. Nita's mother was fully aware of what was happening. Perhaps they don't tell their mothers at first, maybe not for the first surrogacy, but they do find out. Yet many of the mothers are supportive of their daughters once they know what is involved. Then again, it is said that Gujarat is one of the least conservative states in India and is outward looking and progressive. Although when it came to alcohol consumption, it was a dry state. Foreigners had to have a valid liquor permit to legally drink. The state does have a long tradition of emigration, especially to Britain, the USA and Africa, among its merchants, shopkeepers and entrepreneurs. Bina's family is just one example. And many of the Gujarati diaspora avail of surrogacy services in Anand. Nearly all the surrogates at Dr Patel's clinic came from Anand, from an area near the railway station, a five-minute walk from the clinic, or nearby villages. So it's not like they've walked a hundred kilometres from their village or town to avoid the locals knowing about it. But perhaps some women do lie and cover it up, moving away from their town or village, but that could be true of surrogacy anywhere – from India to America to Eastern Europe.

From observing them in the surrogacy house and at the hospital, the surrogates were quite proud of each other. They really do see it as such a gift. And it was not just a case of really poor women opting for surrogacy, though admittedly most are of lower caste. Some of the nurses working at Dr Patel's clinic had even been surrogates. I remember one day having a conversation with Hansha, a lovely nurse in the hospital.

'I was a surrogate mother too,' she admitted.

'Really?' I replied, rather surprised.

'Yes, twice,' she told me.

'Why?'

'Because I could earn money to give my children a better future,' she answered in total honesty.

The surrogacy did not interrupt her life at all. Some of the nurses or surrogates who can speak English never talked about missing their own children during their surrogacy. Whenever I asked, most of them were on their second surrogacy. The first time had not been so distressing or traumatic that they wished never to go through it again. Nita too had no regrets about the surrogacy. Even if society threw her out, she told the BBC reporter, or does not invite her in, she didn't care. It did empower her to a degree because she was no longer scared of anyone.

'I am not doing a bad thing. I am doing this for my children.'

Perhaps after nearly ten years, the Anand townspeople had got used to the practice, and maybe even welcomed it because it brought tourism and helped the local economy. So much so that Dr Patel and several surrogate mothers were presented with awards by the Gujarat Chamber of Commerce and Industry in 2009 when celebrating International Women's Day. None of the surrogates went into the clinic covered up or anything like that. If anything, the only ones entering incognito were local couples attending a gynaecologist/obstetrician for infertility problems. Indeed, infertility in India is seen as a curse. There was no way they would have wanted family members to observe them attending a fertility clinic.

***

Two days after our first meeting with Nita, we met again at the clinic to work out more details. There was also something I wanted to give her, which I had hesitated doing at our previous meeting. Back in Dublin, anticipating the language barrier, I had written a personal letter to her and got Bina to translate it into Gujarati before I went over. It just said who we were, that we lived in Ireland, and that surrogacy was something we had thought about for a long time. We understood how hard the process was for her but we would do everything in our power for her, give her anything she might need, all she had to do was ask. I had heard that some of the surrogates could not read, and so gingerly handed her the letter.

'I can read, I can read it,' she said proudly taking the letter, as if reading my mind.

It was such a relief that she was delighted with the letter. I knew it was going to be difficult trying to maintain contact in the coming months given the language barrier. To be honest, the clinic like many of the foreign couples on the global forum did not encourage it. Perhaps they felt it was easier for the surrogate if there was less contact, less communication, less bonding. So when the time came to hand over the baby, there would be less emotional conflict. It was hard to know what to do; I could only act instinctively. And all my instincts urged me to be close to Nita. Time would tell.

Chapter 9

Life in India

As our short stay in Anand went on, we grew accustomed to life there very quickly. We met so many different people, especially at the clinic. There were couples from Japan, America, Mexico and the UK. Some of the Americans were of Indian origin and opted to return to India for surrogacy rather than have it carried out in the US. I presumed for reasons of culture and cost. All these couples we would meet again when we went back eight or nine months later because we had all started the process at the same time. One of them was a woman called Payal and we eagerly exchanged email addresses and contact details.

During our trip we literally sat with these couples every morning in the clinic. And the talk was mainly about how many eggs, how many eggs. Everyone was focused on that. Aside from egg retrieval, everybody talked about the same things: their illnesses, how much money had been wasted on other treatments and travelling to clinics all over the world, and then finally coming to Anand, and the hotel facilities. Some of the women required egg donors but no one really discussed the donor profiles. These charted characteristics such as age, reproductive history, medical history, marital status, job, place of residence, personality traits, religion, financial status, etc. I heard most of the donors were Indian and some might even have been surrogate mothers before but identities were never disclosed. During our time there, an

African woman came in to collect her new baby born through surrogacy, so we plied her with questions about her experiences.

A kind of bonding goes on too that is very necessary; a club to jolly each other along. Because I'm a chatty person and can't bear long silences, I talked to everyone just to break the ice. The room where we all sat each day was based in Dr Hitesh's office. With his easy-going and approachable manner, you could ask him anything while he worked at his computer. You could share a joke and a laugh with him. And cheering us up was always a priority for him. One day at the request of the Mexican couple, he made a short video of the clinic. As he roved around the office where we were seated, capturing the faces, he gave a running commentary.

'And next we have the girl from Japan and now we have the Irish people – with all the stories!'

So I found I always got on with the couples and Dr Hitesh. The semen analysis time was particularly amusing, but not for the shy and coy. There was no polite whispering in their ears when the time came for the men to give samples. It was a case of delivering the message in the full glare of everyone.

'So-and-so, you have to go up and do your semen analysis now. Off you go.'

If anyone had any shame or embarrassment, then it was best to leave it at the door.

***

There was something about the Indian way of life that started to appeal to us. Niall and I both found it easy to get on with the local people and talk to them. Niall would always say that if you have a good personality, it's very hard *not* to get on with them. Admittedly we ran into a few unpleasant individuals, with their dismissive air, but on the whole there was a gentleness and kindness to the people that was really touching and humbling. At first because of our white skins and Niall's red hair and height – he's about six foot – they stared at us like we had landed from outer space. But after a while we took it in our stride and barely noticed we were a novelty. The great pride people took in their appearance was evident and keeping themselves spotlessly clean must surely have been hard, given how hot and dusty conditions were. The women in traditional saris looked beautiful; the colours so vibrant and attractive seemed to complement the climate perfectly. Usually you think of traditional dress as something old-fashioned or medieval, but these saris and Punjabi suits looked really smart and stylish and I even fancied buying one myself.

We enjoyed getting to know the local people and Uday was instrumental in that. On our first visit to the clinic, Uday showed us around the vicinity beforehand so we could get our bearings. On the corner of Station Road and the lane leading to the clinic was an optician's shop. The owner was a good friend of Uday's and the shop was a perfect stop-off point.

'I don't want you waiting outside in the heat after your consultation,' Uday said considerately.

'Phone me and then sit and wait for me in the opticians.'

True to his word, Uday spoke to his friend who welcomed us to his shop after our business was concluded at the clinic. A charming man in his early fifties, he observed all the comings and goings in the shop and on the street, but left the serving to his son and daughter. Free to talk to us, we learnt about the family business and swapped stories about India and Ireland.

Street vendors were everywhere and brought great colour to the town. There was such a stunning array of fruits on sale, from bananas, pineapples and coconuts to melons and mangos. Coconuts in particular were considered health enhancing by Uday and others. Driving around with Uday one day, he decided that Niall and I needed an invigorating tonic. All the guidebooks say don't touch fruit in hot climates; when getting travel vaccinations, they say don't eat any fruit unless you've peeled it yourself. But much as I tried to bear all that in mind, it was nigh impossible around Uday. Observing some coconut vendors, he rolled down the car window and spoke to one man in Gujarati. Next we saw the men chopping coconuts swarming with flies and the heat beating down upon them. The guys just took out big knives like machetes and swiftly cut up the coconut, finally popping in dusty straws and handing them to us in the car. I could tell by the look on his face that Niall was really hesitant.

'I'm okay, Uday, thanks,' he began. 'I don't really want one.'

'Nonsense,' replied Uday, 'it's good for getting you prepared for the healthy channel of the baby.'

Not wishing to offend Uday, I took a sip and imbibed the coconut drink. It tasted warm which instantly put me off and made me feel a bit sick. Had it been cold I might have felt otherwise as I genuinely liked coconut.

'No, the best bit is the actual coconut,' Uday informed us, observing us just tasting the juice.

Uday was an expert at picking out the lumps of coconut and insisted we do the same. Yet all I could think of was the flies, as we chewed the coconut lumps, and how I was going to be seriously ill in bed the following day. But I needn't have worried. Luckily, we never got sick in India, no matter what we ate. And gosh, we ate everything.

At the hotel one day we met the American couple that Crystal was assisting. The woman, Nira, just had twins born through surrogacy and they were hidden away in her hotel room. I was dying to see them and couldn't understand why she did not invite me up for a look. I thought it an unwritten rule of the universe that all mothers love to show off their babies, but not in this case. Her husband was Indian so I thought maybe there was some cultural differences at play. Then to my surprise one day Nira suddenly struck up a conversation in the hotel foyer.

'You can come up to my room now,' she invited. 'I have a nanny.'

Her hotel room was located right across the corridor from ours and I grew more excited with every step I took in that direction. Inside, the two babies were absolutely tiny and placed in a travelling bassinette on the floor. Tending to them was an older woman, perhaps in her sixties, and dressed in a sari. It was my first experience of being in an environment with an Indian nanny.

'Hello,' I said, smiling at her.

'She's from Anand,' Nira explained, 'she doesn't understand any English.'

The language barrier was something I knew I would have to grapple with while in Anand. It was not in my nature to ignore people, especially when in the same room, so I would have to find ways of communicating through facial gestures and gesticulating. It was time to rely on all those drama classes from my youth!

'Small babies,' I said to the nanny, pointing at them and gesturing their size, in an effort to be friendly.

She nodded politely and smiled again.

'You must be tired, you know, with twins and feeding them,' I said, continuing to talk.

Before long it was obvious the nanny was just delighted to communicate, despite the language barrier. Dealing with all the bureaucracy of getting her babies back home meant Nira was overwhelmed with paperwork and had not a minute to spare. It was an extremely stressful period. At the time the situation puzzled me but nine months later I would understand exactly what she was experiencing.

Anand was buzzing every minute of the day and even night. The sound of horns beeping was a constant and is now an eternal reminder of the place. Throngs of people were forever on the move – cars, motorbikes, vans, bicycles, tuk-tuks – and pedestrians weaving their way precariously across the street. When I close my eyes even now I can still hear the *de, de, de* of the tuk-tuks and everyone talking nineteen to the dozen, at the top of their voices. And, of course, music emanating from every shop, that *ding, ding, ding* I got to know so well. The air too was thick with the aromas of food, tantalising my taste buds at every hour of the day. Everywhere our senses were stimulated and you felt really alive. Back at the hotel, we had down time, it being the reverse, an oasis of calm. But for all its hustle and bustle, Anand felt a very safe and secure place.

Even the monsoon climate was a marvel to us. All of a sudden you would get a torrential downpour that might last ten minutes or so but before long, the ground would be bone dry again from the intense heat. At night the rain and ear-splitting bursts of thunder and lightning often woke me up.

The everyday life of its people felt unusual to us but fascinating at the same time. It was intriguing to see truck after truck laden with green bananas driving to seaports where they would be shipped around the world; raucous monkeys prancing across busy streets; someone dragging a strong-willed camel – that insisted on answering the call of nature – up the road. Being an animal lover, the cows were still catching my attention and also the goats that were tethered to posts or wandering around. Sometimes it felt like the animals were forced to scavenge for food, rooting through discarded rubbish on the streets. And parts of the town were dirty to be honest, especially where collection or disposal of refuse was concerned. The bony bodies of the cows tended to make me feel sad, and I squirmed every time a vehicle careered towards them.

'I really want to feed those cows,' I would say to Uday.

Being sacred animals, the cows were never eaten, only their milk consumed, so there was no need to fatten them up. Around the town you would catch sight of herdsmen tending to them, as well as the goats. They were dressed like a shepherd from biblical times, leading the animals off to be milked or bringing them to the fields. Usually, the herdsmen stayed indoors.

'Uday, there must be a truck going around picking up dead cows every day.'

He laughed.

'The cows are very happy, Caroline,' he would reply, 'they never get hurt here because the cow is sacred and we avoid them.'

Anand, indeed Gujarat, was famous all over India for producing Amul milk by a huge dairy cooperative. Amul parlours were found everywhere, selling milk and other milk products in various flavours from chocolate, saffron and strawberry to coffee and mango. With our affection for the people growing by the day, the poverty in Anand could not escape our attention. Even on the first day arriving in the town and observing from the taxi, it pulled at my heartstrings. The living conditions of some inhabitants were pretty shocking. In the town you might see a big fine building and camped beside it a family in cardboard boxes. Even outside our hotel, the plush five-star resort, with its elaborate wrought iron gates and driveway, there was no denying it.

Just outside the gates on the left-hand side, there was an entire family trying to survive with little or no shelter. They literally had four sticks, a bit of plastic sheeting for a roof and scraps of material converted into a makeshift dwelling. A little girl of about three, attired in nothing but a little top, was lying in the sun on a bed. However, the bed was no bed at all, just metal springs without a mattress. Homemade hammocks made from woven leaves and twine served as their sleeping quarters, while they bathed in big cooking woks. Their main source of sustenance was a goat and cow tied up outside.

'Oh my God,' I said to Uday, as we passed by in the car. 'Can't we stop and give them something, maybe food?'

'No, they're fine,' he would answer, knowing that if you put your hand out to one person, you would be soon be fleeced. Everyone would flock around you within seconds.

When the monsoon rains came I felt for the family, despite the heat and the humidity. The flimsy structure was no shelter against the elements. And I wondered how they could protect their babies, raise their family, living at the side of a main road, with tuk-tuks flying around and motorbikes swerving by. To have extreme poverty and wealth side by side did prick our conscience. The one-hundred-dollar-a-night Madhubhan Resort & Spa must have seemed like a paradise to them. From Niall's enquiries, the owner of the hotel literally owned everything in the town from the local dairy and steel production company to the corner shop and an actual road. Even blades for wind turbines supplied to Ireland are manufactured by his company.

Other days in town I saw people who were physically disabled, with no mobility aids to help them, and in dire need of wheelchairs. With such widespread poverty I wondered how the people could rise above it. With a billion in population, one third of the world's poor lived in India. How could the government possibly improve the lot of all the homeless and underprivileged and malnourished children? It was not like they could rely on social welfare or other benefits seen in western societies. Gujarat, where Anand was located, was in one of the more prosperous Indian states and I dreaded to think what it was like elsewhere. The memory of seeing all those slums in Mumbai was still horrifying.

In hindsight, while the place might have been a culture shock for some foreign couples, I think we kind of revelled in it. Crystal was amazed at how quickly we took to the country. Many of her clients arrived over and hated the food, complained about the dirt, and didn't want to meet the local people.

'I'll always remember you as the people who just loved the place from the minute you walked into it,' she would say.

The reason for this I think was because I always wanted to go there, from being around Bina so much and listening to her stories. Our experience of Indian people before travelling to Anand had been informed by her family. All we knew were warmth, friendliness and great hospitality. And in Anand we met the same kind, good-hearted people, very strong willed too. Although Bina never lived in India she is exactly like the local people and for me she represents all that is good and positive about Indian culture. Like Bina, nothing seemed to get them down. Low spirits would be understandable considering the severe poverty endured there, but Bina would say there is no point in worrying – her famous words. Maybe it was a question of faith and accepting what the universe was throwing at you, but she would never feel sorry for herself or wallow in misery. Instead she believed in facing whatever comes, head on, and being pragmatic. Whatever the problem, it was not going to last forever.

As we got ready for the embryo transfer to take place and my mind raced with 'what-ifs' and 'hopefully nots', I thought about Bina. What she said when I had been sick came back to me.

'This is just a stepping stone, just a path.'

'It's not a path, Bina,' I would wail.

'No, just a stage in the path.'

Chapter 10

The embryo transfer

Back at the clinic everything was going according to plan. Nine eggs were successfully retrieved, after previous injections of gonadotropins, much to our great relief. Niall's semen collection and analysis had gone well too and the sperm were viable. In fact, Uday took the whole business of semen collection very seriously. There was almost a ritual attached to it. He made it his business to find out what day the collection would take place, so that the day before could be spent in preparation.

'Niall, today is very important,' he would say. 'I am bringing you to this place where we will drink special juices and eat special foods to make everything go okay.'

And so we would dine out on the most delicious Indian food and fruit juices. It was all rather funny but delightful too.

'You need to be strong, go to bed early,' he instructed us, 'and I will be at your hotel at 9 o'clock . . .'

Like clockwork, he would be at reception half an hour beforehand and ring through to our room.

'Take your time, relax, eat your breakfast. Today is an important day.'

The following day the eggs and sperm were fertilised in the laboratory on the second floor of the clinic. After that we waited a few days to see if they would make it.

'How are they looking today?' I would ask Dr Patel each day.

Dr Patel and the doctors explained to us beforehand that, say for example, if we started off with nine eggs, as we had, only five might survive after fertilisation. The embryos were sometimes allowed to go to blastocyst stage as these ones have the best chance of a successful pregnancy. On day 4/5, the blastocyst develops from the solid mass of cells produced by the first cell division of the fertilised egg. Blastocyst transfer was more likely to happen if you had several embryos to choose from. In that scenario, the embryos are kept for longer than usual in the laboratory: five or six days rather than two or three days. Luckily for us our embryos were ready on day three.

In the waiting room, all the intended mothers gathered and nothing but eggs and embryos were on everyone's lips. The excitement was sky high.

'How many eggs, how many?' we asked as each woman arrived into the waiting room.

'I have ten.'

'I have twelve.'

However, the news was not always heartening.

'I have one.'

At hearing chances that slim, our sympathies were for the young woman in question. She was so upset, she could barely speak. However, as luck would have it, that day the door opened and in trooped an African woman who told us she was here to collect her newborn baby. There was congratulations all around before the burning question could be asked.

'How many eggs did you have?'

'One,' she replied, beaming.

Gosh, we could have cheered for joy. Hope springs eternal!

Finally, Uday's coconut juice worked its magic and the day was set for the embryo transfer. It had us on tenterhooks and we hoped and prayed everything would go well. By this stage Nita had been medically prepared for the transfer. In the previous weeks, she had been given various hormones to temporarily knock out her normal cycle and suppress ovulation, as well as preparing her womb to accept the embryos. Naturally, she had to abstain from having sex with her husband at this time too. And then there was the wait until Dr Patel felt Nita's womb was ready for the in vitro fertilised embryo. On the morning of the transfer I arrived at the clinic early to get a chance to sit with Nita and wish her luck and just be with her. Her husband accompanied her and she came with her bag packed, ready to go. Having to fill her bladder so her womb would be fully visible on the ultrasound monitor had made her uncomfortable, but she never once complained.

'Are you nervous?' I asked.

'No. This is my gift to you.'

We were given the option of going into the room, the 'clean room' in the sterile laboratory as it was called, where the transfer would take place. On a previous tour of the building we had entered the room through a sliding door and had to take off our shoes and put on a face mask. On the day of the transfer, Dr Patel asked us if we wanted to come in, but did enquire if we were wearing any sort of make-up, perfume, deodorant, or scented lotion. I had a shower that morning and had generously doused myself with shower gel. Technically, you're not supposed to wear any kind of chemicals in the presence of embryos – that's normal practice everywhere. I did not want to risk or jeopardise things in any way, so I reluctantly declined. But I would have loved to have been there.

I found it all rather emotional seeing Nita going in for the transfer. I did feel for her. Even though she had done it before, I could only imagine what emotions she might be feeling. She was human after all and no robot. At the time, however, she showed scant emotion – certainly in front of the staff and me. After some sedation, a catheter containing the embryos was inserted up through her cervix and into her womb and five embryos deposited there. Once the transfer was completed, she would have to continue on hormone treatment for at least three months to support the pregnancy.

As we sat outside the room, I was plagued with fears and worries. Was it going to work? Will I be that lucky? There was Nita's health to think of too.

I prayed she would be okay. And it wasn't out of self-interest because she was having our baby but a genuine wish for her welfare. After the transfer Nita was moved to a room in the clinic where the surrogates usually stay after the procedure. It meant that she would have to stay in bed for fifteen days, with the exception of toilet visits, so that implantation in the womb could take place without any hitches. Dr Patel really left nothing to chance. She had transferred five embryos to Nita to boost the success rate. Although that meant there was a higher chance of multiple births and indeed many of the surrogates at the clinic do deliver twins. Some hours later I went to visit Nita, thinking she might be less woozy from the sedation at that stage. At first, I just popped my head in, not wishing to intrude if she felt unwell, but she was fine and eager to see me. I went in, while Niall stayed outside, thinking that some things are best left to women.

I really just wanted to assure myself that she was fine, knowing only too well how awful hospital procedures can be. What I did not want to do was annoy her with endless questions. Luckily one of the surrogates in the room spoke English and helped interpret our brief conversation.

'I'm praying that we will have success,' Nita told me. 'Everything will be okay.'

I smiled in gratitude and held her hand. Yet it was not the time to linger as she looked quite tired, so I told her I would come and visit her before I returned to Ireland.

'Just lie there, don't move,' I reassured her. 'And if you need anything, just let me know.'

It was quiet time she needed now. However, the two-week wait until we heard news of the implantation would be one of the most tortuous in our lives.

**

Uday's involvement in the clinic had come about through Dr Hitesh, whose friendship stretched back to their schooldays. They were close friends and used to socialise all the time. Knowing the surrogacy process so well, Uday literally took us under his wing, especially the days we spent waiting between procedures, and would never see us stuck. Every day he would bring us to the clinic, wait outside sometimes or else pick us up at the opticians, ask what we wanted to do next, where we wanted to go, what we wanted to eat. Over the years he had assisted so many couples that he could almost anticipate our needs. It felt reassuring to know that when I returned for the baby's birth that he would be there. I would be as safe as houses.

Luckily for me there were several good shops and supermarkets. It was not so much that I was interested in purchasing fashion items, but seeing what was available if I needed supplies when I returned for the birth. I remember D-Mart and a place called the Big Bazaar in particular. D-Mart was like a big supermarket with trolleys and had everything you might need to look after a baby, especially toiletries. Granted, the most up-to-date brands were not available but what they had was absolutely fine. Upstairs in the Big Bazaar clothes were on sale. They may not have been high fashion but at least you would not be stuck for light clothes, especially in the intense heat and humidity.

Niall found the whole experience of being in the Big Bazaar indeed rather bizarre. It was like going into Willy Wonka's chocolate factory for him. Everywhere he walked children followed him around the store in waves. Hordes of them just stared at him, wide-eyed, and full of laughter too. Our fair skins were still proving to be a novelty and of course Niall's red hair. Even adults had joined their ranks. Each time Niall picked up a t-shirt or item of clothing to inspect it, all eyes were on him. Never before had we such a captive audience when shopping.

Not being able to resist the traditional dresses on sale, of course I had to try one on. As I stepped out of the changing cubicle to show off the gorgeous sari to Niall, I was met with a sea of curious eyes. A crowd of people stood around dying to catch a glimpse of what I looked like. It was as good as a fashion show, except I was no willing model. It was a memorable moment and quite amusing, and Niall's comment always sticks in my mind: 'you wouldn't want to have a complex about your colour, race or creed in India'.

While in Anand, Uday tried to make our stay as enjoyable as possible and encouraged us to see a little of India. And so sightseeing became part of our itinerary, something that was largely overlooked by many foreign couples given time constraints. For me, one day I wanted to be able to tell our child something about the place and country where she had been born. Thanks to Uday we got to see some marvellous sights; Laxmi's Vilas Palace was certainly a high point of our trip. The name had particular appeal because Bina's mother is called Laxmi, so as soon as Uday mentioned it, it was a must visit. The palace was not far, located in the nearby city of Vadadora, formerly known as Baroda. Set in over 700 acres of green parkland, the palace and a number of other buildings were the official residence of the Maharajas of the region and indeed, the royal family still lives there. The palace itself was constructed in 1890 by Maharaja Sayajirao Geakwad III and built in the Indo-Saracenic style of architecture. Even though it combined Indian, Islamic and European styles, it looked like an enormous country house in England to me. In fact, they say it is four times the size of Buckingham Palace. Captivated, I took shot after shot of the imposing exterior and the surrounding parkland.

Being such an iconic building, it was swarming with mostly Indian tourists led around by a very enthusiastic tour guide. Uday, of course knowing everybody, approached the tour guide and informed him we were from Ireland. Having foreigners in his midst was a welcome opportunity for the guide to show off the impressive palace. At once, Uday brought us up front with a full view of all the interiors and artefacts on display. On the ground floor, the only section open to the public, we witnessed the most incredible sights: some rooms resplendent in gold furnishings and fittings, glittering chandeliers, with beautiful mosaics and tiles and stained glass windows, and water fountains in a palm courtyard. Sculptures in marble, bronze and terracotta filled the building and courtyards and spoke opulence everywhere. Niall, being a history lover, was in his element. Whether it was 100 or 1000 years old, it did not matter to him – it was all fascinating. Whenever someone asked a question, Uday would translate it so we did not miss any nuggets of information. The guide also showed us metal artefacts taken from the ground that had been dated and carefully preserved over the years.

As we went through the ornate palace rooms, at one point Niall and I stalled a bit and fell to the back of the group. Perhaps the guide thought we had lost interest and wanted to reinvigorate us because he suddenly appeared at our side and started to explain things, while the group waited a short distance away. In our midst was an ancient armoury, with magnificent swords on display, and the guide proceeded to explain all their intricate features and name every single one of their owners. To our embarrassment, it must have taken him about thirty to forty minutes, while the rest of the group continued to wait patiently.

Being out and about exposed us to the delights, or otherwise, of Indian public toilets as well. Laxmi's Palace was my first experience of Indian loos, which were literally a hole in the ground. At Ahmedabad airport, we had noticed signs for Indian toilets as well as European toilets. The latter consisted of a very low bowl but not what you would expect in Europe. The other one was again just a hole in the floor. It was a balancing act that took some getting used to, if at all.

Before we took our leave of the palace, Uday made sure I got a postcard.

'Send it to Laxmi in England and tell her you were in the real Laxmi Palace.'

As I quickly scribbled a message to Laxmi, Uday promised to make sure it was posted. And I knew he would. There were so many small acts of kindness that made Uday more than just a businessman but a friend too. It felt comforting knowing that he would be there when I returned for the birth in nine months' time.

No trip to India would be complete without a visit to the Gandhi house and museum. So we set off with Uday on another hot day, but at least this time I was cool and comfortable in white linen trousers. The house was located on the banks of the River Sabarmati in Ahmedabad from where

Gandhi had sowed the seeds of non-violent protest against British Rule in the years leading up to 1930. Through many photos, paintings, letters and film, we learned so much about him. It was touching to see his writing desk and the small spinning wheel he used. The house and museum were more than just buildings and the place and grounds felt very spiritual and tranquil. You felt close to the spirit of Gandhi.

On the same day we decided to visit the zoo, also in Ahmedabad. Ever since we started dating, Niall and I enjoyed a trip to the zoo and if ever abroad it was a main attraction. Being an animal lover, I envisaged the animals roaming free within a decent-sized enclosure. However, in Ahmedabad, it upset me to see elephants in shackles and the animals squeezed into cages, hardly able to move. After coming from Gandhi's house with the emphasis on freedom and dignity, it was a big let-down. The only attraction at the zoo seemed to be us: two white people among the exotic animals. People kept staring at us, especially Niall. The monkeys admittedly were entertaining; full of mischief with tails as long as ropes. The zoo was also memorable for the enormous manmade lake there called Kankaria Lake, where kings once bathed. With its colourful riverboats and speedboats making a splash, it was a nice slice of Indian life.

***

Housing and construction in Anand was of obvious interest to Niall. Part of the sightseeing for him was the building sites on our travels around Anand and indeed Gujarat. He was quite taken with the massive modern-day building sites, yet one day ten tiers of wooden scaffolding took our breath away.

'You'd go up there on a wing and a prayer,' he pointed out.

When completed, many of the buildings were like huge concrete blocks. During our time in India, we got to see a wide variety of dwellings and often wondered what type Nita would favour. As far as we could tell, it all depended on where you lived and how close you were to the town. At the edge of the town it was all farmland, flat land, with houses built within the farming community. Brick houses were seen as socially desirable so baking bricks was big business in the town. Many of the houses further from the centre were older buildings built in the days of the British Empire. Red-bricked Victorian houses and villas, with sash windows, were something similar to what you would see in Dublin. Run-down apartment complexes were also evident in the town, the kind seen on holidays in the Canary Islands that had not a lick of paint in several years. There was nothing wrong with them, except for lack of maintenance, as Niall saw it. There were many different types of communities there. India's booming economy had seen the rise of new apartment complexes in Anand as well, many aimed at westerners. These upmarket deluxe apartments were not unlike those built in the Dublin Docklands, although we doubted if Nita would opt for that kind. She was more likely to choose something in the community apartments close to family and friends.

The opportunity to visit an Indian home came unexpectedly one day. Uday popped in to see a friend of his while on our travels. The house was very impressive and we could tell his friend was a man of means. Like Uday, he too had servants in his house and was very welcoming, offering us fruit juice to slake our thirst in the heat of the day. The house was a detached, three-storey, colonial-style building with a basement. It was charming with pretty shuttered windows and a verandah, where his two dogs, Tiger and Spider, stood guard. Out front was a lovely big garden with statues and water features that was very pleasant on the eye. We were glad to have stopped by, if only briefly.

Ever conscious of how indebted we were to Uday, we wanted to repay him.

'How much do I owe you?' I would ask each day.

'You're my friends, my friends, we'll talk about money at the end.'

But each day our fears grew that we would be saddled with a huge bill at the end.

'Uday, we would like to settle up,' I persisted. 'We really want to know what we owe you.'

In the end, he charged us a small amount by our standards. It was US$60, which we doubled because he had been so good to us. On day trips we paid for entrance fees and lunches, although Uday would usually decline to eat. But there was no way we were going to eat in front of the abstaining Uday, so we insisted.

***

Before we left Anand, I paid a final visit to Nita. It was too early to tell if the embryo transfer was successful and she was quietly resting in bed in the clinic. Much as I would have loved to stay in Anand, I knew there was no point in looking at Nita in bed for fifteen days. At any rate, Dr Patel would not have encouraged it and preferred for the surrogates to be left undisturbed. Usually most of the intended parents leave India two or three days after the transfer. Some couples prefer not to go near their surrogate at all, before or after, and have a more clinical approach. But not me. I honestly don't know which way is best and who am I to judge. My gut instinct was always to visit Nita. From my cervical cancer experience, I understood how invasive procedures could be and regardless of whether the transfer was successful or not, it was still not nice to be poked and prodded. Fortunately, she was feeling fine and looked comfortable and was chatting away to the other surrogates in the room.

Out and about the previous day I had bought a set of five red, glass-beaded bangles. I loved their colour and it reminded me of everything that was vibrant and alive in India. Without hesitation, I gave Nita two of the bangles. 'I'll wear these other three,' I said, placing them on my wrist.

It was just a small token of my appreciation but also a bond of solidarity. She smiled warmly and slipped the bangles on her tiny wrist too. For the next nine months I wore my bangles every day. Even today, I still have those bangles and keep them safe and close on my bedside locker. It always reminds me of Nita and that day. Our trip had been momentous and exciting and more than I had ever imagined. We had experienced a whole new culture and I knew our lives would be forever bound to India. Something good, I knew, would come of it. I had learnt that Anand means 'complete happiness' in Hindi, one of the official languages in India, and I hoped this would come to pass.

Chapter 11

The pregnancy

Back in Ireland, the two-week wait was proving unbearable. As the month of September wore on, the days began to feel interminably long and more like months. It was a terribly anxious time: I couldn't eat, I couldn't sleep, I couldn't think, I couldn't do anything. I had driven myself demented. In one way I was excited yet totally sick at the same time. I was just hoping and praying that nothing would go wrong. Niall, on the other hand, was much calmer and kept telling me to relax, saying it was all out of our hands now. Heeding his advice, I tried to throw myself into everyday life in Dublin.

As the fifteenth day approached, I knew Dr Patel would contact us by email. So I frantically tried to predict exactly when, taking into account the time difference of 5½ hours. The laptop was switched on all night, waiting for the email to come through. I had half-expected it to arrive around 3AM, but no joy. As I set off for work the next morning, my nerves were completely shot.

When I had heard nothing by midday, I bounced an email off to Dr Patel asking for news. Within minutes, I got a reply. When I first saw it in my inbox, I was almost afraid to open it but quickly put my fears to one side. It was a brief email, one line, as was customary and I suppose you could say it was a standard email. *CONGRATULATIONS, Nita has a positive pregnancy beta.* Dr Patel gave me the beta measurement and indicated it was a good one. After having a blood test on day 15, Nita had a good strong beta. 'Beta' refers to beta HCG, which is the hormone, human chorionic gonadotropin, known as the pregnancy hormone. Needless to say I was on the phone within seconds, sharing the good news with Niall and our families.

Later when I arrived home Niall and I hugged each other, scarcely believing our wonderful news. That evening was spent ringing around, sharing the news of our good fortune. Everyone was overjoyed and genuinely pleased for us, telling us how much we deserved to be happy. And a grandchild on the way was a real thrill for both my parents and Niall's. In my exuberance, I even rang Uday in Anand. As it happened he was out for the evening with Hitesh, driving around, and had heard the good news.

'It's great,' Uday responded. 'But let's pray. It's still very early.'

He was right of course. Next Hitesh came on the phone, offering his congratulations too.

'I can't thank you enough, Hitesh,' I gushed with emotion.

In Anand, they repeated the blood tests two days later to see if the hormone levels were continuing to rise, which thankfully they were. A series of tests and scans then followed to check the health of the baby and Nita. Doing her utmost to keep us informed, Dr Patel emailed all the ultrasound scans and relayed the good news that there were no genetic abnormalities, like Down syndrome, with the baby. From then on, Dr Patel would give me updates from month to month, or whenever I requested information.

***

Now that the pregnancy was a reality, it gave me pause to think more about surrogacy as a method. Given the 'conception' as such took place in the laboratory and Nita would deliver the baby, it was easy for people to think we had manufactured a baby. But we never felt like that. I suppose a lot it might depend on your viewpoint or religious beliefs. As Niall and I saw it, the development of our baby was just the same as a baby conceived in the normal way, only the insertion was different. Our baby wasn't a product but a living human being.

In my eyes, in years to come the controversy surrounding surrogacy will be a thing of the past. After all surrogacy is not a new phenomenon, from what

I've read. It's been here since the dawn of time. In biblical times, Abraham's wife Sarah could not have children so she arranged for him to sleep with her maidservant Hagar and they had a child Ismael. And then there was also Rachel, wife of Jacob, who was infertile and arranged for him to sleep with her servant Bilhah, who gave birth to twins, Dan and Naphtali. Surrogacy is not such a foreign concept to Indians either. The Mahabharata, the religious epic of India over two thousand years old, contains a surrogacy story among many others. It centres on an evil king, Kansa, who after hearing a prediction that he would be killed by Krishna, the eighth-born child of his sister Devaki and her husband Vasudeva, imprisoned the newlywed couple and killed each of their six sons at birth. Realising their plight, the supreme god, Lord Vishnu, arranged for the seventh male child, Balarama, to be transferred to the womb of Rohini, the first wife of Vasudeva, who craved a child of her own. Meanwhile a female child, an incarnation of the goddess Maya, was placed in Devaki's womb. In time, Krishna was born to Devaki and Vasudeva, as an incarnation of Vishnu, and eventually killed Kansa, thus completing the prophecy.

Throughout history surrogacy was always practised, mostly in secret. So nobody can say surrogacy is unnatural and only arrived with modern technology. It's part of human nature. Modern technology has now made commercial surrogacy possible and placed it on a grand scale. It is true it has made it more complicated in that more people, like the intended parents, donors and surrogate mother could potentially be involved. And in some cases, it has reached the stage now where you hardly need the parents to be present for anything. You can just ship sperm or eggs to the clinic in question wherever in the world. Eventually, the controversy over surrogacy will be old news. It's just technology and you can't hold back the advancement of science, despite how hard you try.

***

As the weeks progressed, my curiosity about how Nita was faring grew. I didn't want to plague Dr Patel with emails but one of the couples I had been corresponding with in England encouraged me to contact her. After that, I was constantly emailing Dr Patel asking is everything okay with Nita. And literally half an hour later she would reply. The email was short, one sentence, but it was enough. *Yes, Nita is fine, the baby is fine, looking forward to seeing you.* That's all I needed to reassure me.

Maybe it was because I never asked much of Dr Patel that she used to reply so promptly. On the global forum, I sometimes read complaints from dissatisfied couples but I suppose expectations can vary hugely among people.

Among our families the topic that consumed us most was the sex of the baby. *Is it a boy? Is a girl?* My parents were fully convinced it was going to be a boy. In fact, we all did, even Nita when I met her months later. Bina's brother, a paediatrician, had declared it was going to be a boy when emailed the scan image.

'I know by looking at it, it's going to be a boy.'

Thinking about it now, I really don't know why we all thought that way. All we were basing our judgement on were ultrasound scans and a photo Dr Patel emailed of Nita in early pregnancy. Maybe we thought Nita looked very 'big' in an Indian context, as the people were generally small framed. One way or the other, Dr Patel was never going to reveal the sex of the baby. It was prohibited under Indian legislation; too many cases of female infanticide had seen to that. Besides, all we wanted was a healthy baby and the sex never mattered to us.

***

Another issue demanding our attention was the legalities of getting a passport for the baby. This was far more worrisome than finding out if the baby was a boy or a girl. During Nita's pregnancy we did some preparation work in Ireland and before I returned to India for the birth. We soon learned that Irish couples availing of surrogacy abroad did pose a problem for the Passport Office. Surrogacy was not banned in Ireland as such, from a legal viewpoint, but no money could exchange hands and the surrogate mother was automatically recognised as the legal mother of the child and her husband or partner seen as the legal father. The intended parents were free to adopt the child but would be required to go through the official adoption process and get a declaration of parentage. That avenue was effectively closed off to us.

In October 2010, I contacted the Irish Embassy in New Delhi to enquire about what was required to eventually bring the baby home. We knew the Indian authorities would only issue an exit visa for our baby once we produced an Irish passport or emergency travel document for her. My email seemed to bounce from one desk to another until finally I was told to contact the Passport Office in Dublin. After a while, it looked like the emergency travel certificate might be our best bet. I next rang the Irish Consulate in Mumbai, anonymously.

'I'm just wondering about these emergency travel documents,' I began, 'Are they being issued?'

The official replied they were being issued and as regards surrogacy the office had received confirmation of that from the Passport Office in Dublin. The official just presumed I was enquiring for surrogacy reasons. The document or certificate was only issued if there was cause to believe the child was an Irish citizen. Yet this was only done in exceptional circumstances and certainly not issued in advance but on a case-by-case basis. And of course it would take time, a long time, from what I could gather.

I hesitated contacting the Passport Office directly until I had more information to hand. Through an internet blog I learned of an Irish couple travelling to India for surrogacy that November, though not to Dr Patel's clinic. After making contact, it was such a relief to hear someone in the same position as us and what they were experiencing. The woman had been in touch with the Passport Office in August 2009 and again in June 2010. From emails she forwarded to me, it was obvious there was no clarity. On the one hand, the Passport Office was saying that the position regarding entitlement to passports and consent to issuing of a passport was unclear when it came to surrogacy and the absence of legislation in Ireland. But on the other hand, that we could resolve the uncertainty by getting a declaration of parentage under Section 35 of the Status of Children Act, 1987. As regards consent, we would probably need the consent of all the possible guardians – first the surrogate mother and her husband and secondly the biological parents, i.e. us – or we could seek an order relating to Section 14(3) of the Passports Act, 2008 that dispensed with the consent of any other guardians when issuing a passport to a child. And then of course there was the constant goodbye line. *You should give serious consideration to obtaining further advice from an Irish solicitor.*

At one point I grew so befuddled from all the legalities, I thought it might be easier if Nita was actually registered as the birth mother, thus making her the legal mother. The email from Dr Patel left me in no uncertainty or doubt as to the wisdom of my request. Dr Patel flatly refused; there was no way she would consent to it. After some consideration, I could fully understand why. Nita had no genetic connection to our baby, regardless of carrying her for nine months. Interestingly, the issue of passports had been thrashed out in the Indian Supreme Court with another one of Dr Patel's clients back in 2005. In that case, the German authorities had refused to issue a passport to the baby of a German couple, and the Indian court had ruled that the intended parents were the legal parents.

From listening to all the forums I eventually emailed the Passport Office in Dublin myself and got the same response as the other Irish couple. In the reply, the director of passport services mentioned that his office was in discussion with the Department of Health and Children, which was the department responsible for surrogacy matters. Pending the outcome of those discussions and the issuing of guidelines, the Passport Office would not be issuing any Irish passport to children born through surrogacy. However, we still banked on getting the emergency travel document, at least that's what everyone was saying on the internet forums. Then some doubt arose and we heard that the embassy was not issuing the certificate in the case of surrogacy.

Just before I went to India, I rang the Irish Consulate in Mumbai, again anonymously and without bringing up the subject of surrogacy.

'I'm just wondering about these emergency travel documents,' I began,

'I've heard they're not being issued.'

'Is it for surrogacy?' the official enquired. 'I'm just being honest with you. Are you in that situation yourself?'

I was taken aback, unprepared for such a direct question.

'No, I'm just enquiring on behalf of a friend,' I replied.

But he suspected it anyway, obviously the embassy was finding more and more people in my circumstances. From my first email to the Passport Office they had my name, so I was sure I was on their surrogacy hit list.

During the pregnancy, Niall had discussed surrogacy with a few solicitors personally known to him, more on a friendly basis rather than as a consultation. A lot of family law firms he contacted were unable to offer any advice whatsoever. Most responded with the same opinion: surrogacy was a grey area within Irish law. However, we knew the 2005 report by the Commission on Assisted Human Reproduction set up by the Government had recommended that surrogacy be permitted in Ireland subject to regulation, but by 2011 the Government was still delaying its response and the introduction of any legislation. The Commission had even gone so far as to say that the child born through surrogacy should be presumed to be the child of the commissioning couple. We were caught in the middle while the Government dithered.

In February 2011, Niall did contact one law firm claiming to have some knowledge and experience of surrogacy. However, the consultation proved disappointing. We arrived at their office one afternoon and the solicitor greeted us in a small shabby reception area, and then in a rather officious tone told us to wait in the office.

After explaining our situation, all the solicitor could offer was a number of stories of Irish and non-Irish commissioning parents that were stuck in legal limbos. However, none of those cases had been handled by the law firm. The solicitor was then kind enough to put forward a number of options, in no particular order or importance. The first suggestion was that we would have to attend the High Court and obtain a declaration of parentage and a declaration of guardianship. This seemed like a reasonably straightforward process, until a bombshell was suddenly dropped. We would need in the region of €30,000 to obtain a declaration of guardianship and up to €250,000 for a declaration of parentage.

The second suggestion was that we should research orphanages in India, and when we found a suitable one, we should relinquish all legal rights to our baby and leave her in the orphanage of our choice. Needless to say, it was not the type of reassurance we expected to hear from a professional specialising in this area. The shock left us reeling in our seats.

'Do you have any questions?' the solicitor enquired, perhaps seeing our shell-shocked faces.

The question of issuing a passport to what we saw as the child of Irish citizens was the nub of the matter. For months Niall had been reading up on various pieces of Irish and European legislation relating to children and to citizenship and posed several questions to the solicitor.

'But doesn't that contravene the Irish Nationality and Citizenship Act, the Passport Act, the Guardianship of Infants Act, the Constitutional rights of the child, the European Convention on Human Rights, and the UN Declaration on the Rights of the Child?'

'I agree with you,' said the solicitor, though obviously not expecting to hear the arguments Niall presented. 'Are you going to challenge the Courts?'

Niall shrugged, knowing the costs involved would be astronomical. The thirty-minute consultation, at a cost of €350, ended and left us in a far worse frame of mind since the entire surrogacy procedure had started.

With all the talk of exploitation in surrogacy, Niall sometimes felt the ones who were really exploited were the commissioning parents and their child by some legal firms. The cost of advice was proving expensive, if not exorbitant, by firms who had little or no experience of surrogacy. If anyone was going to be exploited it was the child rather than the surrogate mother who at least got paid. It often ended up that Irish parents were running around in circles, while their children were in legal limbos.

I have to admit the whole legal area energised Niall. His grasp of the law and all its complexities astounded me as indeed both our families. And like a dog with a bone, Niall would not give up and just go on to the next stage, undeterred. It was as good as a military campaign. Since 1995, because of running his own business, he had engaged the services of the legal firm, Lavelle Coleman, especially whenever the issue of non-payment of invoices by his customers arose. They were helpful and put him in touch with one of their young solicitors who dealt with probates, deeds and some aspects of family law. By her own admission, this solicitor knew nothing about surrogacy and we appreciated her honesty. Not stopping there, Niall next contacted the firm of Willie O'Grady Solicitors on Percy Place, whose business he was acquainted with. Again it wasn't something Willie dealt with but, willing to help, he asked his son Ronan to look into it. True to his word, he did. Ronan contacted us with the name of a young dynamic solicitor, Deborah Kearney, who worked for Leman Solicitors in the same building in Percy Place.

When they met, Deborah listened attentively to everything Niall said, sympathising with our predicament. Fair play to Deborah, he would say afterwards, she knows her stuff. She was indeed well informed but more importantly for us, she was able to see a way around the complications that other solicitors saw, especially after scrutinising the case from every angle. We decided to follow the route that any Irish-born citizen or their children would be expected to follow. We would apply for a passport as set out by the Passport Act, 2008. As far as we were concerned, we met all the required criteria set by the Irish authorities so there should be no issue with the baby's citizenship or the issuing of an Irish passport. Our child should be afforded all the legal rights and privileges of an Irish citizen. In readiness, Deborah prepared all the paperwork and we hoped it would work.

Not content with just accepting the word of officialdom, we were constantly testing the waters. Twice I visited the Passport Office on Molesworth Street in Dublin along with my mother on what we called our dry runs. Nervously I approached the counter when my turn was called.

'My child is going to be born in *India*,' I said, choosing my words very carefully. 'What will I need to get a passport?'

I explained my husband would apply for the passport in Dublin while I stayed with the baby in India. The official held up the passport application form and signalled the relevant areas to complete. Obviously Niall would bring along the birth certificate and photographs and the appropriate fee, when applying.

'Yes, that's all you need,' the official said. 'You just get this part signed in India and your husband gets this part signed here in Ireland.'

'Are you sure that's all I need?'

'Yes, that's it,' she replied confidently.

On both trips it was the same reply, no matter how much I kept repeating 'my child is going to be born in *India*' over and over again. Niall too phoned up the Passport Office in Cork, just to see if he would get a different response. Again, he emphasised that our child would be born in India. It was the same reply; there would be no obstacles once all the documentation and fee were received.

In addition, back in February 2011, we started to crusade far and wide. Election fever was in the air as the Fianna Fáil government battled to stay in power in the midst of one of the worst recessions the country faced. Niall and I contacted public representatives in our Dublin South-West constituency, while my father did the same in Dublin Mid-West, since my parents were still living in Palmerstown. Though sympathetic to our plight, none of the politicians really did anything to assist us. My dad even went out canvassing for the Labour Party, but to no avail.

Though it was never said, I knew for some TDs the topic was too hot to handle and might upset the views of the electorate, especially those that had moral and ethical oppositions to surrogacy.

At the time we were worried we would receive neither a passport nor emergency travel document. To his credit, Conor Lenihan TD, then a Minister for State in the outgoing Fianna Fáil government, did raise the matter with the Department of Foreign Affairs, after we contacted him by phone. By way of background information, I had forwarded on emails received from the Passport Office in Dublin. He expressed the view that the position taken by the Passport Office was ridiculous and an embarrassment to the State and should be resolved as a matter of urgency. However, the Department in its reply reiterated the same official position we had heard from the Passport Office: that when dealing with any passport application, it had no alternative but to apply existing Irish laws applicable in the areas of citizenship, guardianship and other parental rights. Aware of the report of the Commission on Assisted Human Reproduction, the official said it was up to the Government or a member of the Dáil or Seanad to bring forward any proposals for legislative change.

So it was back in the politician's court, yet few of them seemed to have any appetite for change, despite hundreds of Irish couples being in legal predicaments.

***

In the midst of trying to sort out the passport difficulties, I was busy preparing for motherhood too. Every time I glanced at the red bangles on my wrist, it was a reminder of how time was moving on. Nita's due date was around late May 2011 but I was thinking of going out in early April just to spend time with her and get used to the idea of motherhood. Being in Ireland, I suppose I felt a little cut off. However, I knew the situation could not be helped. Even without a bump to show I was pregnant, I was always thinking ahead to the practicalities: imagining the night feeds, nappy changing, cuddling the baby in my arms, bathtime and dressing. By constantly looking at the scan images and photos of Nita with her proud bump that Dr Patel had emailed, it made the pregnancy all the more real for me. There was something so captivating about Nita's smile, warm and welcoming, as if saying this is your baby too.

As I counted down the months, there was so much to consider. Christmas approached and I imagined what it would be like the following year with a baby in the house. It was just too good to even believe it could be possible.

'What do you want for Christmas?' Niall asked shortly before the day itself.

'Money for the baby!' I answered, without a second thought.

The vouchers from Mamas & Papas that awaited me on Christmas morning were as good as a diamond necklace. Armed with the vouchers I descended on the shops for the January sales and went crazy stocking up on baby stuff. For a change it was wonderful to be buying baby items for my baby and not as presents for others. I knew I could get used to it very quickly. My mother, Bina and Niall's mother, Marie, were a godsend with tips of what I might need or anything I might have overlooked. I kept in touch with Payal, whom I had met in Anand the previous August, and we eagerly made our to-do lists, wondering had we covered everything. It was hard to know what supplies I might actually need once over in Anand but at least I could rely on the supermarkets surveyed on our last trip there. Because we would be staying in a hotel, I had to think about what the baby would need to sleep in: a petite bassinette travel cot and maybe a breathable mattress because of the heat. There was also what was required to carry the baby home safe and sound to Dublin. In the house, there was the bedroom to prepare, choosing a colour, buying a cot and of course a buggy for outdoors. The baby's bedroom was the last thing to be done. Just before I went over in April we started to decorate the room, painting it in neutral creams to suit a boy or a girl.

During Nita's pregnancy, I received a request to take part in a radio series called *Window on Your World*, broadcast by the BBC World Service. Back in India the topic of surrogacy was very much in vogue and no doubt the BBC wanted to capture that and had chosen Dr Patel's clinic for their documentary. It would be broadcast in July 2011 as *Your World: Womb for Rent*, a title that never goes down too well with intended parents. However, I hoped that by July everything would be sorted out with the passport and so agreed to participate in the programme.

Supposedly following Nita and myself over a nine-month period, the radio crew arrived at my home in January to record the first part of the programme. At first, it felt strange to be talking about the pregnancy when Nita was thousands of miles away, but I knew it was as real for me as it was for her. I just hoped it would depict Niall and me as ordinary decent people and not some cold-hearted couple from the west intent on exploiting under-privileged Indians.

Niall and Caroline on their wedding day, September 2002

Caroline at the Madhubhan Hotel in Anand

Dr Nayna Patel

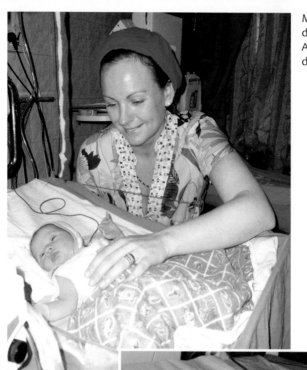

Mum and
daughter,
Ava at one
day old

Ava in the
neonatal unit
at one day old

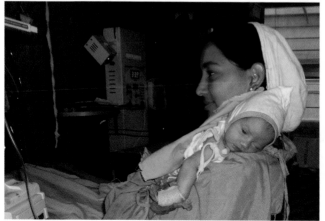

Ava and her
nurse at the
neonatal unit
after her first
feed

Ava finally leaving
the neonatal unit but
still no Daddy or
passport in sight!

ur nanny, Vimla,
feeding Ava

Vimla all dressed up
and ready to attend
a family wedding

Caroline and Ava as
the family finally
begins the long
journey home

Above: Ava in her uncle Philip's house with that first toy doggie from her Daddy

Right: Ava with great grandmother Nolan

Ava's christening, at six months

Mum and daughter back home in Ireland, July 2011

at fifteen months

Niall and Ava on
a family holiday
in 2012

Above: Niall and Ava at the Natural History
Museum, Dublin in September 2012

Left: Ava, July 2012

In her seventh month of pregnancy Nita had a baby shower in the surrogate house, as was customary. Although I suppose it wasn't exactly a shower but a welcome to 'channel a healthy birth', as the girls called it. The intended parents normally foot the bill, so I was asked to pay US$100, and we happily obliged. From photos of the event emailed to me, they all seemed to have enjoyed themselves thoroughly. There were loads of guests in attendance at the Hindu ritual, all dressed in their best saris or suits. The surrogate mothers and their families were present along with other guests, Dr Patel and Dr Hitesh included. Seated in the centre of the room, Nita took pride of place, where she wore an orange blossom garland and her hands were decorated with Mehndi. Prayers for a safe delivery were said by a priest dressed in white robes and Nita was given a kind of blessing, while all heads were bowed. Another important Hindu ritual that took place was the breaking of the coconut. This happens before starting any new venture in life like a birth or wedding. I thought it was a wonderful custom, having seen it performed at Bina and Philip's wedding years before. During the ceremony in the surrogate house gifts of fruit, bangles and sweets were distributed, as so often happens at Hindu ceremonies, and a special lunch was held afterwards. It was brilliant to get the photos and I only wished I could have been there.

Chapter 12

Returning to India

With a wet and gusty start to the month of April, I dashed around putting the house in order and finalising the packing. Already, two suitcases were filled to near bursting point. Packing was proving difficult as I had to take clothes and items not only for myself, but also for the baby, as well as all the paperwork. With my usual checklist in hand, I ticked off all the items and scaled them back to only the most essential. The plan was to spend about a month with Nita before the baby was born, while Niall looked after the dogs at home and obviously met his heavy work commitments. At first it was hard to decide exactly when to go over. Obviously, I wanted to be there for the birth; there was no way on earth I wanted to miss that. The question of maternity leave was problematic because the baby would be born abroad and surrogacy was not officially recognised in Ireland. But meeting Nita again and preparing for the birth of the baby were important to me, so I took leave from the GP practice where I was working. Luckily, my employers were very understanding and sympathetic. The plan was that Niall would join me in Anand after the birth and by which time he would have received a passport for our baby, all going well.

The day of my departure for India, Wednesday, April 13th, arrived and with it a great feeling of excitement. That said, it was tinged with trepidation because I didn't know how the passport business would pan out. Nevertheless,

I couldn't get to the airport quickly enough that day to let it all begin. My outward journey was the same as the previous time, flying Dublin/Heathrow, Heathrow/Mumbai, and Mumbai/Ahmedabad. As I locked the front door and bid the dogs goodbye, I thought to myself that the next time I step over the threshold will be with a baby in my arms. And the next time I see family, friends and neighbours, I'll actually be a mother.

On the way to Dublin airport, my mind was racing. I was worried about leaving the dogs, imploring Niall to make sure they were okay in my absence. By the time we arrived at the airport our plans nearly came undone. In fact, it was the start of a series of mishaps before my plane ever touched down in Mumbai, amusing in hindsight but which upset me at the time. To begin with, at the Aer Lingus check-in desk, my two bags weighed in at 19 kg and 21 kg, respectively. I had booked an international flight with the Indian carrier, Jet Airways, and had checked in two bags online and was given a baggage allowance of 40kgs. Nonetheless, Aer Lingus forced us to pay €300 euro in excess baggage, despite misleading information on their website. All our attempts to resolve the matter, explaining I was travelling on to India, were met with deaf ears by a very unsympathetic stewardess. The easiest solution from her viewpoint was to leave the suitcase full of baby items behind. That would have horrified me. In desperation, we had even offered to buy a second ticket to Heathrow, which would have been a cheaper option, but that was not going to work unless Niall actually flew. At that point Niall even considered flying over to Heathrow with the suitcase and back again empty handed. In the end, the least hassle was to pay up. Hurriedly we made our way to the security screening area and I psyched myself up for the long trip ahead on my own. As we kissed each other goodbye, we grew excited again, knowing we were on the verge of truly starting a family.

However, in Heathrow there was more calamity in store. In the Duty Free shop, I tried to pay for a few small gifts with my credit card but it had been inexplicably cancelled. With no sterling cash, I couldn't even buy myself a cup of coffee in a restaurant. And then when I tried to ring Niall, my mobile phone would not work. Tearful, I slumped into a seat and wondered had the world gone mad and was I jinxed. Luckily, an Indian gentleman, a fellow passenger, came to my aid and let me use his mobile phone to contact Niall, who in turn sorted out the credit card.

As I boarded the flight to Mumbai that evening, I was hyper-aware it was my first time travelling alone outside of Ireland and Britain. While it did give me a huge sense of independence, admittedly I was nervous too because of my fear of flying. That reality hit me as I buckled up and prepared for takeoff. Whenever I get nervous I'm compelled to talk to the nearest person, as it does tend to calm me down. But without Niall beside me, there was no family or friend to speak to and comfort me. In an attempt to distract myself, I looked around and saw that everyone was black haired and dark skinned. The passengers were predominantly Indian and I wondered were they travelling home or visiting relatives or on business trips. I imagined their homecomings, judging the scenarios by their faces and body language.

'I hope the flight's not too bad,' I murmured to an Indian gentleman sitting beside me, not capable of staying silent any longer.

He nodded but I guess conversation was the last thing he wanted. It was a night-time flight and sleep was probably foremost on his mind. I settled back as the plane took off, thankful the crew were not anticipating any turbulence. If they had, I probably would have got off the plane there and then. But I soon regretted putting the idea in my head in the first place. Flying somewhere over Europe we experienced turbulence so bad I thought the plane would actually go down. I was seized with fear and clenched my fists, digging my fingernails deep into my skin. Finally, I could bear it no longer and turned to the man beside me, now slumbering, and actually tipped him on his shoulder until his eyelids flickered open.

'I'm really sorry but I have to wake you because this turbulence is really bad.'

'I've flown to India and back so many times and I've never seen it this bad,' he said quietly and calmly like a Buddha.

After that he just closed his eyes and went back to sleep. That left me feeling even more terrified because I knew I couldn't disturb him a second time. I had to distract myself so I asked the stewardess could I go to the toilet, thinking the walk down the aisle might help. Luckily, she allowed me.

'This seems really, really bad,' I confided to the stewardess as I left the toilet.

'It's just the area we're going over,' she replied soothingly. 'Nothing is going to happen.'

Calming down, I struggled to return to my seat, trying to regain my balance as I walked back along the aisle. In my mind, I started to break the journey up into stages. *Stage 1 is done, stage 2 is nearly done.* It was the only way I would make it all the way to Ahmadabad.

Inevitably, anyone I met on the flights or in transit lounges would ask was I going on a working holiday to India, seeing that I was travelling alone.

'Kind of,' I would answer, hesitating to elaborate on the real reason for my journey.

Surrogacy being a delicate subject for many people was not exactly a small-talk topic. There was no way of predicting people's response to it. But thinking about the baby helped me to focus on the real purpose of my visit and cast thoughts of turbulence aside. I convinced myself it would be just another story to tell our baby when she grew up. So it was with absolute joy that I greeted Uday in Ahmadabad airport at about 3 o'clock the next day. It felt so good to be back on terra firma and to see a familiar face. Within hours he had driven me to the Madhubhan Hotel, another familiar sight. Seeing that I was visiting on my own, my family and Niall's were anxious that I stay somewhere safe and secure. There was no telling how long my visit would last, especially with the uncertainty of the passport.

***

Next morning, refreshed from sleep, the first thing on my mind was Nita. After breakfast, Uday, ever so helpful, drove me to the clinic. There seemed to be no end to the journey, negotiating all the pedestrians and animals along the way. One item I needed in particular was a new mobile phone now that mine had given up the ghost in Heathrow Airport. I wanted to be in touch with the clinic if anything happened to Nita, no matter how trivial, or if she went into early labour.

'If anything happens, I don't care if it's the middle of the night,' I had told Dr Patel. 'I want somebody to call me.'

Thankfully, Uday offered to arrange the purchase of a new phone, which was a great relief for me. Being back at the clinic felt good and I noticed some changes since my previous visit. Dr Hitesh's office was now located in a building adjacent to the main block complete with full air conditioning and a small comfortable, leather sofa. His old office had been converted into a waiting room for couples.

'We've come up in the world,' Hitesh explained, showing me his new office.

We all laughed. After greeting Hitesh, he introduced me to a lovely, young petite Indian woman standing in his office, telling me she was from Mumbai and here for a meeting with me. This was news to me and I was totally puzzled. However, she explained she was from the BBC World Service and there to record more interviews for the documentary. Straightaway, I texted the producer of the show, who confirmed her colleague's identity. The reporter asked if she could follow me upstairs to Nita's room. At first, I was reluctant but she promised to keep at a distance and not intrude in our conversation in any way. After seven months of pregnancy, Nita had been moved from the surrogate house and was staying in a small ward upstairs in the clinic.

Once in the clinic proper, it was wonderful to be remembered by Hansha and all the nurses, who were as friendly as ever.

'Where's Nita?' I asked, barely able to contain my excitement.

'She's up on the third floor,' replied Hansha.

'I can't wait to see her.'

'We'll just tell her that you're coming.'

Giving Nita time to prepare herself, I made my way to the new waiting room. Inside there were new couples, intended parents, like I had been back in the previous August, some of whom were British. My face lit up at seeing all the couples and I couldn't stop beaming as I took a seat.

'Is this your first time here?' enquired one woman.

'No, but my baby is going to be born soon,' I replied, grinning broadly.

Gosh, I was just ecstatic. Everyone of course was dying to hear my story, as I was further down the process than they were. The queries just kept coming. *How many eggs did you have? How many embryos were transferred?* Back in August when I had met other couples nearing the end of the process, I remember saying if only that were me. It was so hard to believe that I had now reached that stage, the much-longed for stage. I could feel the exhilaration rising.

'Did it work first time?' another enquired.

'Yes, it did,' I answered, remembering my great relief at the time.

After ten minutes, Hansha arrived back with a young man called Jenti Boy, who worked at the clinic and spoke very good English. He dealt with office administration and divided his time between the clinic and the surrogate house. Hansha led us to the third floor where she opened a door on the dim corridor. Inside the room were about five beds accommodating five surrogate women, all lying down relaxing and periodically rubbing their bumps. In one corner, Nita sat on her low bed, a small metal frame with a pretty blue tartan-style bedspread. Aside from the surrogate mothers there were several visitors in the room, even young children. Another surrogate mother, Tina, lay on the adjoining bed and had a good grasp of English and so helped translate our conversation, as did Jenti Boy. But sometimes it was easy to tell what Nita was saying just by her gestures and motions.

'Hello,' I said, greeting Nita. 'How are you?'

'Thank you,' said Nita in English.

'You look so good.'

'Yes,' agreed Tina.

'I came at last,' I said to Nita, thinking she must have wondered about my long absence, even though I had sent a message to say I was coming some weeks before.

'I'm happy to meet you,' said Nita.

'I was waiting for months and months to meet you, so long,' I said, 'I have your photograph at home.'

She smiled as Jenti Boy explained about the photograph while I stood by and observed her. Her smile was just the most beautiful smile I could imagine, beaming away, looking so happy.

'We are so thankful to you, Nita,' I said. 'You have made our dream come true.'

'Thank you,' she replied politely.

Seeing her bump in the flesh for the first time made everything so real. It left me rather emotional. My hands ached to touch her bump, but I wouldn't have been that forward, not unless invited. Instead we gave each other a warm hug and then Nita gestured for me to touch the bump. The joy I felt was indescribable and I cherished that precious moment. We then sat on the bed together; the physical proximity felt so good and helped bridge any gap. By all accounts the baby was very active. Very active indeed. Definitely an O'Flaherty, I thought.

'It's keeping me awake at night,' Nita said, making kicking gestures. 'It must be a boy!'

I'm sure the heat and high humidity did not help matters either. The room was very warm, though a gentle breeze blew in through the open windows, billowing the dark heavy cotton curtains. The women preferred to have the curtains drawn to keep the heat out, which left the room quite dim. I suppose it was inevitable the women would get hot during pregnancy given the climate. I had arrived in April, in the middle of the summer season, with May being the hottest month when temperatures would soar above 40°C. It would be mid-June and the arrival of the monsoon rains before there was any relief from the heatwave. Luckily, a large portable fan was positioned in the corner near Nita's bed.

'You've a good spot,' I said to Nita, pointing to the fan nearby.

'It's hot but it's going to get hotter,' she said.

I soon learned that the women, and indeed all the locals, were not looking forward to the month of May at all.

The word had gone out that a foreigner was visiting one of the surrogates. So, curiosity being what it is, it wasn't long before the door was inched open and left sufficiently ajar for other surrogate mothers to peek in. I was within earshot of some snippets of their conversation.

'Nita.'

'Ireland.'

'Not England, Ireland.'

It made me smile. For anyone speaking English, it was automatically assumed they were from Britain. When I met Nita on the last trip, I used to say 'Not England, Ireland', when explaining where I was from.

'Another plane to Ireland,' I would gesture, indicating a second plane ride.

My curiosity and novelty value was also evident among the many children of the surrogates who were visiting that day, none of whom were Nita's. Several of them were just standing about beside one wall, quiet and well behaved but taking everything in. I couldn't resist waving to them, which sent them into hysterics of laughter, and the delight on their faces made me repeat it over and over again. Not wishing to tire Nita out, I left after a while. It was a great relief to see her looking well and comfortable, aside from the heat. By this time, I had forgotten all about the BBC reporter whose presence in the room I had barely registered.

When I left the clinic that day, I remembered that Uday had said to ring him whenever I wanted to return to the hotel. I decided to pop into the optician's and wait for him there like we had done on our previous trip. However, the proprietor was nowhere to be seen and the shop felt strangely empty in his absence. Without seeing his face, it just wasn't the same. His family members were preoccupied with the business of the shop and had less time to chat. I got the distinct impression that something had happened. When Uday came to pick me up, I mentioned it to him in the car.

'I got a call one day,' Uday began, 'and they told me my friend was dead.'

It appeared the man had had a massive heart attack, despite being only in his early fifties, and died suddenly. As it turned out, there was an epidemic of coronary artery disease in India that seemed to be claiming the lives of a lot of relatively young men.

'It is very sad,' Uday said mournfully. 'Every time I drive by the optician's, I think of my friend.'

Yes, it was very sad, particularly after making the acquaintance of the man, and I felt for Uday. However, Uday was such a tower of strength, though sometimes his attentive manner ran against my independent streak. His help was always invaluable, whether it was bringing me dinner, sorting out a new mobile phone after the Heathrow Airport mishap, getting my camera fixed, or loaning his laptop when my own broke down.

***

In sari and pearls and occasionally a bindi mark on her forehead, Dr Patel was as busy as ever. Answering the phone and emails, dealing with people in the clinic, performing scans, checking the surrogates upstairs in the clinic, and delivering babies, there seemed nothing she was incapable of doing. But one thing was certain; she was always in control of the situation, knowing exactly what to do. As the weeks wore on, I couldn't believe just how phenomenal and super focused she was. With so much work, she must go home exhausted at night, I thought. I even asked her husband Hitesh how does she switch off.

'She just doesn't switch off,' he replied. 'I can tend to switch off but not Nayna.'

In my experience Indians tended to wear gold jewellery but Dr Patel in her trademark pearls stood apart. Because I loved pearls myself, it was something I particularly noticed and admired. Perhaps being a woman, the different saris she wore fascinated me too; all so very beautiful and made from the finest material. She must have had 365, one for every day, and I imagined a servant in her house selecting one each morning. I wondered too, as I saw the women constantly fix their saris, tossing the top corner over their shoulder, if they were a hindrance to wear at work. But Bina assured me they were quite comfortable to wear, especially in warm weather. Naturally, Dr Patel wore a gown and cap for surgical procedures.

Shortly afterwards the sonographer performed an ultrasound scan on Nita. It was my first time to be present at the scan and also incredibly thrilling.

'Oh my god, it's amazing to actually hear', I gushed, rather overcome with emotion.

The sound of the heartbeat, the thumping *whosh, whosh, whosh* filled the room. For those few moments nothing else existed.

'Gosh, it's strong,' I said.

The sonographer nodded and smiled. I thought of Niall and wished he could be here to witness it.

'My husband is very tall. It's probably a long baby.'

Later I visited Nita upstairs in the clinic. The time we were spending together was becoming very precious to me and I enjoyed the company of the other surrogate mothers too. The solidarity among the women was plain to see, much of it forged from their time at the surrogate house. None of them felt isolated or cut off at all and I was pleased to learn that Nita had been happy at the house. With my laptop I could make contact with the relevant intended mothers from around the world, when requested, and pass on any messages for the women or vice versa. Because I had time on my hands, I was also free to run errands for the women in the room. At that time of year, the most important thing was keeping cool and hydrated. In the room a large fridge contained soft drinks and water to keep their thirst at bay. Every day I would go to the shops and stock up on soft drinks or fruit for them. Like many Asian shops, the vendors would be on their doorsteps trying to entice customers in.

'Come in, come in, come in,' they would chime as I passed by. 'We have make-up, we have jewellery, we have clothes in here.'

After a while, one shopkeeper became familiar with my requests and would automatically ask how many soft drinks I wanted that day. Nita's ward was also a hive of pregnancy stories and even of customs and practices. After the embryo transfer many of the women continued to avoid any chemicals in shampoos, deodorants, scented soaps and not wash their hair for a month. If they could wait longer, two or three months, so much the better. A shower room and toilet adjoined the ward and was for the use of the five surrogates only. When showering, they just used water and possibly a plain soap.

***

When I arrived in April, the topic of surrogacy was growing more popular by the minute among the Indian media, if not internationally. Part of that was due to the Bill on artificial reproductive technology making its way through the Indian parliament at the time. The Bill promised to radically overhaul the practice of surrogacy in the country, since there were hundreds of clinics offering surrogacy services with widely varying standards of care. In some cases, not Dr Patel's I hasten to add, the surrogate mothers were not treated as well as they should have been. In fact, there were rumours that some were being exploited from a financial viewpoint, not receiving the amounts agreed in their contracts. Many measures in the Bill were designed to protect the surrogate mothers, not only financially but physically and psychologically. Because Dr Patel's clinic was known internationally, she became the focus of surrogacy. And because her clinic had nothing to hide, she was prepared to speak to the media and dispel the myths that the surrogate mothers were being exploited wholesale. Two or three days after my arrival in Anand, the clinic was swarming with reporters: even the local TV station, IBN7 – the India version of CNN – were doing a big programme on Dr Patel. And because I was one of the foreign couples, who spoke English and liked to chat, they all wanted to speak to me. Aside from the BBC documentary, I was reluctant to get involved, preferring to wait until we got the passport issue sorted. In fact, I did not want to jeopardise my situation in any way. Aside from that I wanted to make sure the baby was alright first. I felt slightly superstitious talking about the baby before she actually arrived. It was a case of not counting your chickens until they're hatched.

For someone unused to media contact, it was weird for me, especially since I was over in India on my own. Dealing with the media, whether turning down requests or postponing interviews, I did feel a little vulnerable without Niall at my side. Also, I had no idea what other people in the clinic or surrogacy house would say about me and about our situation.

***

With my daily visits, the bond between Nita and me continued to grow. God only knows if the other surrogates or nurses grew sick of looking at me in the clinic, but I have no regrets. In a way, bonding with the surrogate is somewhat discouraged and I suppose I overdid it a little. In India, some intended parents never get to meet their surrogate but I obviously did. Not only did I get to spend a great deal of time with Nita but also her children. It became the norm for her mother to visit the clinic each day and bring the two children along. Some days the five of us walked to the nearby shops, sometimes limiting our time outdoors because of the extreme heat. Eight months pregnant with a highly visible bump, Nita took it all in her stride. It was clear that she had nothing to hide while strolling around. The children, bright as buttons, were fascinated with me because I was white skinned and I suppose exotic-looking from a child's mind. They gazed wide-eyed at photographs I brought from Ireland and gingerly touched my laptop like it was a wondrous creature.

Since I knew I was disrupting her home life for nine months, it was comforting to know that Nita's children looked happy and well cared for. For me it was natural to buy them toys and clothes or whatever Nita requested when out shopping together.

***

When not with Nita I had a lot of time on my hands. At first, staying at the luxurious Madhubhan Hotel was charming and I loved it, but its appeal soon wore thin. Normally I would get up early because I'm usually full of beans and not the kind to lounge in bed. But that made the day very long indeed. All attempts to occupy myself came to nought and after a while I found myself getting very lonely. That said, in one way it was nice to be on my own and get my head around the impending birth of the baby.

The hotel and spa resort prided itself on the peace and tranquillity it afforded. If anything, it was a retreat from the hustle and bustle of life, which meant if you were on your own it was going to be rather quiet. The hotel was set in twenty acres of the most beautiful grounds, perfect for strolling around and unwinding. However, there were only so many times a day you could do that before straying into boredom territory. Anticipating the need for diversion, I had brought some books with me and reading them in the shade was the best option in the oppressive heat. It was very restful sitting beside the swimming pool with a Patricia Scanlan novel in hand, while to one side a beautiful ornate swing was suspended from a tree. Throughout the grounds an army of grey squirrels scarpered about and if you sat still long enough, they would playfully run around your feet. I got quite used to this and would sit pretending to read but secretly watching their every move. Sometimes I used to feel guilty that in the midst of such comfort, I just couldn't appreciate it. Its loveliness after a while kind of pressed in on me.

'What on earth am I doing here? I'm like a lady of leisure and here I am moaning about how bored I am.'

Not too far away there were distinctly uncomfortable lives. From the hotel, I would catch sight of the homeless family that had set up camp just outside the grounds. I remembered them vividly from my first visit. A well was located just inside the hotel driveway and, in the mornings, the mother of the family would religiously arrive in with a bucket and draw water from the well. It always amazed me how people's lives could be so vastly different at such close proximity.

But for the staff of the hotel I literally would have had no one to talk to. Nobody. They were always very attentive, seeking me out in the gardens or swimming pool and enquiring was everything to my satisfaction or did I require anything else with my dinner or other meals. Each morning at break-fast I would sit alone in the restaurant surrounded by about twenty waiters, all staring in my direction. Not impolitely of course but just making sure that I was not kept waiting between courses. The service was impeccable but I was unaccustomed to such close attention. I literally felt like a princess in her palace yet with nobody to speak to.

Only for my laptop and mobile phone I think I would have felt completely cut off. They were invaluable at keeping me in touch with Niall, family and friends and all the news and goings-on back in Ireland. Close friends and family in Dublin were very good at texting me and asking how I was getting on. My Facebook page had no details of the true purpose of my trip to India, other than letting friends know I was on holiday.

Sometimes I would relieve the boredom by opening the baby's suitcase and laying all the clothes on the bed, all the tiny little babygrows in neutral whites and creams. And then I would inspect the heat-resistant mattress I had brought, as well as the mosquito nets and the steriliser. I figured out the best place to set up the travelling bassinette and where I would position everything else in the room whenever the baby was discharged from the clinic. As I fingered the tiny vests and babygrows, I could scarcely believe that soon a little body would be dressed in them. Our little baby. It all seemed so unreal that I had to pinch myself just to believe it was happening soon. The staff at the hotel obviously knew why I was there and after two weeks I got to know them so well. Even the cleaners would come in and I would try to converse with them, telling them I was waiting for the baby to come and showing them all the baby stuff. They seemed as excited as I was.

Lucky for me, Uday would phone every morning at 10 o'clock without fail, in case I needed anything or wanted a lift to the clinic to see Nita. And I knew, although I was on my own, I had him at the other end of the phone for absolutely anything. Because I had to pay separately for dinner at the hotel, my stay was working out to be quite expensive. Also, the experience of eating alone with just one or two guests in the restaurant and the staff all watching to see what I had eaten left me feeling uncomfortable. I mentioned this to Uday and he suggested it might be cheaper to eat out in Anand for dinner. On one or two occasions he did bring chicken biryani or some other takeaway to the hotel for me but in the hot climate it was not safe to keep it in my room without proper storage.

After about a week at the hotel I had had enough and had started to imagine all sorts of things. I grew nervous at the constant knocking on my door by the staff. Did I need anything? What would I like for breakfast or lunch? Would I like my bed turned down?

'No, thank you,' I would reply. 'I really don't need the bed turned down any more.'

As the days went on I grew more and more uneasy. Having no one to converse with, especially for me since I never stop talking, was becoming a problem. More than anything, I wanted to be in a good frame of mind when the baby arrived, not stressed out and anxious. The honeymoon murder in a luxury resort of Tyrone bride Michaela McAreavey on the island of Mauritius in January that year was playing on my mind. If anyone attacked me, I would have no one to come to my rescue. Clearly the isolation and heat had got to me.

The breaking point came the day I got stuck in the lift. Earlier I had updated my Facebook page, posting *Just conquered my first fear – I've done three flights in 24 hours.* At that, my cousins and friends were cheering me. But then my second fear struck – the terror of being trapped in a lift. It happened as I was going down for dinner in the Madhubhan one evening. I was alone in the average-sized lift, when all of a sudden I was plunged into total darkness and silence. Pressing the button furiously, I screamed like some wild animal.

'I'm stuck. Get me out of here.'

I was probably trapped for less than a minute but it felt like ten hours before the back-up generator kicked in. When the lift reached the ground floor, I was met by about five workers in overalls.

'Oh my god, what happened there?' I asked, trying to compose myself but still in a state of shock.

'The power, it goes sometimes,' they laughed.

It turned out that power outages were common in India. With millions of households and a growing economy, the demand often outstripped the supply.

'You are okay, have a glass of iced lemon water,' they suggested.

'I'm not using the lift again,' I replied, still in panic mode.

'It's okay to use during the day but maybe not in the evenings.'

'No, I won't be using it again.'

And I never got back into the lift again.

A few days later I moved into the Rama Residency Hotel. It was close to the clinic and while it was basic compared to Madhubhan standards, it did accommodate many foreign couples. The hotel was relatively new and scrupulously clean with bright airy rooms and corridors and was good as a three star hotel back in Ireland. And just at the entrance to the lobby, opposite the lift, there was a shrine to Ganesh set within a recess in the wall for good luck. Soon my isolation was a thing of the past. And luckily for me it had no lift. Admittedly, the power outages did knock out the air conditioning system for half an hour or so each day, but I could live with that.

I got to meet all sorts of couples there, Indian and foreign, and I enjoyed the interaction and cultural diversity. Within days I was overjoyed to see Payal and her husband check in, the birth of their baby imminent. By this stage, after months of correspondence, we had really clicked and I had been eager for her to arrive. Living in the hotel was also a window into other people's problems. For example, I met an Indian couple whose IVF had failed a number of times. It was a very difficult period for them and they nearly had an argument in the hotel one day. Dr Patel had advised the woman it was time for a donor because she had attended the clinic unsuccessfully so many times before. But engaging a donor, whose caste and colour would not be disclosed, was posing a challenge. The couple sat with me and another girl over lunch one day and discussed it.

'Well, we're Indian and this whole caste system, different colour and all, is a problem for us,' the wife revealed.

However, as much as we sympathised with them and heard them out after a long discussion, we knew they could not pick and choose donor characteristics at Dr Patel's clinic.

'Look, surrogacy may not be for you, if there is a problem with skin colour,' I suggested.

'You don't go picking,' added the other girl. 'You don't go into Dr Patel saying I want a light-coloured baby or a dark-coloured baby.'

It was true. Dr Patel was very particular, caste system or not, about straying into the area of designer babies. The only reason she would take on a case was if there was a medical reason why you could not bear a child. Women with a host of medical issues from leukaemia and cancer to paraplegics found themselves knocking on her door.

**

As we entered the last week of April, my thoughts constantly turned to the actual birth. There was about another four weeks to go and I wondered if the baby would arrive early.

'When do you think the baby will come?' I asked Nita one day, as we sipped cool drinks.

'Nayna will tell me,' she replied. 'She will come up and talk to us all this afternoon.'

All the surrogates placed their trust in Dr Patel, or Nayna as she was known by her first name. Every afternoon, regular as clockwork, she would arrive upstairs to see them and check their progress. As the time drew near, I wondered how Nita was feeling about the baby. All those months in her womb, that precious time, she must have grown attached to the baby, despite there being no genetic connection. It was only natural she would. Did she feel it was hers? Again, I suppose it would be normal to feel that too. I wondered how Nita would feel or react when handing over the baby. Would it be painful, a terrible wrench? Would she have doubts? I presumed at one level that she would be glad to deliver the baby and get back to her husband and children and make up for lost time. But on a human level it would take some adjusting, getting used to the idea that the baby was gone from her. I consoled myself thinking that because she had no genetic connection to the child, maybe in time it would be easier for her to let go.

In one way, I suppose I didn't have any great fears that Nita would not hand over the baby. In India, unlike other countries such as America, there was no legal provision for the surrogate changing her mind after delivery. It was all bound up in the surrogacy contract. Although that might all change in the future if new legislation was passed to protect the rights of the surrogates in India. At a practical level, it was widely accepted that Indian surrogates did not want to keep the babies and have another mouth to feed, clothe and educate in a country still ravaged by poverty, despite a booming economy. It was one responsibility they felt they could do without.

Chapter 13

The birth of Ava

After spending two weeks in Anand and expecting a leisurely end to the pregnancy, it came as a shock when Nita went into early labour. The baby arrived a month early, a month premature, on 25 April 2011. The previous day I had no inkling of what was in store as I arrived at the clinic to see Nita. It was Easter Sunday back in Ireland and Anand seemed a world away from the chocolate eggs and bunnies feasted on at home. I doubted if chocolate could even withstand the heat in Anand for too long. The temperatures had soared to 40°C and beyond and we all struggled to keep cool along with our sanity. At the clinic that afternoon, Nita and I were just doing our usual thing, chatting and laughing with the other surrogate mothers. Loath to annoy her, I had resisted asking her on a daily basis when did she think the baby would come. I just wanted to let her be. On that Sunday, however, she was shifting uncomfortably on her bed and rubbing her belly, wearing a pretty Punjabi suit.

'Are you in pain, Nita?' I asked, concerned.

'Just uncomfortable and very hot,' she admitted. 'I can't sleep.'

'Is there anything I can get you?'

'No, I'm fine.'

'Maybe the baby will come . . .' I suggested.

'No,' she hesitated, still trying to fix herself into a comfortable position. 'Nayna will check.'

I nodded. Meanwhile Tina was lying down and watching an Indian soap opera on the tiny television in the corner along with the other surrogates. Turning from the drama, she cast her eyes in my direction.

'You know the baby is going to come tomorrow,' she said calmly. It was so matter of fact that she could have been informing me of the weather forecast.

'What!'

'Yes, Nita is kind of in labour.'

I was incredulous. With my experience of women going into labour, I had absolutely no idea if it was true or not.

'Hold on, Tina, ask Nita is she in labour?'

'She's been having pains.'

'Yes, it will be tomorrow,' the other surrogates agreed, still engrossed in the larger-than-life domestic drama. Family squabbles looked familiar the world over, except none could beat the colour, glamour and excess of an Indian soap.

Finally, even Nita agreed it would probably happen the following day. By now my curiosity and excitement had reached fever pitch. The first person I got hold of later was Jenti Boy. I had got to know him better and sometimes he would translate for me if the surrogates were in need of drinks or required anything from the shops.

'Jenti, I think Nita is in labour,' I said.

'Oh, it will be Madam who will decide,' he replied in his very precise manner. 'Madam will decide.'

Madam was the title Jenti reserved for Dr Patel and clearly he was not going to hazard a guess on the timing of the birth, outside his sphere of knowledge. Still concerned for Nita, I next phoned Hitesh to tell him Nita was possibly in labour.

'Who knows, who knows,' he said, laughing at the other end.

'Well, I'll be at the clinic first thing in the morning. I think this baby is coming tomorrow.'

That night back at the Rama hotel, I frantically emailed everyone – my parents, brother, friends. *I'm telling you the baby is coming tomorrow!* Needless to say the advice not to get all worked up because Nita could be having false contractions, false pains, came thick and furious. It might not happen at all, they counselled. Keep calm was the overriding message. Niall, being a typical guy, liked things in black and white and could not understand the commotion.

'Is she in labour or is she not in labour?' he asked, when I got him on the phone.

'It's not as easy as that, Niall. I don't know really,' I said. 'I'll wait and see.'

I could tell it was going to be a sleepless night.

***

By 9 o'clock the following morning, I was at the clinic, having showered and dressed at lightning speed. My first port of call was Dr Patel's office. Inside she was poring over her desk, busy with paperwork.

'The baby will come today,' she announced, smiling at me, immaculate as ever in her pearls and sari.

Though half-expecting it, her words still took me by surprise. I could feel my heart racing and I inhaled deeply. Seeing that the baby would be premature Dr Patel informed me that she would probably need to be cared for in a neonatal unit at first. There were two suitable paediatricians that provided services to the clinic and we agreed that one of them, Dr Anita Kothiala, from the nearby hospital, Apara Nursing Home, would attend the baby.

'I'll call Dr Anita and tell her to come,' said Dr Patel.

'Okay.'

All this news, though exciting, left me distracted and wishing only to see Nita. By this stage, Nita was downstairs in a small room in the labour ward, lying on a bed and hooked up to a drip. At first I got a fright because she wasn't her usual, happy smiling self. I had never seen her like that before. She was in the throes of pain and very uncomfortable, but at least her mother was at her side, holding her hand and soothing her. I stared at the nurse fixing the drip, not sure if they were hydrating her, inducing her, or giving her painkillers. The clinic was hectic that Monday morning and everyone too busy to tell me what was going on exactly.

'Miss Caroline, very exciting day for you,' the nurses would say as they hurried by.

I could not believe the day had finally come and it felt so strange, so surreal. I was nearly having a heart attack at the thought of how soon the birth was. Slowly, I inched closer to Nita's bed.

'Are you in pain, Nita?' I whispered softly, though it was obvious by the look on her face.

'Yes, but I am excited for you.'

I smiled at her gratefully. It was sad to see her in pain, especially after we had spent so much time together. Even though I knew that pain was a natural part of childbirth, in one way I found it upsetting and I felt a little guilty because Niall and I were partly responsible. It was a sobering thought and whatever exhilaration I felt initially, it had given way to concern for Nita.

'Do you want me to stay?' I asked, not sure if I should be there or not.

'Stay if you want to,' her mother answered, still rubbing her hand softly.

It was an awkward moment. On one hand, I didn't want to leave, not wishing Nita to think I had no interest in the birth. I also felt it was my place to be there and, of course, it would be a truly wonderful moment witnessing the birth of my baby. But at the same time, it felt a little intrusive. That time was important to Nita and her mother too and they needed privacy, especially since Nita would be giving up the baby. Aside from that, I didn't want Nita to have to put on a smiling face for me just because I was sitting there like a spectator. What could I do at that point anyway? I couldn't keep plying her with questions. *How far apart are the contractions? Is it coming? Is it coming?* Having to make an effort to be polite to me when in the throes of childbirth, and unable to speak English, would have been very unfair to her. From my time in hospital after the cervical surgery, I knew I wanted to be left alone to deal with the pain and discomfort. But at least, Nita wasn't alone, her mother was at her side.

After a few minutes I took my leave and made my way to Hitesh's office. In fact, I spent the next two and a half hours there, cocooned from the heat and listening to the sounds of the street filtering into the office. Life was going on in all its abundance yet time stood still for me. Having missed breakfast, I was starving but couldn't eat and tried to occupy myself. The office over the course of the morning bustled with couples from all parts of the globe: the USA, India, Britain and Germany. On their way to the shop the couples would offer to get me food or drink but I declined each time. I was beside myself with anticipation. Amid dealing with the couples, Hitesh did his best to humour me through the nail-biting hours.

'I feel like the father,' he confessed, entering into the spirit of things. For effect, he paced up and down like a frantic dad. His rapport not only with me but with all the other couples was a great support.

'I can't even go for my lunch,' he joked. 'I'll have to wait and see this baby.'

The time passed, interspersed with hilarity and tension. At one point a young English couple arrived in and gingerly sat down. The wife appeared rather quiet, while her husband turned to me.

'Oh, are you from England?' he enquired.

'No, I'm from Ireland and I'm all excited,' I blurted out.

'This is our first trip, we've actually made a trip to see what the place is like,' he explained. 'We're not even starting treatment.'

I nodded, having met quite a number of couples who had travelled thousands of miles just on spec to see what the clinic was like.

'How have you found the clinic?' he continued.

'Well, my baby is going to be born any minute now.'

'Did you hear that?' he said, hastily turning to his wife. 'Please I don't want to annoy you but can we sit with you for five minutes and just ask you a few questions?'

'Of course,' I replied, though probably too exuberant to form coherent sentences.

Soon all the couples were waiting and waiting for our baby to arrive, especially when we heard Nita had been taken to the delivery suite. Outside the room we waited and held our breaths. Every time a nursed passed by, we were on tenterhooks and I broke out in a cold sweat.

'Not yet, not yet,' they would say, as they saw us raise our heads in expectation.

'Oh, my nerves are gone,' Hitesh exclaimed.

'Your nerves are gone, Hitesh!' I cried out. 'My nerves are totally gone.'

By half past one in the day, we were put out of our misery; one of the nurses appeared, smiling broadly. We held our breaths as she started to speak.

'Girl!'

At first I was kind of confused, not sure what she meant.

'Me?' I said, pointing to myself. 'You did say a girl?'

There were cheers and congratulations and claps of joy, but I was still a bit shaken. Immediately after that Nita's mother came out of the room and took my hand.

'It's a girl,' she said, squeezing my hand.

Finally, it started to sink in. The feeling was like nothing I had experienced before; all the years of pain and suffering had finally come to an end. I could hold it back no longer. Tears of joy started to stream down my face. It was just wonderful news. Unbelievable. Blissful. Surreal.

Nita's mother had come to fetch me so I could see the baby. It was only a short walk but I was weak with every step I took. The euphoria seemed to have sapped my energy. As I entered the room, I got a fright because Nita was lying on the treatment table and Dr Patel and the other doctors and nurses were busy stitching and cleaning her up. Lying there, she looked limp and exhausted. Meanwhile the baby, purple in colour, was being lifted up and spirited away by Dr Anita and her two neonatal nurses from the nearby Apara Nursing Home. Dr Anita was very much in control. Though I had never met her before, she had come highly recommended from the other couples on the forum. Amid all the action, my immediate concern was for Nita.

'Is Nita okay?' I asked, turning to her mother at once.

It came as a shock to see just how drawn and lifeless she looked.

'Your daughter, your daughter,' she rejoiced, still holding my hand, and pointing to the baby.

The nurses reassured me that Nita was fine, much to my relief. From then on, everything happened at breakneck speed. The nurses immediately wrapped the baby up; there would be no touching or holding her for me until her condition stabilised.

'Is she okay?' I asked Dr Anita, almost too scared to ask.

'Come with me,' the doctor replied briskly.

There was no time for chitchat or social niceties. The baby needed to get to the neonatal unit straight away. I literally left the room with Dr Anita, still in her surgical attire, and raced behind the nurses. Within seconds, we were in a waiting white-coloured car, parked just outside the clinic door and on our way to the hospital across the street. The hospital was separate to Dr Patel's clinic and had a paediatric wing while caring for adult patients as well. At that point I rang Niall to let him know the baby had arrived, conscious I only had seconds to fill him in.

'The baby's here but she's not breathing.'

He was dumbstruck, not knowing what to make of my jumbled news. All I could do was stare at the baby's tiny face and watch while the nurses held her and listened to her fighting for breath; struggling to live. There had been no big cry, the roar you normally heard in movies when newborn babies arrived. One of the nurses was gently shaking her.

'She will be okay,' Dr Anita reassured me. 'But she's just having difficulty breathing.'

'She's not breathing!' I kept repeating, on the verge of panicking.

I could not even bear to think that she might not make it. After everything we had all gone through, these were scary moments. Amid all the mayhem, however, Dr Anita and the nurses remained very calm.

'She will be fine,' Dr Anita repeated in a heartening tone. 'We are just going to the clinic.'

The hospital, situated beside a shopping centre of sorts, was undergoing considerable renovation at the front of the building. The noise of drilling and construction only added to the chaos of sounds from the street, the incessant chatter and horns beeping. I remember mounting the dusty marble stairs and everyone staring at me as we made our way to the neonatal unit. On each floor, long Florence Nightingale-type wards were crammed to capacity with sick adult patients. It really brought home to me just how densely populated India was. Some patients were even lying on the floor. The neonatal unit was located at the end of a corridor, and admitted only Dr Anita along with the baby and the nurses.

'Let us do our work,' said Dr Anita, before vanishing behind its closed doors.

'Okay,' I replied, not allowed go any further.

Standing outside, breathing in the smell of disinfectant, I tried to take stock of things. It had been such a whirligig, everything happening so quickly in the end. I was at a loss what to do or even think or feel. Looking around the white tiled corridor, the clinical setting did not offer any inspiration. After about two minutes, Dr Anita suddenly reappeared.

'What is your little girl going to be called?' she asked.

'Ava.'

'Oh, Ava Gardner,' she responded humorously.

To be honest, I didn't know where the name Ava had exactly come from as Niall and I had only picked it the night before. But for everyone, like the couples in Hitesh's office, it seemed to bring to mind the image of the famous American film star from the 1940s and 50s. It felt surreal thinking here I was in India and Dr Anita was remarking on an American actress. But then again Indians were such great film lovers with thousands of Bollywood films to prove it. And maybe the film *Bhowani Junction*, set in India in 1947, with Ava Gardner as the half-caste heroine had been memorable to the Indian population.

'Ava is fine,' Dr Anita continued. 'She is having some oxygen.'

Slowly I started to breathe easy and get some oxygen into my own lungs, relieved that Ava's condition was stable.

'You can go home and have your lunch,' Dr Anita suggested. 'Do whatever you have to do and then come back.'

'Is she really okay?'

'She is fine. We'll do our job.'

At that Dr Anita disappeared behind the swing doors again. She was a straight talking, no-nonsense doctor and I put great trust in her doing a good job. But for now there was nothing I could do. I just had to follow hospital protocol; the priority now was Ava's health. Slowly I made my way back down the stairs. Near the exit there was a stone balcony overlooking the street and I stopped to survey all the cows that seemed to have assembled outside. It still amazed me that every time I left a shop doorway I was met head on by a curious cow. The scene was such a far cry from the hospitals of Dublin. Thinking of Dublin, I rang Niall immediately with a proper update.

'It's a girl, it's a girl, it's a girl,' I cried, brimful with happiness this time.

'She's alright, is she?' he asked, half-afraid to hear bad news.

My last phone call to him, frantic and incoherent, had left him in a state of anxiety.

'She's fine, she's in ICU. They told me she's going to be fine.'

'Okay,' he replied, the relief evident in his voice.

After that it was time to place a quick call to my parents, which was answered by my dad.

'Well, hello grandad,' I laughed. 'You've a granddaughter!'

'A girl,' he said slowly and pensively, the surprise plain to hear.

I laughed to myself. Everyone had said it was going to be a boy and they were now dumbfounded she was a girl. But the shock was short-lived and outweighed by sheer delight. My phone calls at an end for the moment, I now had to exit the hospital. This was no straightforward matter with construction in full swing. Clad only in shorts the construction workers were now standing barefoot in wet cement at the end of the stairway smoothing it out. At ground level, the front of the hospital was literally being held up by sticks and I had to walk across a plank to get out. An old wizened man in a wheelchair was being carried head high by several people who had gathered to help bring him upstairs. And all in front of an audience of bored hungry cows. It was quite a bizarre scene.

***

Back at the Rama Residency Hotel, a two-minute walk away, I was bursting to tell Payal and the couples I had got to know over the past week. It was such great news I had to physically share it, especially since Niall and my family were half a world away. Knocking on their doors, within minutes all the couples had learnt of Ava's birth. Their reactions were just wonderful, hugging and kissing me.

'Hold on, let's celebrate,' one couple suggested. 'Let's everybody have something to drink.'

Usually we would gather in someone's room to chat or in the stylish cafeteria on the ground floor. This was something I really enjoyed about staying at the Rama, the camaraderie was a joy. That day, everyone wanted to mark the occasion, knowing just how precious the birth of a baby is to an infertile couple. The tea arrived as I finally sat down with the others in the cafeteria. My face just beamed with joy, though I was wet from perspiration. The heat was growing more intense by the day and I was glad to relax in the air conditioned hotel.

After a while our celebrations attracted the attention of a much older Indian couple, guests in the hotel. They soon approached our little group.

'Oh, all this great excitement going on,' the Indian woman remarked in English.

'Yes,' I said. 'I just had a little baby girl. I'm so excited.'

'Do I hear an Irish accent?' the woman enquired. 'Are you Caroline by any chance?'

I looked at her with quizzical eyes, curious that she would know my name. 'Yes.'

'You were speaking to my daughter who lives in England,' she explained.

'Oh, my God,' I said, amazed at the coincidence.

India's connections with the rest of the world seemed to get closer all the time. 'I'm Sharmila's mother.'

About three weeks previously, a woman called Sharmila had posted a message on the global forum saying her son had just been born prematurely in Anand and that she herself was in England and had no way of getting over yet, what with arranging visas and so forth. She enquired if there was anybody in Anand who could give her information on her baby's condition. Naturally, Dr Patel and Dr Anita had been in touch, but Sharmila wanted more minutiae and did not like to bother the busy doctors. At that stage, I was about to depart Dublin for India and only too happy to help. I told her as soon as I got over I would get details for her and pictures if she wished, which I did.

Despite residing in England, Sharmila's family were Indian and her parents and in-laws lived in another state in India. So the grandparents actually came to see the baby before Sharmila and her husband managed to get over. Now meeting me, the person who had helped her daughter, was as good as meeting actual family for her mother.

'This is so funny because I am now sitting here with Caroline and I will have to ring Sharmila and tell her,' the mother announced, highly amused.

The connection was amusing but incredible too. A bond and community spirit existed among the intended parents, always willing to help out, put minds at rest, and ease the burden with enlightening tips and advice. Though we were strangers online, we were also one big family, clichéd as it may sound.

'We all know each other virtually online but we don't technically at the same time,' one woman remarked as we sipped our tea.

'Ava is in Dr Anita's?' Sharmila's mother then asked, having gathered as much from our conversation.

'Yes, Ava is in ICU,' I replied woefully.

Knowing the situation at first hand, she sympathised with me. Her grand-child, Ravi, was at Dr Anita's hospital too. Before long, I was calling the woman Auntie, a term of respect reserved for older Indian women. And in one way, she became a virtual mother for the remainder of my time in India.

'Would you like us to go with you after dinner to Dr Anita's?' she asked. 'We will stay and walk you back again to the hotel.'

At that moment I was filled with such gratitude; even though the hospital was a stone's throw away, I struggled to recall the exact street turn. I felt a little guilty about imposing on the woman and her husband. As if reading my mind, she added.

'We'll go with you because we are going to see our grandson anyway.'

That put my mind at rest. As it turned out she mothered me, mothered us all as the days went on and while she waited for her daughter and son-in-law to arrive.

It was with some nervous excitement that I returned to the neonatal unit that evening accompanied by Sharmila's parents. Before stepping inside, we had to remove our flipflops and put on surgical gowns, caps, gloves and galoshes. Only after scrubbing our hands and drying them with neatly cut sterile newsprint were we allowed to enter.

In the first section of the unit I passed about five babies in incubators before reaching the area where Ava was located. Here about seven more tiny babies were being cared for. And there, right beside Ava, was the premature Ravi. He was absolutely teeny, almost barely formed lying in his incubator. Definitely, arriving two months early, he was the smallest baby I had ever come across in my life. Meanwhile Ava was lying in a type of open cot that looked like a Perspex box. Her face was kind of swollen with oxygen prongs and tubes coming from her nose and a drip in her hand. The poor little mite looked so tiny and defenceless wrapped in a light blue cloth with a pink vest peeking through and a blue-rimmed cap on her head. The clothes were hospital regulation ones, as we were not allowed to bring in our own. I wondered when I would get the chance to actually dress her myself. Behind the cots were large portable fans blowing on the babies.

'Is that okay?' I asked, pointing to the fans, unsure if the babies would be chilled to the bone.

'Yes, it's so warm in here,' Auntie replied.

I had forgotten about the climate. It was not like back home where you would have to protect the babies from our harsh cold, wet weather.

'I'll leave you for a minute,' Auntie then whispered.

I nodded but all I could do was just stare at Ava. Here was my little girl, but I couldn't just pick her up and cuddle her. I was afraid to touch her in case it caused her any discomfort.

'Talk to her,' Auntie nudged, seeing how helpless I must have looked.

It was good advice. By getting used to the sound of my voice and touch, I knew I could comfort Ava. Luckily, the cot was open and I was free to touch her. As I gazed at her I scanned her face for any family resemblance, thinking maybe there were traces of Niall. But it was too early to tell. Her hair caught my attention and what looked like a tiny piece of afterbirth stuck to it. My brother had asked earlier what colour was her hair and at the time I couldn't recall but now I reckoned it was black like my own yet then again couldn't really tell the colour. Maybe if I had a photo I could scrutinise it back at the hotel and send it on to Niall and my brother.

'Can I take a picture?' I asked one of the nurses.

'Yes, but no kind of flashing bulbs or flashes,' she advised.

There was so much to learn about caring for a premature baby. I realised how much I needed to rely on Auntie and the nurses and doctors for advice. A kind of system had evolved for all the inexperienced intended parents in Anand; every time a premature baby arrived in the neonatal unit, the mother learned the ropes from the couple already there with their own baby. That said, not all babies arrived prematurely at the clinic, most went to full term.

'What do I do tomorrow, Auntie?' I asked, wondering what to expect.

'We get up and have a shower and we immediately go to the unit and come back and have our breakfast,' she replied. 'Then at lunch we go again and then at dinner time we go again.'

She had recited it pit pat like a timetable printed indelibly on her mind.

'So we can all go together,' she added, smiling.

Her kindness to me was really touching and I felt so relieved as we all left the building. On the street my thoughts turned to Nita and I wondered how she was faring. The image of her lying exhausted on the bed after delivery was still fresh on my mind. Instinctively, I went straight to the clinic to visit her. This time she had been moved to a smaller room, which she shared with another surrogate in an advanced stage of pregnancy. And the room had the bonus of being fully air conditioned, which I'm sure would please Nita. Thankfully, it was a very different Nita to the one I had seen earlier. She had revived and was back to her former smiling self, though still a little tired. All the surrogates were there, having travelled up from the surrogate house to see her. There was a real celebratory atmosphere in the room, with all the surrogates cheering and congratulating her.

Nita looked relieved it was all over. I later learnt that she had not been nervous about the birth at all, accepting the pain of childbirth as something natural to be expected. One thing she had been particularly pleased about was having a normal vaginal delivery. Many of the surrogates do end up having Caesarean sections, often because twins or multiples are expected. A Caesarean for a surrogate mother would have meant stitches and the physical evidence of childbirth, something that might invite prying questions later. However, Ava just slipped out – all five pounds and seven ounces of her – so there were no telltale stitches and people would have been none the wiser that Nita had had a baby. In the BBC documentary Nita would say that her family had only found out about the surrogacy in the fortnight before the birth. Obviously from my perspective this didn't include her mother who knew from the start. I presumed she was talking about her in-laws and extended family. *Now when I go home, I won't tell them anything. They didn't see me pregnant. I will say I'm not pregnant. Did you see me pregnant?*

In all the excitement that evening I didn't get a chance to ask Nita how long she would be staying at the clinic before being discharged. I was unfamiliar with the protocol and the procedures, especially now that Ava had arrived early. One of the reasons I had expressly gone out earlier was so that I would know exactly what to expect when the baby arrived. Now, I would have to learn things on the hoof.

***

The following morning, Auntie was as good as her word. She rang my hotel room to check if I was ready and off we set. It was the start of a system of ringing each other daily at dawn like comrades in arms. Shortly after dawn we stepped out onto the street. The shopkeepers were up already and out cleaning the street with long-handled brooms in readiness for a day's trading. As the day wore on the streets would be filled with dust and rubbish, attracting animals and especially cows who loved to root through it. Though less people were around at that early hour, the sounds of motorbikes and tuk-tuks still filled the air in the buzzing town.

'She'll have her sponge bath too before feeding,' Auntie explained as we made our way to the neonatal unit. 'It's really nice to see that.'

'She's going to have a sponge bath already!' I exclaimed.

'Oh yes, and a massage with coconut oil,' she added.

Once in the unit, I looked for Ava but in vain. I just couldn't recognise her at all.

'Where's Ava?' I asked the nurse.

'She's there,' she said, pointing to the same place where Ava had been the evening before.

But this time she looked completely different. For one thing, the swelling had gone from her face.

'She looks different,' I remarked.

'Yes, they always look different the next day,' she informed me.

This time I noticed a sign over the cot with my name and Ava's below it. At least next time, it would be easier finding Ava. The sponge bath, when I finally got to witness it, was lively and entertaining. From Ava's roars, you would think she was being battered to death. The paediatrician on duty that morning was wearing thin red decorative strings around his wrist, celebrating the brother and sister day in India, Raksha Bandha. It obviously was appealing to Ava too, whose tiny fingers tugged at the strings.

'Look at that,' he said, 'she's grabbing already. She's going to be a very strong baby.'

It was during the sponge bath that I got to hold her for the very first time. It was a prized moment but terrifying at the same time because she was so tiny. At first I was even afraid to touch her to be honest.

As it turned out Ava did not have her first feed that morning. In fact, for the first two and a half days of her life she was on a drip. The nurses had asked that I bring along my own sterile bottles to the unit, which I did in readiness for the feeding. But it would be several days before she was strong enough to suck from a teat. When Ava was three days old she was given breast milk to suck from a syringe. The sight was so endearing I took a video of it, which everyone loved because of the slurping noise she made. I presumed it was Nita's milk that had been brought from the clinic. The nurses subsequently enquired whether breast milk was available for Ava or not, as they were running low on the pooled breast milk in the unit. I was unsure, as no one had ever mentioned it before.

'Nita did not come with the breast milk,' the nurse told me.

'Have you got breast milk here?' I asked the nurse, not familiar with the protocol.

'Yes, for a day or two.'

Seeing as she was premature, I knew that Ava would eventually be starting on formula milk for low birthweight babies and left the matter at that. I had ordered some but it would take a while to arrive and the hospital had plenty of supplies. In the meantime, Sharmila and her husband had finally arrived over from England and we then accompanied each other to the unit. Of course, she was just over the moon to see her baby for the first time. Side by side with Ava and Ravi in adjoining cots, we talked to the nurses about the babies. That's when I learnt there was no breast milk available in the unit.

'Hold on a minute,' Sharmila interrupted. 'She's supposed to be having breast milk.'

The protocol was that Nita's milk should have been brought to the unit from Dr Patel's clinic. In fact, it should have been organised well in advance. I suppose events had happened so quickly that some things had been overlooked. To be honest, not having breast milk did not seem a problem to me. Formula milk could have been used instead. Coming from Ireland, where more mothers bottle feed than breast feed, it seemed a logical solution. I had been bottle fed myself and most of my generation. However, the tradition was different in India and breast milk was the norm. Even Dr Anita had advised that it would be good for Ava to get it for the first few days. Sharmila was insistent, however, going on about the many benefits of mother's milk. It was all true, I knew, but I didn't know where to start or what to do.

'What do you think I should do?' I asked her, hesitantly.

In the end, we went over to Dr Patel's clinic and found Nita. She was pleased to see us and looked quite relaxed and back to her old form. I was so glad she didn't look dejected or unhappy. I knew she must be feeling low trying to adjust to being without the baby. This time Sharmila translated our conversation and asked Nita about the breast milk. After a while, I could tell by Sharmila's voice that she was getting worked up.

'Sharmila, please be nice about it,' I pleaded, not wishing to offend or upset Nita in any way.

It pained me that I couldn't have that conversation with Nita myself. With little or no Gujarati, I was helpless. It brought home to me the real disadvantage of the language barrier. Up until then we had seemed to develop a way of communicating: smiling and nodding, having a basic kind of conversation, getting around things. But this time it was different.

'Does Nita need a pump or anything to express the milk?' I enquired.

'Look to be honest, I'd forget that whole scenario,' said Sharmila after a while, 'because she has told me about ten different stories at once.'

Not able to get any clarity from Nita, I reluctantly left and we returned to the neonatal unit. I let the nurses know I was happy to go with formula milk, if that was okay. It was fine with them and they would supplement it with breast milk whenever it was available. In the end, I was prepared to go along with whatever the nurses recommended.

Gradually I got used to Ava being in the neonatal unit but I suppose I did have some niggling questions about her progress. Luckily in the meantime, I met an Indian couple from Mumbai back at the hotel, who were attending Dr Patel's clinic for infertility treatment. The wife Jaya was a paediatrician back in Scotland.

'Look, I'll come in with you,' she said, offering to accompany me to the unit.

'Do you mind?'

'I don't really want to go in and start asking loads of questions because it's not my place,' Jaya continued. 'But I'll know a lot just by going in and looking.'

There were no visitors allowed in the unit other than parents, or grandparents in Ravi's case. However, I did ask the nurses was it alright if I brought my friend in with me. The staff was aware that Niall was still back in Ireland and probably felt sorry for me.

'No Daddy, no Ava Daddy?' they would ask each day.

'No passport, no passport,' I would keep saying. 'He will be coming soon, probably this week.'

Knowing the nurses would not appreciate someone interfering with Dr Anita's work, Jaya was as discreet as possible. After taking a quick look at her chart, she whispered to me.

'Within the next 24 hours they're going to tell you that Ava has jaundice.'

'What!' I exclaimed.

'I can tell by looking at her and that a few other babies in here have it as well.'

I did calm down when I learnt that jaundice was fairly common in premature babies. Before long, as Jaya predicted, Ava was treated under blue lights and had to wear goggles to protect her eyes. Attached to a drip and a monitor, the little one was exposed to the continuous beep, beep, beep of the machines. By the looks of it, Ava was given a lot of vitamins as well. Jaya too had advised me that Ava didn't absolutely need breast milk and it was up to me to decide. Her words gave me a lot more solace.

Back in Ireland, Niall and my family and friends were in constant touch, boosting my spirits and taking the edge off my isolation. I knew I would be on my own until Niall managed to get a passport for Ava. As the days went on and people rallied to help me, my gratitude grew deeper and deeper. Auntie was such a lovely woman and I enjoyed our conversations, filling her in on my own medical history. Through her, I learnt more about what the older Indian generation felt about surrogacy.

'When Sharmila first told me she had been here, in Anand, I could not really understand it,' she confessed. 'But when I hear that you had cancer and of course Sharmila had a kidney transplant – her father donated his kidney – I can understand why.'

'Everyone who has been here has had an illness of some description,' I agreed.

The situation made more sense to her and her husband when they were physically present in Anand and could witness at first hand what was actually involved. By meeting infertile couples and hearing their stories it put it all in perspective.

***

In all, Ava spent about six days in the neonatal unit and her jaundice started to resolve itself. I relished being a mother with every passing day. My confidence grew and I just loved to hold and feed her. Everything was provided for her from the hospital stores, in fact the only items I could bring in from the outside were sterile feeding bottles. I was billed each day for items like nappies, coconut oil, cotton wool, formula and so forth. Fortunately, Meenakshi, an Indian lady living in California, who was also staying at the Rama hotel, translated the lists for me and helped me get supplies from the hospital stores. Not knowing how long Ava would spend in the unit, I hoped it would not be a huge expense. But I need not have worried, the cost was minimal.

The day before Ava was due for discharge Dr Anita discussed her after care.

'Has your husband arrived?' she enquired, aware of our passport situation.

'Not yet,' I said, shrugging my shoulders.

'Are you going to get a nanny?' she asked.

'I've been thinking about it.'

It was true; I had talked to Sharmila, Payal and Meenakshi about it. My main concern, being a private sort of person, was sharing a room with someone I didn't know. But I knew I would have to put my reservations to one side and be practical and realistic. The girls all impressed upon me how much I would need someone to help me, since Niall was still back in Ireland.

'You are going to be on your own in a hotel room,' Dr Anita finally spelt it out. 'That won't be happening.'

And she was right. The realisation of being on my own with a newborn baby sank in at last. After our conversation I went straight over to Dr Patel to discuss my predicament.

'Niall is not here. I don't know when he's going to be here,' I explained. 'The baby is going to be out in a day or so.'

'So you want a nanny,' she replied sympathetically. 'That's no problem.'

Within hours Hitesh had made the necessary arrangements. I was told to come to the clinic first thing in the morning. I was to collect the baby and the nanny would be there. However, as it happened there was a false alarm on the day. They decided to keep Ava in for one more day. When informing Hitesh of the situation, I got a chance to meet Vimla the nanny. She was sitting in his office, looking very serious, prim and proper, dressed in an immaculate sari and holding a small dainty bag.

'This is Vimla,' said Hitesh, introducing her.

At about twenty-four years of age, Vimla was an old hand. She had been married since the age of thirteen and had one son. Luckily for me, she could speak a few words of English.

'They're after telling me that Ava is not coming home until tomorrow,' I told Hitesh.

'Do you want Vimla to come with you to the hotel now so you can get used to each other,' he asked.

I hesitated, unsure what to think and overwhelmed by all of it.

'I can go home for today and come back tomorrow,' suggested Vimla.

That settled it. It would also give me some hours to get used to the idea and to prepare for bringing Ava home.

Chapter 14

Discharged from the neonatal unit

Now that the month of May had arrived, the weather had soared into the high 40s and even hit 50°C on occasion. Those who told me, when I had arrived in Anand, that it would be unbelievably hot were not exaggerating. During previous sun holidays abroad, the heat would make my legs swell, in particular my right leg, the one that suffers from lymphoedema. However, the heat in Anand was a different case entirely. The morning after meeting Vimla, I noticed that my right ankle had started to swell.

'Oooh, oooh,' Dr Anita exclaimed, when I arrived to visit Ava at the neonatal unit. 'Did you get a bite?'

'Oh God,' I replied, looking down at my leg.

I had never seen my leg quite so swollen. It was huge but I knew it was no insect bite.

'Look, it's fine,' I continued. 'I know what it is.'

'No, my husband is a doctor,' she said, still alarmed. 'You must go and see him today. I will get my driver to come and bring you.'

Awaiting her driver back at the hotel, I bumped into Jaya, the Indian paediatrician with whom I had become firm friends. As always she was wearing a beautiful top with matching earrings – her trademark style, as I had learned. Quickly, I explained what was happening.

'Look, you won't be able to speak to them at the clinic,' she said. 'Do you need someone to go with you?'

'It's fine,' I replied, not wishing to inconvenience her. 'I'll just go myself.'

Finally, the driver turned up and we started for the clinic. I had no sooner arrived than I met Jaya and her husband sitting there, waiting for me. She was such a lovely woman, so considerate and compassionate, as was her husband too.

'We decided to come and wait for you,' she started to explain, 'because we knew you would need help with the language when you got here.'

Eventually, the doctor arrived to examine my leg, with Jaya present. I spilled out the long saga of my lymphoedema. At first he was overcautious, perhaps because I was a foreigner.

'Are you sure you don't need a scan on this leg?' he asked, quizzically.

'No, I don't. I know what it is. It's the heat.'

At that he sent some poor fellow off on a bike to get a special compression bandage that was out of stock in the clinic stores. It did the trick but I had to wear it from thigh to toe and keep my foot elevated. It confined me to the hotel as well. But with heat that intense you just couldn't go out anyway. When I first arrived in Anand, the climate was more a dry heat and very dusty. I would come in filthy all the time, especially my feet, from the dusty streets. When the weather got really hot and humid, the locals went around with cloth handkerchiefs over their mouths. On the streets women in saris would stop and pour water over their heads. Or else they would wet the corner of their saris and wrap them around their heads to keep cool. Occasionally, I might pop out of the hotel, hatless, for literally two minutes only to have the locals on the street warn me.

'Oh, no, no, cover head. You get headaches in heat.'

If I walked only a short distance I would come back with such a headache. *Boom. Boom. Boom.* It was like being in a fire. So the heat, that intense pressure and humidity, generally kept me off the streets.

***

The next morning, Ava's homecoming, or rather hotelcoming, turned out to be yet another hot and sultry day, as I arrived at Hitesh's office. Trying to keep abreast of the weather and mounting laundry, I had bought several sleeveless decorative *kurta*, the traditional tunics worn in India, which were in plentiful supply and inexpensive down at the Big Bazaar. I found them cooling and easy to wear and could mix and match them with my own light trousers. Mostly I wore tops and trousers or the occasional cotton dress during my time in Anand, not feeling comfortable walking around in shorts, unlike many of the Americans staying there.

The previous night was spent deciding which baby clothes to bring to the unit for Ava at the request of the nurses. At first, I couldn't make up my mind, laying out several items carefully on the bed and scrutinising them. Finally, I decided on a white babygrow and white hat along with a white little blanket – white would definitely be cool in all this heat.

Arranging the room was also another matter. There would be three of us living in the room, an average-sized hotel bedroom which, though reasonably spacious, would have to house us for God knows how long. Niall was still battling to get the passport sorted out back in Ireland. I placed the travelling bassinette close to the bed in the far corner of the room and away from doors, draughts or air conditioning outlets. It was hard to believe that within hours Ava would be discharged from the neonatal unit and I would have sole responsibility for her care. As the days had passed, admittedly I had grown in confidence but still was relieved that Vimla would be on hand to show me the ropes. Thinking about Vimla living at such close quarters did give rise to some panic on my part initially. I didn't know how I would fare living with someone I really did not know. As it turned out, I need not have worried.

At the clinic that morning, Vimla had returned and was pristine in her sari and burnished black hair. Aged about twenty-four, she was taller than Nita and held herself very erect.

'Ready?' she asked, when we met at Hitesh's office.

'Okay,' I said, as we proceeded to leave the clinic together.

Seeing that Vimla had a small bag containing personal items with her, we stopped off first at the hotel, a short detour on the way to the Apara Nursing

Home. Like Nita, Vimla was pleasant and friendly and we tried to converse given the small amount of English she had. The Rama Hotel was familiar to her and she had stayed there several times before as a nanny to foreign couples. I got the distinct impression that Vimla could be relied upon and was very trustworthy. She was quite accustomed to the whole surrogacy process and had in fact been an egg donor a number of times and a surrogate mother on a separate occasion.

In the hotel bedroom, one of the first things she did was to lay a kind of tartan rug, brought from home, neatly on the tiled floor.

'I will sleep here,' she said, pointing to the blanket.

'No, Vimla,' I replied at once, thinking how cold and hard the surface would be for sleeping.

'Okay, Miss Caroline, where would you like me to sleep?'

'You can't sleep on the floor,' I replied, laughing. 'I'll ask the hotel staff for another bed.'

When I enquired from the hotel staff about another bed, they were rather mystified. Even more so, when they found out it was for Vimla.

'She won't need a bed, but do *you* need a bed?'

Most of the nannies, especially if hired by couples of Indian origin, were expected to sleep on blankets on the floor. I supposed it was a caste thing but it was something which I didn't feel comfortable with. In the heel of the hunt the bed never arrived and Vimla ended up sleeping in my bed. The double bed was enormous and could in fact comfortably sleep three adults. So it transpired that I took one side of it and Vimla the other, and sometimes we placed Ava in the middle. By that stage I didn't care, as we had kind of developed a rapport and were getting on well together.

Another thing that fascinated me was what the nannies were supposed to wear. This too emerged on the first day at the hotel.

'Will I stay in my sari?' Vimla asked, touching her dress.

'Make yourself comfortable,' I replied, not sure what she meant.

Later I noticed that many of the other nannies were in saris every day, depending on who hired them. Saris were considered more formal wear, more official. I presumed, in the case of surrogacy, worn to pay respect to the employer as such. When out on the streets of Anand, I would see many women bustling by in their saris, whereas the kurta was considered more relaxed wear. In conversation, Vimla told me that when her mother-in-law and in-laws came to visit, she would always make sure to wear a sari and even drape it over her head as well. During my time in Anand I had come across women wearing Punjabi suits too. This was a three-piece outfit consisting of a tunic called a kameez, trousers called a salwar, and a long scarf called a dupatta. Traditionally, the kameez was a long-sleeved, knee-length, flowing kurta with side seams left open below the navel. You could literally buy thousands of kurtas in Anand because they were on sale everywhere, made from cotton or thin silk, and quite cheap to buy. For my part, I was quite happy for Vimla to wear whatever she liked. Fairly soon, she learnt that I wasn't going to be fussy over what she was wearing in comparison to an Indian family. As long as she was comfy and content, it didn't bother me. As the days went on Vimla settled into the Rama Hotel and mostly wore vibrant kurtas with a kind of leggings. But clothes were always a talking point for us. Strolling together by the shops, Vimla, with her eye for clothes, and I would discuss fashions and different styles of saris.

Once discharged from hospital Ava was brought straight to the hotel. I had been given her medical records to take away and the neonatal staff were very warm in their goodbyes. Needless to say, there were still endless enquiries about Niall's whereabouts.

'No Ava daddy?'

'No passport today?'

'Still waiting for the passport,' I would dutifully reply.

There are no words to describe my gratitude to Dr Anita and her staff. They were absolutely fantastic and the care Ava received was truly amazing. In fact, all the newborns were treated royally. I learnt that some of the babies there were actually full terms waiting on their intended parents to arrive from whatever overseas destination they hailed. If babies were born prematurely or just before their due date, the parents at home often had to scramble to book flights and make arrangements to leave at short notice, which in some cases took time. Their babies were perfectly healthy and accommodated in the neonatal unit in the meantime.

Uday, as dependable as ever, had arranged for the car to be right outside the hospital, so there would be no delay or impediment to her safe transfer. Vilma accompanied us and Ava was as good as gold during the short journey from the hospital to the hotel. Back at our room, it was wonderful to hold Ava, this time without the backdrop of beeping machines and drips and bright lights. I was still a little scared holding her because she was so small and defenceless. But it's funny really because I felt like I had given birth to her myself. There was no other feeling. There was no 'have I done the right thing' or 'what have I let myself in for'. Immediately it felt so natural, so normal. As I stared into those big eyes that eventually turned steel grey, stroked her jet-black hair and touched her milky white skin, I knew she was our child. All I could think was that I was a mammy. This was now my job and I had responsibilities. Everything else just disappeared. After that Vimla and I tried to create a routine of sorts, as all mothers of newborns do. The endless cycle of feeding, sleeping, nappy-changing, bathing, and cuddling became the norm. But I relished it all. Hours were spent just gazing at Ava, even fast asleep, noticing tiny flickers of movement or the rise and fall of her chest when breathing.

It soon became clear that Vimla was quite an experienced nanny and did everything with such ease. She made it all look so simple, whether bathing or feeding Ava. I loved to watch her comb Ava's black hair, surprisingly plentiful, all over with coconut oil. It was an Indian tradition that kept hair dark and glossy and in good condition. Indeed Vimla put it all over Ava's body and I still do to this day. Even Bina would put it in my nephews' hair. Always oil your hair became Vimla's mantra.

The long hours spent with Vimla in the hotel were also an opportunity for us to get to know each other better. Before long, she was regaling me with stories of her donor experiences. Most centred on keeping her husband in the dark; he was completely unaware that she had been a donor so many times before.

'Because I keep the money and say nothing,' she told me with a nod.

Good for you, I thought, having your own little stash.

'Would your husband have had a problem with it?' I wondered aloud.

'No,' she replied, and then added matter of factly. 'But you need to have your own money.'

From what I could gather she used it wisely and discreetly on her children. During our stay at the hotel, Vimla was also an egg donor. It was nearing the time for her egg retrieval and she was taking hormone injections to trigger their release. It was never a big deal for her or her compatriots because Indian women seemed to be super fertile. One day, she got an urgent phone call from Dr Patel saying it was time and she was off like a rocket.

'I got a call,' she exclaimed excitedly. 'I'm going!'

Through Vimla I learnt just how small indeed the surrogacy world was. By sheer coincidence, when I was first interested in surrogacy the year before, Dr Patel had supplied me with the email address of a couple who had been to Anand and had a successful surrogacy. The woman, whose name was Emily Jane, had provided so much valuable advice that we remained in touch. One day, in the hotel bedroom, her name came up in casual conversation.

'Emily Jane, I had their baby!' Vimla exclaimed.

It was such an incredible coincidence that I got on my laptop straight away and started Googling. By another coincidence, Emily Jane and her husband had done a magazine article some months before and it was still available online, which I proceeded to read to Vimla and show her pictures of the baby and the parents. Her deep delight and excitement were so touching. I could see that the baby still had a special place in her heart.

While at the Rama Hotel, I made the acquaintance of a few nannies that had been surrogates and were training some of the other girls to be nannies as well. It was a curious sort of career path in one way. If you didn't want to be a surrogate any more, you could move on to being a nanny, a job which they all loved because it meant staying in nice hotels and often getting to meet foreign couples. With so much experience, Vimla was frequently in demand. When Sharmila's baby was eventually discharged from the neonatal unit, it was Vimla who came to show her how to bathe him, seeing that he was so small.

During my time at the hotel, Sharmila and her mother continued to help me out as well and told me what I needed in the way of sterilisers, especially Sterilin hand sanitizers – bought in bulk from the hospital stores – and baby creams and so on. Her surrogate had been discharged home but used to come to the hotel every morning with expressed breast milk for Ravi or else the woman's husband would bring it. It was a separate arrangement to the surrogacy agreement, whereby Sharmila had organised and paid for it herself. Sharmila and I were both very conscious of hygiene, given the heat and humidity of the climate. In fact, we probably went a bit overboard at times, being first-time mothers. Whenever I entered her room, I would douse my hands in Sterilin and put on my indoor flipflops without a trace of outdoor dust or dirt. We tried to keep everything scrupulously clean, sterilising bottles and utensils. Thankfully, everything worked out fine and Ava never picked up a bug.

When cabin fever set in, Vimla and I would take Ava outside for a quick stroll or to buy essential baby items. The Seven Eleven baby store was fantastic and supplied just about everything I needed. I had to laugh at my previous misconceptions that I would be unable to buy even a nappy in Anand. The store could order in anything you needed from Sudocream to Dr Brown's bottles, you name it, they could get it. Speaking Gujarati, Sharmila would often phone the store for me and order stuff if I was stuck. And it was all delivered to you at the hotel with a beaming smile.

Crossing the chaotic streets in Anand was something I was slowly growing accustomed to. At first negotiating the traffic used to petrify me, so much so that in the early days Uday had to steer me across.

'Uday, I can't cross this road, I'm terrified.'

'Take my hand,' he would say, proffering his arm.

And then he would lead the way, reciting 'vom vom', as if to stop the traffic in its tracks. I would half close my eyes and just go with him. I soon learned from Uday and Bina too that you just have to walk out in front of the traffic and they will avoid you.

'That's the way it is done.'

But in the intense heat, we never stayed out for very long. Wearing the compression bandage for my lymphoedema put an end to any longer excursions as well. I had bought a small, black baby carry nest, fitted with a coolmax mattress, popular with foreign couples in Anand, which was perfect for moving about. It was designed almost like a small rucksack and had a mosquito net to cover and protect Ava. It also meant that her face could barely be seen. This suited Vimla no end, as I was to learn. One custom important to Hindus, as indeed in other cultures, is fear of the Evil Eye. It is a common belief that all kinds of illnesses, pains, fits and handicaps are caused by the evil eye, or because someone is possessed by an evil spirit. A person is said to possess the evil eye if whatever they look upon is harmed. This person is not necessarily deemed wicked themselves and usually the effect of the evil eye is unintentional. Good-looking children, in particular, are considered most susceptible to the evil eye. For this reason, Vimla insisted on carrying Ava when outdoors to ensure no one saw her. Unlike in Ireland and the western world, you're not supposed to look at babies in India. There was certainly no oohing and ahhing and doting on them by all and sundry. Through Bina and other Indians, I had already known of this custom.

'That's not right because of the evil eye,' Bina's mother would say.

As a result, there are all sorts of practices to ward off the evil eye or else rid the effects of it. For starters, children have to wear special, protective charms and lockets. Black kohl eyeliner is applied to their eyes and a small black bindi dot to their foreheads.

'We'll put a black spot on her because when we go out she is too beautiful,'

Vimla informed me, 'and people will look at her, and that's the evil eye.'

The kohl and black bindi are believed to mar the child's beauty and make them unattractive to the evil eye. As for charms, Vimla wanted Ava to wear a black bangle.

'Vimla, she's not wearing a bangle,' I exclaimed. 'She's too small.'

But whatever I thought, it didn't matter because people purchased presents of black bangles and bracelets for Ava anyway.

Nita brought along a black bracelet when she paid us a visit at the hotel. It was such a comfort to see her because I still felt bad about the misunderstanding over the breast milk. However, another issue had arisen that had upset her in the meantime. After Ava's birth, she had remained on in the clinic for several days; her stitches were removed in due course and she had recuperated well. During her recovery, I had returned to see her after the visit from myself and Sharmila. I wanted to see her and let her know that Ava was doing well and on the verge of being discharged from the neonatal unit. I also nursed the hope that she might think again about supplying breast milk. Having had a change of heart and seeing how breast milk is considered like gold over there, so full of nutrients, I thought it might be good for Ava. But before I could begin, the issue of the nanny emerged.

'I heard you are getting a nanny,' she began.

'That's right,' I said, explaining what Dr Anita and Dr Patel had advised. 'I need a nanny.'

'Me, me,' she kept saying.

This was the first inkling I got that Nita wanted to come to the hotel and be the nanny. I was not sure of the protocol, but the first thought that entered my head was maybe it was a bit too close to home for me. Culturally, it didn't feel right to me, but perhaps in Indian culture it would be perfectly acceptable. As far as I was concerned, there had to be a cut-off point at some stage, but there were no hard and fast rules about when that should be.

'Can I come and be the nanny?' Nita repeated.

Though my initial reaction was reluctance, I did want to be fair to Nita all the same. My appreciation and debt of gratitude to her were as deep as ever and had not changed one iota. And perhaps she wanted to do it out of the goodness of her own heart. I sought out Dr Patel and Hitesh and explained Nita's request. By that stage, all the arrangements with Vimla were in place and they were not prepared to change them, expressing doubts about Nita into the bargain. Even though some surrogates do end up being nannies for foreign couples while sorting out their paperwork, Hitesh did not think it would be for the best in my case. I think he and Dr Patel felt I was vulnerable on my own, without Niall, and needed someone neutral to help me care for Ava.

Despite the nanny setback, I visited Nita briefly once more at the clinic before she was discharged. But there was still tension in the air. Whenever I brought up the subject with the other couples at the hotel, they were sceptical.

'I think it's time to step back a little bit here,' one girl advised. 'You can't be with Nita now all the time.'

It was true I did feel vulnerable and didn't know exactly what was going on because of the language barrier. Only for the fact that there were people in the Rama Hotel who could speak both Gujarati and English, I would have felt very lost, trying to communicate with everybody. I suppose in one way, if Ava had gone to full term, all of these things, like breast milk and nannies, would have been ironed out beforehand. We could have planned things much better, at least regarding the aftercare. That's where I felt really stuck.

From Dr Patel's point of view, she felt that the surrogate mother should not have any expectations of being close to the intended parents or treated like a family member once the baby is born, and vice versa. In fact, about a tenth of couples that attended the clinic did not want any contact whatsoever afterwards. Yet despite not wishing Nita to be the nanny, it did not mean that it was the end of the road; that everything was over like a business transaction. It was always my intention that we would keep in touch and that we would return to Anand to see her one day when Ava was older.

For this reason, I was really pleased when Nita, her mother and her little daughter and son turned up at the hotel shortly after Ava had been discharged from the hospital. Lying on the tan-coloured bed cover and swaddled in a white blanket, Ava was fast asleep. She looked the picture of contentment.

'Oh,' exclaimed Nita, a broad smile appearing on her face. 'My gift, my gift to you.'

'My angel, my angel,' I said, pointing to Ava.

Nita was so happy to see Ava and there seemed no trace of bitterness now. As she sat on the bed and I placed Ava in her arms, she certainly didn't get upset or sad. It was such a beautiful sight, especially Nita in a gorgeous patterned aquamarine and cerise sari. Nita's daughter hopped on the bed as well, a quiet pretty girl dressed in pink leggings and a pink and black latticed top. Her bright brown eyes were just like Nita's and darkened with kohl eyeliner to ward off the evil eye. Needless to say, my camera clicked merrily, capturing the moment. Then Nita's mother took my place at the lens and I joined the three ladies. All I could say to Nita's mother was that her daughter was like a god, giving me the wonderful gift of Ava.

There was also another important reason for Nita's visit. Normally six days after a baby is born in India they hold a short ceremony to ward off the evil eye. Because Ava was still in the neonatal unit at that stage, this had been postponed. Now Nita and her mother conducted it, presenting Ava with two bracelets – two little chains with alternating black and silver beads. It made them happy to know that the ceremony had taken place and that Ava was safe and sound.

Seeing Nita with Ava, I imagined what it would be like if she were the nanny. Perhaps everything would have been fine and I would have got over being uncomfortable and feeling the set-up was inappropriate. By this stage I was well used to Vimla and because she was so experienced, I willingly took instruction from her. I soaked up her advice about the dos and don'ts of motherhood. Maybe it would have been harder to accept that kind of advice coming from Nita. At least I knew for certain it was not a trust issue. I never felt that Nita was going to run off with the baby or anything like that. It was just too close for comfort in my eyes. And I wasn't the only one who felt that way; the other couples at the hotel used to say it was ridiculous and why would I have Nita as my nanny.

After that Nita returned to the hotel three or four times to see us. Then requests for personal items began, like clothes and toys for the children, and a mobile phone for herself. We would all go shopping together and there was always something that she needed urgently. At first I willingly bought her the items, but gradually eased off. Perhaps she was a little bit pressurised by other members of her family to ask for things. I wasn't sure. I didn't think it was coming from Nita personally. All the monies owed to her had been paid over by Niall and me. There was no shortage of opinions from my family, friends and the other couples on the matter. Some would suggest the demands had arisen because she was still sore over the nanny issue or that it was the Indian way of life. Looking back on the experience, I don't know if there was a right or wrong way to act. I suppose being a foreigner in a strange country, it was a bit scary. Being on my own, I didn't really know how to handle the situation.

***

Another intended mother I got close to while staying at the Rama Hotel was Meenakshi, a Californian of Indian origin. She had arrived over early from the US and was awaiting the birth of her twins through surrogacy. Her fluency in Gujarati helped me out of many a sticky situation. So I was only too happy to return the favour whenever she needed company, support or advice. Finally, one afternoon, not long after Ava was born, Meenakshi got a call from Dr Patel to say her babies would be born that day. In high spirits, we dashed over to the clinic and into the room where Meenakshi's surrogate, Rani, was lying. It was similar to the one that Nita had been in before delivery. The babies were to be born by Caesarean section but there had been a delay. What was really remarkable about the situation was that Rani was there with her pregnant sister who was a surrogate for another couple. Beside them, tending to their needs, was their mother, who looked equally as young.

'Oh my God, your two daughters!' I blurted out, totally amazed.

A warm smile rested on her face, as Meenakshi translated our conversation. You could tell the mother was very proud of her family.

'You are like your daughters,' I said, noting the resemblance.

She nodded and explained that it was the first-time surrogacy for Rani, while her other daughter Esha, who spoke perfect English, was on her second surrogacy and due to deliver within a week or two as well. As it turned out, Rani was supposed to go to theatre some hours earlier but had eaten a sandwich, forcing Dr Patel to postpone the surgery for a few hours. We sat with her in the meantime. By her own admission, she was very nervous, never having had a Caesarean section before. Reassuring her and asking how she was feeling, I think we grew more nervous by the minute. The waiting is the worst, no matter whose child it is!

Eventually Dr Patel entered the room and sat down at the side of the bed. It was pretty obvious that Rani was anxious.

'Everything is going to be fine,' Dr Patel soothed.

There was one thing I had noticed about Dr Patel during my days in Anand. She had a very good bedside manner and this time was no exception. In chatty and reassuring tones, she put Rani at ease, asking how she was and how were things; anything to distract her or at least think about the positives and benefits of the pregnancy.

'This is exciting, how do you feel?' Dr Patel asked, getting more animated.

It was no wonder the surrogates had huge respect for her, seeing that she often put their interests and concerns first.

***

One of the advantages of staying at the Rama Hotel was there was no scarcity of couples to talk to and eat with. Meenakshi, Payal, Sharmila and her parents were just a small sample of those I could dine with each evening. Indian food being a particular favourite of mine ensured I never went hungry. And because I don't really eat meat, vegetarian foods were top priority. But unlike elsewhere being a vegetarian in India was rather a source of good luck and the food really scrumptious. It was not to everyone's taste, however. Deeply ravenous, some of the Americans used to trek to the local D-Mart store and buy up tins of meat and ask the kitchen staff to prepare them. In times like that I was glad I was not a steak eater. My favourite dish at the Rama was chilli paneer. In fact, I liked it so much that I had it every single day and the staff had my order off by heart. Chilli paneer is basically a spicy dish of cottage cheese cut into cubes with finely chopped onions, chillies, coriander, ginger, garlic and spices. It looks like you're eating chicken yet doesn't have a cheesy taste. It's a weird taste really but absolutely delicious with chapati breads.

Yes, there was no fear I was starving myself at the Rama. Mindful that I was on my own, Uday was always putting me in touch with hospitable, kind-hearted Indians. On one occasion, he introduced me to a Sikh family he had been friends with since childhood and invited me to their home. On arrival, three generations of the family greeted me and Ava – from the widowed grandmother down to a young boy wearing a patka, a head covering to keep his long hair in place. It was a friendly, relaxed atmosphere and everyone was dressed casually in t-shirts and shorts. The family, or rather Bindu the daughter, had kindly prepared chapatis and a selection of traditional Indian food followed by delicious mango ice cream – the fruit freshly picked from their garden. It was all delicious but a surprise was in store when we sat down to eat. I was the only one served any food and all eyes were on me as I took each mouthful.

'Are you not going to eat?' I enquired gingerly.

'No,' Bindu replied. 'You eat first.'

'Please eat,' I implored.

'You are the guest.'

My discomfort increased with every morsel and I wondered how to end it.

'I really have to get Ava back to the hotel soon,' I said, thinking fast.

'She is under the fan with grandmother in the garden,' Bindu replied, insisting I take my time and enjoy my food. 'Please eat.'

I came to learn that Sikh hospitality is legendary all over the world, and this was no exception. It was a big part of their culture to assist travellers and especially feed them. Their generosity and kindness to me was very much appreciated.

On the other hand, Vimla had a separate eating arrangement, unique to the nannies at the hotel. I learnt about it when we first brought Ava home from Dr Anita's clinic.

'Do you want to eat in the hotel?' I asked her, thinking we hadn't eaten in hours.

'The Tiffin Man will come.'

'The who?' I uttered, completely bewildered.

The mention of Tiffin sounded like a chocolate bar, but I was sure that's not what Vimla had meant. The Tiffin Man was the guy who brought meals in special metal containers called Tiffin boxes. Made from stainless steel, they came in three separate tiers for different parts of a meal, hot or cold, that were locked together for easier handling. They were opened by unlatching a small catch on either side of the handle and removing it. The food in the different tiers, anything from rice to curries, vegetables or chapati breads, could stay warm for up to two or three hours.

When I saw the boxes I remembered I had actually seen them before. They were the same ones supplied to Nita and the surrogates when staying in Dr Patel's clinic in the latter stages of pregnancy. I had spotted them on the floor of the room but never got an opportunity to enquire about their purpose. The clinic organised the Tiffin boxes for the surrogates and nannies and the cost was factored into the overall surrogacy fee or nanny fee. Vimla's fee worked out at about US$100 a month. From her point of view, the food was plentiful and delicious.

'I'll be going home twice the size,' she wailed after one meal. 'I'm eating so much.'

In all our time spent together we had grown fond of each other. It was a far cry from our initial meeting with Hitesh in his office when I was still uncertain about having a nanny at all. Vimla had even confided much later that she did not know what to make of me after that first day. How we both laughed at that. I knew I would miss her when we eventually returned to Dublin. But how long we remained in the region entirely depended on bureaucracy, both in India and back in Ireland.

Chapter 15

The birth certificate

Right from the moment that Ava was born getting her passport was paramount. As soon as I had gotten over the initial shock of her premature birth and transfer to the neonatal unit, I swung into action. The first thing to be done was to register her birth and get the birth certificate as quickly as possible. Fortunately, I was aided in the matter by Hitesh. The day after Ava's birth he rang me.

'I want you to come over,' he requested, 'and write down Ava's name as you are going to spell it.'

Hitesh supplied all our details on the birth notification form, which was sent to the local authorities. In India, births have to be registered within twenty-one days, unlike the three months given in Ireland. I had heard that it could take up to ten days to get the birth certificate. Though I was obviously in a big hurry for it, I didn't want to push the issue with the Indian authorities in case it backfired. In any event, Hitesh was aware of the urgency of the matter and acquainted with our plans. At that stage, we hoped Plan A worked. If not, we were into Plan B. The principal plan was that once I got the birth certificate I would courier it and the passport application over to Niall in Ireland so he could apply to the Passport Office in Dublin. Plan B was a more serious step, involving solicitors and barristers.

About two days later, Hitesh phoned and asked me to come over to the clinic, saying he had something for me to sign. I was there in a shot, thrilled that things were moving quickly. In Hitesh's office, another employee helped him out with the paperwork, who spoke good English and was tall and stocky. He too was present when I turned up and asked me to look over the document to ensure all was correct.

'Make sure the spellings are correct,' he advised, inviting me to sit and read it.

After checking the document, which was the actual birth registration form, I signed it. From the clinic it then went to the local civil registration office. By all accounts, the Gujarati civil registration system had a pretty good reputation. Having upgraded its electronic infrastructure in recent years, it now offered one of the fastest registration processes in India. The registration was also free of charge, as was the birth certificate.

Three days later the birth certificate was ready. Again I had to read the document closely to make sure it contained no mistakes. I went through it, line by line, and thankfully everything was in order. The certificate recorded Ava's forename and surname, her gender, time and date of birth, place of birth, registration number and place of registration, i.e. Anand, and the signature of the issuing officer. As well as that Niall and I were registered as her legal father and mother and our address in Ireland recorded. There was nothing about our nationality, dates of birth, marital status, or professions, and more importantly, no mention of surrogacy. The certificate was bilingual – in Gujarati and English – and issued by the state of Gujarat. And with its distinctive Gujarati script with cream paper and red writing, it could be immediately identified as a foreign birth certificate.

It was just fantastic that we had received it within a week. It was probably just as well that Ava was being cared for in the neonatal unit, and later by Vimla, because it meant I was free to sort out the paperwork and I could give the matter my wholehearted attention. Filling out the necessary parts of the passport application required all my energies. All the envelopes were written and ready to go. Prior to this Niall and I had done up mock documents with mock names, of boys and girls, so we knew exactly where to fill in the actual information when the time came. Even so, with all the heat and excitement

I didn't want to make a mistake that would cost us precious time or jeopardise the application. My dad, who so wanted to come to India and be of help to me as indeed did my mother and brother, rang with advice. He knew I had to put myself into the right frame of mind for tackling the bureaucracy.

'Ava's in ICU so you don't have to worry about her. Concentrate,' he advised, 'Focus on this. There's no point in you couriering your documents if they have to be redone.'

'Okay, this is it,' I said, preparing for the task at hand.

I sat in my hotel room and took the phone off the hook for an hour. That way I could concentrate completely on the Irish passport application form and see what items were required at my end. I personally could not apply on Ava's behalf because that would mean stating I had given birth, which obviously was not the case. We were careful not to do anything illegal; everything on the application form had to be true and correct. Fortunately, you only needed details of one parent when applying for an Irish passport for a child. So parts of the form were left blank for Niall to fill in back in Dublin. As Ava's father, Niall would be the parent making the application, since he personally would have to present himself at a Garda station to get the form signed and later at the Passport Office. He would supply his own birth certificate and our marriage certificate as proof of Irish citizenship. As we needed a witness to sign the form, Uday brought me to an Indian solicitor in Anand. She duly signed and stamped the form for a small fee and also signed the back of Ava's photos. Finally, I got Sharmila's husband to read through all of the instructions to make sure I had left nothing out.

For several days, I had been trying to take passport photos of Ava. I knew we needed them pretty quickly but the fact that she was in the neonatal unit and so tiny had posed a number of problems. Uday too was well aware of the situation and did his best to help me acquire them. It was no mean feat, as it turned out. In recent years very strict instructions had been issued by the Department of Foreign Affairs regarding passport photos of babies, so I knew it was not going to be easy. I tried to figure out how best to include her ears and keep her eyes open and mouth closed in a close-up shot. I knew it had to be done right first time, as having to redo the photos if they were rejected could delay the application by weeks if not months. Time was definitely at stake.

It proved very difficult getting a good-quality shot of Ava in the unit. For one thing she was sleeping so much you just couldn't frame her. Even the nurses got in on the act, helping to position her, taking her little hat off and adjusting the lights. The fact that Ava was jaundiced did not exactly give her the natural skin tone they were looking for either. Panic sometimes set in when I thought about the delay. Fortunately, I wasn't alone. Sharmila was in the same boat applying for a British passport, but her little boy Ravi was so teeny, it was almost impossible. Her husband went to such great lengths to photograph Ravi, who was so severely premature he barely looked formed. His ears were practically non-existent as his father folded them forward to be included in the frame. In fact, Ravi's whole head was like an egg in his father's hand. And of course hands holding the baby were not allowed to be visible either. All our attempts at photography were comical in hindsight. Finally Uday intervened.

'Look, I know it's delaying it a few days,' he began, 'but I have a professional photographer who can come to the hotel room when she is discharged and take a proper photo of her.'

He was right. Despite my anxiety over a further delay, there was no point pursuing it while she was in hospital. Over the phone I poured out my fears to Niall and my dad. They too agreed that it was far more important to get the right kind of photo rather than send any old one because it would be duly sent back and waste more precious time. And the cost of packages going back and forth around the globe by DHL would be no joke in the long term either.

So I held tight until Ava was safely installed in the hotel. True to his word, Uday arrived around with a photographer the following morning and knocked on our door. By this stage Ava was a lot more alert and awake so Vimla and I laid her carefully on the bed while the photographer stood over her and took the shot.

'I'll have them back for you in one hour,' he promised as he left the room.

I breathed a sigh of relief, thinking at last we were getting somewhere. As ever I was so grateful to Uday, who honestly never let me down. Bang on sixty minutes or so, Uday returned. It was lunchtime as I remember. In his hand, he had little folders with holders for the photos, all neatly ordered and perfectly shot. The quality was excellent and worth every penny or rather rupee spent. Typical Uday, ever my protector, asked me to look over the passport application information to make sure all the instructions had been met. *Have you got this? Have you got that? Make sure everything is filled in and signed.*

Finally, as Uday and I dropped the package, addressed to Niall, at the DHL office in Anand, I crossed my fingers and hoped we would have the passport without any hitches. All that was left was for Niall to get the application and photos signed at our local Garda station. In truth, we were not saying anything other than the baby in the photos was one given birth to and declaring that Niall was the father. There was also the passport fee of €31.00 to be included, as Ava was under three years of age.

***

My world was completely overshadowed by getting the passport. It began to consume every minute of my day and many a sleepless night. I could barely eat for fear things would not go according to plan. However, one event that was to make headlines worldwide knocked it off my radar briefly and inspired fear of a different kind. A week after Ava was born, Osama bin Laden was killed in Abbottabad, Pakistan by American Special Forces. The world's most wanted man was no longer at large, yet it brought great uncertainty to the region. A region I was now residing in and for how long I just had no idea.

I remember the day very clearly, Monday, 2nd May. In the hotel that morning Vimla was on her mobile phone to someone, obviously speaking Gujarati, when I overheard her saying *Osama bin Laden*; I was puzzled his name would crop up in conversation.

'Is he dead?' I suddenly asked for no good reason.

'Osama bin Laden dead!' she exclaimed, putting the phone down.

Luckily, we had cable TV in the hotel room and quickly turned on CNN to watch the news unfold. Vimla was worried. A wave of terrorism led by al-Qaeda had struck India in recent years, especially Mumbai in 2008 when over 160 people were killed and luxury hotels targeted. The state of Gujarat bordering Pakistan was a cause of unease too. Being in close proximity was not such a good thing. I was sure there would be more security restrictions, especially for tourists. Within hours of bin Laden's killing, the Pakistan branch of the Taliban threatened reprisals. Tensions were high and Americans were seen as legitimate targets.

I rang home to let Niall and my parents know that bin Laden was dead. Immediately my dad had my security and welfare at heart.

'You want to be careful now going out because of this,' he warned.

To be honest, at first I was not unduly concerned but then remembered what it was like out and about in Anand. If you're a tourist or visitor, everyone thinks you're American, especially if fair-skinned. I used to be mistaken for an American all the time. Suddenly, it all felt unsafe. I knew I needed to be extra careful now. At least I could rest assured that the modest Rama Hotel was highly unlikely to be attacked. I did feel very secure there and relieved I had moved from the Madhubhan Hotel, recalling their strict security measures. Long-handled inspection mirrors had been used for checking the underside of cars and vehicles every time we had entered the hotel grounds, usually by taxi.

'What is this for?' I had quizzed Uday one day, as we waited while our taxi was inspected on our way into the hotel complex.

'To check just in case there are bombs,' he replied.

'Jesus Christ, are they going to blow up this hotel because there's loads of Americans?'

Never once had a bomb or explosive device been found but they had to take precautions nonetheless. These thoughts began to haunt me, especially after bin Laden's death. Admittedly, there was no radical activity in Anand, no terrorism at all. However, that was no reason for complacency. Even Uday told me to be careful and not to go anywhere unless he was accompanying me.

'Don't just jump into taxis and go anywhere alone,' he advised.

The turmoil made me wish all the more that things would run smoothly in Dublin and that we could leave the region soon. Every minute of the day I wondered what progress Niall might have made.

Chapter 16

The Passport Office

By the time I received Caroline's package from India later that week, my daughter Ava was about a week and a half old. Before I could submit the documentation to the Passport Office, I first had to get the photos and passport application form signed at our local Garda station. After that, the earliest opportunity to get to the office was the following Monday, 9 May. But at least things were in motion. For so many months this scenario had been rehearsed in our minds but now the moment had actually arrived. At the time my work schedule was frenetic and in an effort to beat the crowds, I arrived in Molesworth Street shortly after 5AM on Monday morning. It was probably the worst time of year to apply because of the legendary summer backlog and queues, but it could not be helped.

It was hard to believe that Ava was already two weeks old and I still had not seen her, or rather not held her. Thanks to Caroline I got to see photos of her regularly by email. I eagerly awaited each one; every picture of our beautiful tiny girl was like seeing her for the first time. More than anything I wanted to be with them in Anand, to share the joy of her birth, to protect them and to ease the stress burden, but I knew the priority lay with sorting out the passport here in Dublin. The news of Osama bin Laden's death had left me apprehensive about them being alone in India. Even though Anand was considered relatively safe, you still couldn't take any chances in that region of the world. In the UK, Caroline's brother Philip had been in contact with the British Foreign and Commonwealth Office regarding the security situation in India. A senior official had advised him that Caroline should change her hotel room every couple of days, should not enter any public areas of the hotel she was staying in, and to limit any trips she took to the local shop unless absolutely necessary. Hearing that was cold comfort indeed. But at least the Commonwealth Office were concerned enough to ring her and check that she was okay and offer further advice. It was more than could be said for the Irish embassy in India.

The Passport Office did not open until 9.30AM but a queue was about to form at 5AM. One gentleman stood outside the office yet I wasn't sure if he was coming home from a night on the town or just anxious to be first in line. I decided to wait in the car and allow a small queue to form, thinking fourth place or thereabouts would be good enough for me. Eventually I joined it and claimed eleventh place. Caroline had already been on the phone that morning and I knew she, as indeed her father, was in a sweat with worry. I went over all the documents in my head that I had brought to support our application, just in case they were needed – long birth certificates of Ava as well as mine, Caroline's and both our parents'; our marriage certificate; the signed photos of Ava and the signed passport application form from witnesses and the Gardaí. You name it, we had it. I had also been in touch with our solicitor Deborah, who was trying to cover every angle and ensure everything was above board.

By 9.30AM, the queue had started to snake along Molesworth Street, maybe about thirty people in all. When the doors finally opened, I felt a sudden rush of blood to my head. I grew dizzy and my heart was beating like crazy. This was it, D-day. When my number was called, I walked calmly to the public counter, hatch number three, and was greeted with a grunt from the female civil servant. I presented our application in silence. She quickly flicked through the application and glanced at the Indian birth certificate.

'Why does the baby have an Indian birth cert?' she asked.

'Because she was born there,' I answered.

'Is the baby Irish?'

'Yes.'

At that, she walked away from the counter to consult her superiors. After all our dry runs and telephone exchanges with the Passport Office in Dublin and in Cork months previously, choosing our words carefully and emphasising our child was going to be born in India, none of the officials had raised an objection at least at that stage. And then on the real run, I suppose seeing the actual foreign birth certificate, in appearance so different from an Irish one, made them sit up and take notice.

Almost twenty minutes passed before she returned to tell me that the application could not be processed and handed me back the forms. Yet she was unable to offer a single reason for not accepting it. Instead she referred me to hatch number one, which was a private cubicle. Behind closed doors, I spoke with her supervisor, a pleasant and sympathetic lady.

'Why was the baby born in India?' she enquired.

'The baby was born in India, to myself and my wife, due to medical reasons,' I explained. 'She's our biological child.'

I further explained that my wife had had cervical cancer, had consulted with her own doctors here, who had suggested we attend a fertility clinic in India, which we did. The reason we had chosen India was because Caroline had a family connection with the country, and also because of costs. At that, the official requested additional information like medical reports to show whether Caroline had actually been pregnant. For example, prenatal scans, medical reports, letters from the doctor, and so on. Now I had never stated if Caroline was actually pregnant or not. The woman just assumed that Caroline had carried the baby.

'We have to be very careful when processing application forms because a number of children born outside Ireland are born through surrogacy,' she added. 'It's not as straightforward as a normal passport application.'

With that, I didn't mention anything about surrogacy but thanked her, calmly took the forms and left the building. It was all very confusing since no other additional information should have been necessary. I had presented all the required paperwork according to the Passport Act and guidelines set down on the passport application form. To be honest, I was taken aback. It was not a case of us being naïve, thinking all would go well, because there was genuinely nothing wrong, nothing untrue or illegal, on our application form. It was only later we learned anecdotally that there were in fact Irish couples, number unknown, whose child had been born through surrogacy abroad, and who had quietly applied for an Irish passport. The Passport Office had duly issued the required passport, none the wiser of the true circumstances.

Despite the setback, I knew that we had right on our side. I immediately contacted Deborah so we could get to work straight away on the legal end of things. Plan B was to get a court order facilitating the issuing of a passport by the Passport Office. Later Caroline and I talked. Not wishing to upset her, I held back on the extent of what had happened. In truth, it was not a case of them refusing us a passport but rather dismissing our application, handing it back, until we supplied additional information.

'Go on, it did work, didn't it?' she said, thinking I was messing with her.

'They just need more information,' I said.

I tried to make light of it, knowing that Caroline would by nature worry. It was not my style to give negative news, either to Caroline or to our families. For me it was best to remain positive, in the face of all that uncertainty and upheaval. Although from the viewpoint of both myself and our legal team additional information was not legally required.

'Everything is going to be okay, Caroline,' I assured her. 'Look, we have Deborah and a barrister working on it now.'

The fact that we did not get the passport that day nonetheless hit Caroline hard. I cursed the fact that thousands of miles separated us. She felt lost because we had done so much preparation work in vain and instinctively knew that the next stage, whatever it was, was going to be difficult and unpredictable. So much for us testing the waters. She was kicking herself that she had emailed the Passport Office at all, seeking information in the first place so many months before. It had only drawn attention to our case, as she saw it. But it was easy to say that in hindsight. The disappointment of our families was plain to see as well. Regardless of how positive I remained, I knew from the way they inhaled sharply and their tone of voice that they felt we had huge hurdles ahead of us now.

***

The more I thought about it, the more I believed the Department of Foreign Affairs was in violation of legislation governing the issuing of Irish passports as well as European legislation concerning the welfare of the child. But all that did not seem to matter to them. They were well aware that the issue of surrogacy was an escalating one, given the number of Irish couples enquiring about it, yet they still chose to bury their heads in the sand. The manner in which the Department dealt with our application was totally unsatisfactory. The truth of the matter was that they had no procedures at all in place to process an application based on a child born through surrogacy. That said, as far as I was concerned, it was not required by law, as it should be a normal application if the parents were Irish-born citizens.

Surrogacy, to my mind, had always been our best option. Perhaps Caroline was more committed to exploring the IVF and adoption routes than I had been at the time. I suppose I even went along with them because they weren't worth having an argument over. So when she lost faith in them, it did not bring too much upset or disappointment my way. I understood her concerns about IVF at the time and the adoption course had been a dismal joke as far as I was concerned. But I could sense over the years how much she longed for a child and would not rest until we had a family. Initially with surrogacy, I had lukewarm feelings admittedly but as the pregnancy became a reality, I felt differently about it. And of course with the actual arrival of Ava, I was thrilled, and only regretted that I was absent for her birth, though there was nothing I could do about that.

Signing up for surrogacy in Ireland was never going to happen for us. Reports first surfaced in 2009 in the medical press that a child had been born through surrogacy the previous year – the first ever in Ireland. But the intended parents would have to adopt the child, because the birth mother – the sister of the woman – was considered the legal mother. Surrogacy was starting to become a reality, yet only possible down the adoption route within the State. Yet from legal firms to support groups like the National Infertility Support and Information Group (NISIG), nobody really knew much about surrogacy, especially international surrogacy. Maybe that's all changing now; certainly our surrogacy experience was a trip into the unknown.

Because there were no laws governing surrogacy in Ireland, domestic or international, we had to look at other legislation. During Caroline's second trip to India, I continued to research all relevant laws relating to Irish citizenship and the welfare of children as set out by the State. During my research and from earlier discussions with Deborah our solicitor, I was unable to find any official documentation stating that surrogacy was a 'grey area' or any mention of surrogacy whatsoever. The Government had turned a deaf ear to the Commission on Human Assisted Reproduction and its 2005 report had been left to gather dust. None of its forty recommendations, including those on regulating surrogacy, had been legally implemented. From all this I concluded that Ava would be afforded the rights that all Irish citizens and children born to Irish-born parents would be entitled to. In the absence of legislation governing surrogacy, Irish citizenship and child welfare laws did apply in Ava's case and the State would not be in a position to contest our passport application.

I had printed off copies of so much legislation that our home was beginning to look like the Law Library. After immersing myself in these laws, things started to look clearer. To be honest, it all seemed black and white to me. There were about five essential pieces of legislation that supported our position as I saw it. The first one was the Passport Act, 2008, which contained about seven parts applicable to our case.

As far as I could see Ava met all the requirements as set down by the State. To begin with, her birth certificate complied with the definition of a birth certificate cited in Section 2(e). It was a document issued in accordance with a civil system of registration of births in the place where the birth occurs. Her birth certificate had been issued by the Indian state and was all legal and correct. As an Irish citizen, Ava was entitled to a passport and had the right to apply for one, in accordance with Section 6(1). As her father, I was entitled to apply for a passport on her behalf, as stated in Section 3(a). The question of parental or guardian consent was covered in Section 14(1), and I was most certainly giving my consent, as her father, for the issuing of a passport to take place. But even if I did not give consent for whatever reason, the law, in Section 14(6)(a)(b), stipulated that a passport could be granted in exceptional circumstances if there was an immediate and serious risk of harm to the child's life, or if her health or safety required her to undertake travel for which a passport was required. So in the interest of securing the welfare of the child, a passport should be issued to her. This was highly pertinent to our situation. Ava had been in the neonatal unit and needed a lot of care and attention. If she were denied a passport or emergency travel certificate, she would be unable to obtain an exit visa from the Indian authorities and come home to Ireland. Caroline was permitted to stay in India on a three-month tourist visa that could not be extended. Or at least it was a nightmare to reapply. If Caroline were forced to return home after her visa expired, who would look after Ava – a defenceless baby all alone? We dreaded to think what would happen to her if abandoned in an Indian orphanage. As it was, there were about 25 million orphans in India, according to UNICEF, who fell victim to a variety of social ills, especially girls. From exclusion, illiteracy, malnutrition, illness, especially HIV, to exploitation and physical and sexual abuse. It was too horrifying to think about it. If Caroline chose to outstay her visa, she would be deported and could jeopardise obtaining a visa in the future.

The issuing of an emergency travel certificate was also covered in Section 15(2)(a)(b)(ii) of the Passport Act, 2008. An emergency travel certificate could be issued to a person when there was a reasonable cause to believe that the person is or may be an Irish citizen. Or if there was a reasonable cause to believe that the person does not hold a valid passport. As far as I was concerned, there was no doubt that Ava was an Irish citizen, even if I had to take a paternity test to prove it. The question of Ava's citizenship could also not be disputed, when you looked at the Irish Nationality and Citizenship Act, 2001. In Section 3(7)(1), it stated that a person is an Irish citizen from birth if at the time of her birth either parent was an Irish citizen, or would, if alive, have been an Irish citizen. Everything rested on this citizenship by descent rule. Because Caroline had not physically given birth to Ava, it was always going to be difficult to say that she was her mother legally. However, as Ava's father, where my sperm had fertilised the egg, it was more straight forward that I was her biological father.

Even the emails from the Passport Office that Caroline had received, directly or indirectly, always mentioned who qualified for Irish citizenship. The standard reply sent to everyone appeared to be:

> The department has obtained legal advice and is in the process of drafting an information note on the issues. This note will have to be cleared by the Attorney General's office prior to its issue. In the meantime, I shall endeavour to answer your questions. However, the position is subject to change and I should also add that each passport application has to be considered on its merits. Before issuing a passport to a person, the Minister for Foreign Affairs must first of all be satisfied that the person in question is an Irish citizen.

In our emails, we just kept highlighting the same sentence. *If either of your parents was an Irish citizen, you are automatically an Irish citizen, wherever you are born.* If your father is an Irish citizen but died before you were born, you are also an Irish citizen. It did not matter whether your parents were married or not. If you were born outside Ireland to an Irish citizen who was born outside of Ireland, or any other grandparents born in Ireland, you are also entitled to become an Irish citizen as well. If you live outside Ireland, your birth must be registered through the local Irish embassy or consular office. You are entitled to register your Irish citizenship beginning the date of registration and not the date of your birth. It could not have been any clearer, as I interpreted it. By those declarations, Ava definitely was entitled to Irish citizenship and to avail of the same rights afforded to all Irish citizens.

One positive aspect of the adoption course was that we had to familiarise ourselves with some Irish legislation relating to citizenship. So the Irish Nationality and Citizenship Act, 2008 was foremost in my mind when we looked into getting a passport for Ava. Another piece of legislation we were familiar with was the Guardianship of Infants Act, 1964.

Section 3 of the 1964 Act was relevant to our situation because it put the welfare of the infant as the first and paramount consideration in any proceedings before the courts. We knew it would be in Ava's best interests if she were allowed to travel home to Ireland with us, her parents, rather than abandoning her to an uncertain fate in India. Section 5(3) also dealt with the jurisdiction of the case. The jurisdiction was in addition to any other jurisdiction, for example European or Indian, to appoint or remove guardians or as to the wardship of infants or the care of infants' estates. All legal dealings relating to children would take place in the Irish High Court or Circuit Court. It was plain to see that guardianship has many rights, including the right to apply for a passport for the child. Section 10 (2)(a) set out the role of the guardian, stating that he is entitled to the custody of the infant and entitled to take proceedings for the restoration of his custody of the infant against any person who wrongfully takes away or detains the infant. He is also entitled to the recovery, for the benefit of the infant, of damages for any injury or trespass against the person of the infant. I could see that if Ava was denied a passport and forced to stay in India, I would be entitled to take proceedings to get custody of her. However, being forced to abandon Ava in India could also leave us open to another charge. In Section 246 of the Children Act, 2001, it was an offence for any person who has custody, charge or care of a child to wilfully assault, ill-treat, neglect, abandon or expose the child, or cause or procure or allow the child to be assaulted, ill-treated, neglected, abandoned or exposed, in a manner likely to cause unnecessary suffering or injury to the child's health or seriously to affect her well-being. In this case, Caroline, if forced to leave Ava in an orphanage, would be in violation of this Act, through no fault of her own. It was just an impossible situation to comprehend.

There was also the question of human rights at stake. The more I read and thought about it the more I realised our human rights were being infringed. It was crystal clear that the Department of Foreign Affairs, through the Passport Office, was violating the UN Convention on the Rights of the Child and also the European Convention on Human Rights, both of which had been ratified by the Government. By refusing to issue travel documents for Ava, the Government was going against its own laws, namely the European Convention on Human Rights Act, 2003. The Convention also superseded all other legislation to ensure the child's welfare is protected. Several articles were applicable to our case. Article 8 protected the right to respect for private and family life. Article 12 protected the right to marry and have a family. Certainly, Caroline and I, as a married couple, were entitled to have a family. Perhaps the method of birth was unorthodox, but we were a family nevertheless.

You could also argue that Ava, born through surrogacy in India, was being discriminated against by reason of her birth, if not her place of birth. Article 14 prohibited discrimination and stated that the rights and freedoms set forth in the Convention should be secured without discrimination on any ground. This included sex, race, colour, language, religion, political or other opinion, national or social origin, association with a national minority, property, *birth* or other status. Those who availed of surrogacy, as I saw it, were being discriminated against in this country. In Article 17, the Act prohibited the abuse of rights. This clearly was where the Government was at fault too. It expressly stated that no one, including any State, group or person, could engage in any activity aimed at destroying or limiting the rights and freedoms guaranteed in the Convention. And, finally, Article 53 safeguarded existing human rights, so that nothing in the Convention should be construed as limiting or detracting from any of the human rights and fundamental free-doms that were agreed under international agreements.

In essence, all I did was read what was in the legislation. There was nothing tricky or complicated about it. It was right there, in black and white, for all to see. But what no law took account of was the sheer stress and mental anguish of the entire situation: the fear of the unknown, the terror of losing Ava, and Caroline forced to struggle on in India on her own.

***

Only for our legal team, I hate to think what the outcome might have been. Deborah Kearney was just brilliant and couldn't have provided better direction. As an associate solicitor at Leman Solicitors, she had built up considerable experience in family law over the years. Hailing from County Kerry, she was naturally astute and particularly good at anticipating obstacles. We were lucky to have made contact with her so many months in advance and thus could prepare for any eventualities. Despite genuinely hoping to obtain the passport first time round, it was just as well we had laid the groundwork with Deborah. And I suppose the advance warning that the Irish Embassy in New Delhi or the consul in Mumbai were not issuing emergency travel documents put us on high alert. The situation was bleak when Ava's passport application was dismissed, but it would have been a lot worse if we had to start from scratch at that point.

Despite few Irish barristers in Ireland having experience of surrogacy, we did get in touch with several during Nita's pregnancy when we were looking into the matter. Contact was mainly made through family connections or friends, and the barristers appeared to have a genuine interest, possibly because they knew the demand for surrogacy was skyrocketing around the world. It was general legal advice, given pro bono to us, over the phone. One barrister told us about our legal rights; another had a lot of dealings with India, especially regarding visas and setting up new businesses and enterprises. Indeed, there were also barristers in India that were prepared to offer us advice, though I got the distinct impression they were trying to exploit us. Some provided services at extremely cheap rates so you had no way of assessing if they were any good or not. As it turned out, we didn't need their assistance in the end. Our case was helped no end by Nuala Evelyn Jackson, barrister-at-law, who was retained by Leman Solicitors. One of Nuala's areas of expertise was children and family law and we could not have come across a better barrister than her. Indeed Deborah had consulted with Nuala before I ever went into the Passport Office, asking about our rights. Everybody was prepped, ready to go.

***

While Deborah and Nuala were busy advancing our case, I was busy launching my own campaign. The setback at the Passport Office forced me to contact politicians and various bodies who I thought had a vested interest in the matter. I sprang into action and sent emails off to anyone I thought relevant, various ministers and Government departments, quoting the appropriate pieces of legislation. My central argument was that my daughter had an automatic right to Irish citizenship by birth through descent. That week, I wrote to the Tánaiste and Minister for Foreign Affairs, Eamon Gilmore, the Minister for Children, Frances Fitzgerald, the Minister for Justice, Alan Shatter, seeking assistance in our plight and asking them to respond in person. I explained how Caroline was stranded in India with our newborn baby as the Irish passport authorities were refusing to issue any travel documents for the baby to return home. We were the parents of the baby and had conformed to all the legal requirements set out by the Indian authorities. In fact, I explained that commercial surrogacy was a legal practice in India, recognised by their Supreme Court in 2002, and the so-called commissioning parents were the legal guardians of the child. In addition, as her biological father, I was also her legal father.

Even the security situation in the region was highlighted to show how precarious our position was. By now the American and Australian embassies were issuing warnings to all their citizens to be vigilant regarding their personal security and to avoid crowds and areas of large gatherings. The threat of anti-western violence was escalating at a scary pace. Even the local media in Anand were also reporting terror threat possibilities. All I could do was just beg Caroline to confine herself and Ava to their hotel room until I arrived over. There was also the worry that Caroline's visa would expire and she would be forced to leave the country without Ava, if the matter was not satisfactorily resolved. On May 13th, I again wrote to the Tánaiste, outlining our critical situation and informing him of the less than adequate cooperation and assistance from the Department of Foreign Affairs. The department had refused to issue travel documents for my newborn daughter, I pleaded, and I requested an urgent meeting with him.

In my letters I outlined the great deal of stress that Caroline was under, while stranded in a foreign country and uncertain of what the future held for our family. I pleaded how imperative it was that both she and Ava return to Ireland, for the sake of their health and well-being. Any additional stress caused to Caroline could be detrimental to her health, given her previous health issues, and especially the trauma of being deported and separated from the baby, should that happen. I knew the heat and climate were playing havoc with her lymphoedema condition as well. She had never experienced it quite so badly before and I prayed it would not get any worse. Another area of concern was the media attention that Caroline was getting in India. Because she was stranded in Anand with no passport for Ava, the two of them became a big news story. They were dubbed the 'Woman and Child Not Allowed Home'. Because Dr Patel's clinic had delivered sensational headlines in the past – the first clinic in India to deliver a surrogate baby and the dilemmas surrounding the divorced Japanese couple and the stranded German couple – reporters were always nosing around looking for the next scoop. International and domestic news crews were becoming as common as the cows in downtown Anand.

It was no fun for Caroline being confined to her hotel room, even if it was for her own safety, but the media pressure had rendered her almost a prisoner. All this publicity was drawing attention to Caroline and I could see she was becoming a vulnerable target. The media attention was a further complication given the security situation in the country. Although Caroline was more likely to be fleeing the local media rather than some al-Qaeda terrorist, neither prospect made me happy. The media had already badgered her for an interview on a number of occasions, in particular at the clinic.

In addition to the first batch of emails, I also wrote to TDs and MEPs and key personnel in various organisations in relation to our legal rights being infringed: namely, the Irish Human Rights Commission, Office of the President and the Council of Europe, the European Commission, UNICEF, the Department of the Taoiseach, the Ombudsman for Children, the Labour Party, and Fianna Fáil's Micheál Martin as leader of the Opposition.

It was with high hopes that I put together all those letters. Foremost in my mind was that someone would have some shred of human decency or respond at a humanitarian level. After all, we were citizens of the State as were our parents and grandparents and the generations before them. It was not as if we were non-nationals involved in some scam or other to get a passport and defraud the State of social welfare payments, as some would imagine. We came from hard-working families who paid our taxes like everyone else. Whatever about anyone actually doing something about our situation, I was shocked that I barely received acknowledgments of my emails and letters. Despite my pleas for the individuals to respond in person, they never did. Admittedly, there were verbal communications from Micheál Martin's office through a third party, to say that he was looking at it closely, had been in contact with the Department of Foreign Affairs to push it along, and the matter had been elevated to highest priority.

To be honest, my letters felt like a waste of time. That said, the exception was the Ombudsman for Children, Emily Logan. In her reply, she said dealing with the passport situation was not really within her remit, but if the matter was not successfully resolved, her office would pursue it further on our behalf. In the main, my pleas to official Ireland fell on deaf ears. They were too busy opening schools or envelopes or meeting the Queen or President Obama or God knows what!

The experience of petitioning public officials was a real eye-opener for me. It made me realise that the Irish State appeared to have more compassion and consideration for non-EU individuals than an infant born to an Irish citizen. I felt very much aggrieved that the same week that saw the passport application for my daughter dismissed, the Minister of State for Equality Kathleen Lynch announced with great fanfare that Ireland would be one of the first countries to accept Libyan refugees. The previous week, Minister for Justice Alan Shatter had announced a new visa waiver scheme where visitors with a valid permit for the UK would not need a separate visa for Ireland. Interestingly, this would allow Indian nationals to freely enter Ireland. Not for a minute would I begrudge Libyan refugees coming to Ireland, given the turmoil and civil war in their country, but it was ironic that Ireland at the same time could not even look after its most vulnerable citizens abroad.

Chapter 17

Living in limbo

The day Niall rang with news that the passport application had been dismissed left me reeling. It was like being dealt a body blow. My world seemed to be crumbling just when I thought we had finally put the past behind us. At first I thought he was winding me up, like he sometimes would, but the sheer fact that they had returned our application alarmed me. As usual, I knew Niall was putting a positive complexion on things by saying the Passport Office just needed additional information.

Despite our initial fears, I genuinely believed that because we had gone to such great lengths to make sure all the documents were supplied and even notarised, we would be issued with the passport. That's when it struck me. Would it all end in the High Court? Oh my God, what was going to become of Ava? Would I be forced to leave her behind? The advice of one Irish solicitor, whose offices we had sat in the previous year, reverberated in my head. *Research orphanages in India and when you find a suitable one relinquish all legal rights to the baby and leave her there.* The terror of that scenario almost paralysed me. It gave me many a restless night, tossing and turning in bed. But I knew too I would never be able to abandon her, no matter what. All our hard work had been in vain and the next part was going to be very difficult, if not impossible.

In desperation, I rang the Irish consulate in New Delhi, informing them of our predicament.

'What are you going to do now?' I asked. 'I'm stuck here. What's going to happen?'

'There's nothing we can really do from our end,' the official explained, knowing he was powerless to act until clarification and instructions had been received from the Passport Office back in Dublin.

'Are you okay where you are?' he then added sympathetically.

'No, I'm not alright here, and especially now that terrorist, Osama bin Laden, has been killed,' I retorted. 'What are you going to do about an Irish citizen stuck here in India?'

However, my pleas went unheeded; they just didn't seem to make much difference. And so when everything went wrong that Monday morning, I cried and cried. Sharmila and her mother could only look on in pity and comfort me as best they could. I was inconsolable.

'I just cannot believe it,' I said, still dumbfounded.

'Look, you've come this far, don't give up now,' Sharmila urged.

Offering me some coffee-flavoured Amul milk, holding my hand and hugging me, they did everything they could to help. Payal and Meenakshi too witnessed my tears as I told them the news.

'What am I going to do?' I wailed, wringing my hands in despair.

I was grateful for their emotional support, feeling lost and alone and wishing that Niall were with me. Uday too urged me to keep positive, trusting that everything would work out in the end. I could scarcely believe that I was left in limbo while everyone else was getting on with their lives. All I could do was watch enviously as other couples in the hotel got their paperwork sorted, some at a rapid rate. One American couple descended on Anand and occupied the hotel room next door to me. But within three days they had left with their newborn baby, the paperwork all completed and legitimate. Other couples I was friendly with spent a few weeks in Anand, dealing with their paperwork, but knew exactly their date of departure as no problems or hitches were anticipated. That I found really hard. For their part, the people could not understand the mentality of our culture.

'What kind of country do you come from that would do this to its citizens?' Sharmila's mother asked in amazement.

All I could do was shrug my shoulders, too embarrassed to say anything. There was one thing I did know for certain however, if I had stayed in the Madhubhan Hotel on my own, I probably would have lost my mind from the sheer isolation. After that day, everyone knew me as the girl without the passport or the mother and child not allowed home. Even the hotel staff would ask where is your husband, over and over again. Back home, my family and friends were worried about me too. Several family members, such as my mother, who like me was terrified of flying, and Niall's sister Alison, had hoped to join me in India but as soon as the legal battle began, they knew they had to stay put in Dublin and be of whatever assistance to Niall. Getting the passport was the total priority. They all kept in regular contact, however, trying to cheer me up and telling me everything was working out. I felt as if nothing was happening with our case, though they assured me the solicitor and barrister were busy preparing the court applications.

'Look, Caroline, don't worry,' Niall said, in an effort to calm me down. 'We'll know more in a few days.'

It was only after I returned to Ireland that I learnt the full nature of the court dealings. Anxious about my health and isolation, my father and Niall deliberately did not mention any setbacks for fear it would upset me more. Looking back, I'm rather glad they did.

One of the biggest nightmares became the media attention, especially when the passport application was dismissed. No longer my cheerful chatty self but seriously crestfallen, I grew more and more reluctant to talk to anyone. A check-up visit for Ava at Dr Anita's hospital left me agitated when a local TV network appeared in the waiting room and wanted to film her. Finally, Vimla had to get stroppy with them before they backed off. On another occasion at Dr Patel's clinic, I had Ava placed in the baby carry nest but her head was covered by an attachable mosquito net. You couldn't see her but it was obvious the carrier contained a baby. A Japanese photographer went to remove the netting but Vimla stopped her in mid-action and bolted with Ava. This came not long after being ambushed by another news crew. Earlier I had gone into Hitesh's office along with Vimla and Ava to get various papers signed and organise for the medical files to be couriered to Ireland. My mood was totally different from before. An American news crew was upstairs in the building as we went in search of Nita, but she had gone at that stage. While in the surrogate room, I chatted to Tina and the other surrogates to see how they were getting on and if they needed cold drinks or anything else. In fact, Tina was still pregnant with twins and feeling unwell that day. Nearing the end of her pregnancy, she was sweating profusely and her back was very sore. Before long the American crew entered the room in surgical gear with cameras to interview the surrogates or anyone else deemed interesting enough to them.

It was not a sight I welcomed. I just wasn't in the humour to talk about my situation. Immediately, the crew grew excited and angled the cameras at us. I could feel the anger and frustration rising within me.

'Get that camera out of my face now,' I demanded.

I suppose I was really rude to them but they continued filming neverthe-less. As they panned the camera around the room, the running commentary was plain to hear.

'And now we have this person from . . . '

A microphone was pushed in front of my face.

'Where are you from?' they asked.

'Hold on a minute,' I replied. 'I have not said I want to be filmed here.'

'Can we see the baby?' they enquired, pushing things as far as they could.

One of their crew, a young woman, started to photograph Ava on the bed, where Vimla had placed her. I was livid.

'Hold on!' I yelled. 'I told you I didn't want my baby photographed.'

'I'm just clicking the general room,' the photographer responded.

'Don't!' ordered Vimla before turning to me, 'I will go with the baby outside.'

At that Vimla hurried from the room with Ava. There was just no backing off with them and they persisted in filming the surrogates.

'Have the surrogates here agreed to be filmed?' I asked, getting really snotty with the crew.

'Yeah, of course.'

I knew that Dr Patel allowed film crews into the clinic at quiet times for public relations purposes, keen to present the acceptable side of surrogacy. But I suppose I was just furious and stressed with them that day.

'So what's your situation?' a journalist asked me.

'Look, I can't talk to anybody at the moment,' I explained. 'I'm having trouble with a passport.'

'Oh, we heard someone is having problems with a passport,' he replied.

Yet that snippet of information only whetted their appetite even more.

'This will be a great story. Can we talk to you?'

'No,' I replied, adamant that I did not want to talk.

I could feel tears pricking my eyes and I started to get upset. Not that that was any real deterrent for them but just more human emotion to be filmed. By now I was really worn out.

'Just let me be.'

All I could think of was the previous phone conversation with my dad. *Be very careful who you talk to. You can't have a hiccough at this stage.* Fearing repercussions back in Ireland, he urged me to shut down any Facebook or Twitter accounts or whatever I had. He was terrified media coverage or social networking might threaten our passport application. And he was right. My brother Philip had even set up a Facebook page, GET AVA HOME, and there were hundreds and hundreds of people on it. *My sister is stranded in India with a baby . . .* Many of the comments by Irish citizens revealed their shame of being Irish. My friends wanted to know what they should do to help. *Let's march on the Dáil, let's start campaigning.* It was incredible stuff.

But back to the media in India. Try as I did to avoid them, restricting myself and Ava to the confines of the hotel, there was no getting away from them. Later that day a CNN India crew turned up at the hotel. To be honest,

CNN were only interested in my case because they saw me as the white girl with the white child, abandoned by her own state, a supposedly democratic European country. Even Japanese television wanted to get involved in the story – I presume after the Manji case they still took a keen interest in surrogacy.

At the time my friend Meenakshi was trying to comfort me in my hotel room, as I dabbed tears from my eyes with a paper tissue. All this passport business was getting under my skin. The more I talked about it, the more I got upset. *Any news? Any news?* If I heard anyone else asking me that, I would explode.

Suddenly there was a knock on the door. Meenakshi opened it, only to find the CNN crew outside filming.

'We want to speak to Caroline.'

From the room, I said no very firmly and emphatically, but still they persisted.

'You don't have any respect,' chided Meenakshi. 'She has told you that she doesn't want to speak to anybody. Please respect this girl's decision. She does not wish to speak to anyone. She has just told you.'

'But can we just see her for one minute?'

'No.'

'Can we take a picture of the baby? Can we just see the baby? Can we see her for one moment?'

'Please, no,' insisted Meenakshi.

'We have a legal person who may be able to help you,' they replied, offering a carrot, an inducement, for me to talk. But it was the last thing I wanted to be involved in and said no.

'No,' repeated Meenakshi and quickly closed the door.

The ordeal was over and I was so grateful to Meenakshi for handling them. She was a real trooper. But my gratitude to her stood in sharp contrast to the anger I felt towards the hotel staff for permitting the crew to come to my room in the first place. Up to this point I had felt reasonably secure at the hotel but not anymore. Making my way to reception, I confronted the guy at the front desk.

'How did they know what room I was in?' I demanded. 'I can't have this. I'm going to have to move hotel if this carries on.'

He apologised profusely and assured me that no more film crews would find their way to my door.

'I'm under enough pressure as it is. I just can't have people at the bloody door now, waiting to take pictures.'

It was the fear of them taking pictures of Ava that really freaked me out as well. Flashing her face all over the world. Being known as the baby stuck in India. That fear in turn spawned another fear. The fear of opening my bedroom door. I grew afraid that photographers and film crews were lurking in the shadows ready to pounce once my door was opened. Even the slightest sound outside the room, guests or staff walking by in the corridor, made me suspicious and I imagined all sorts of noises. A knock on an adjacent door or others nearby was as loud as hearing a knock on my own door. Luckily, the media pulled back and never returned to the hotel but I still had to run the gauntlet of media attention at Dr Patel's clinic. It was an intense two weeks.

Meanwhile I wondered what was going on back in Dublin. By a bizarre coincidence, Ireland featured prominently on television for hosting the first state visit of Queen Elizabeth II. Every channel in India was broadcasting the visit and royal fever was at an all-time high, especially after the wedding of Prince William and Kate Middleton only two weeks previously. History was in the making, but I wished more than anything it was for Ava. Livid friends would email me about all the pomp and ceremony going on in Dublin, yet Irish citizens stranded abroad in India seemed to count for little.

Chapter 18

Issuing the passport

In the third week of May, there was much excitement in the capital at the visit of Queen Elizabeth, the first British monarch to set foot in Ireland in one hundred years. Ireland may have been all agog with the visit but the only thing claiming our attention that week was the action down at the family law courts. It was the most crucial period of our lives. At the time I had a hectic work schedule in Blackrock and spent the week travelling in and out of the city's legal quarter. However, road closures as well as traffic and parking restrictions meant it was difficult getting around.

Our complete focus was on getting Ava into the country. In that, we were faced with a tough challenge. How could our legal team overcome the Passport Office's resistance to issuing a passport to Ava? Was there any measure overlooked or unknown to us? Some alternative we had not considered before? Some legal loophole? It soon became clear that we would have to approach the courts. There was much to think through, to scrutinise from so many angles, all involving court applications. Everything hinged on establishing a legal connection between Ava and me, her biological father. Could I get a declaration of parentage? Could I get a guardianship and custody order in my favour? And then there was the question of the surrogate mother's rights; since she was most likely considered the legal mother in Irish law, could I get an order dispensing with the requirement that she give consent for the issuing of Ava's passport? Whatever was decided, I trusted Nuala and Deborah completely and had full confidence in them. We knew there was no magic solution and nothing was guaranteed but at least we had a plan of action.

We set about establishing that we were Ava's parents and gathering as much documentation as possible to support it right away. This included Ava's medical file being sent over from India. Granted the Passport Office did not directly request her medical files as such, but with so many medical questions being asked, Dr Patel's clinic decided to break with hospital protocol and release the file. It contained details of Ava's conception, the laboratory tests, surrogacy, and so forth. Despite her exasperation, Dr Patel had agreed to hand it over.

'I can't believe this country you live in,' she exclaimed. 'Give them the file.'

At one point, a friend advised me to get a DNA test to prove paternity. When I enquired at one state-recognised clinic in Dublin, offering paternity services, I was told the cost was €800 for a next-day turnaround. After supplying them with all the information about Ava and myself, everything looked good. That was before they told me I needed the mother's consent. This was going to be problematic since Caroline was not recognised as the legal mother. We were certainly caught in a bind here.

'The State does not recognise that Ava has a mother at this stage, only that she has a father,' I explained.

'I can't do anything,' the guy replied, 'she has to have a mother.'

Despite my pleas that she did have a mother, but I would have to prove it in court, there was no budging him.

'I can't do that. You'll have to get a court order.'

God, I wondered, how many more hurdles could we possibly endure? In any event, we did not need Ava's DNA profile as it was possible to prove paternity through the comprehensive medical records which had been kept from the outset. It would have proved difficult to obtain it in any case because that specialised service was not available at Dr Patel's clinic. Anyhow, as I saw it, no parent who applies for a passport for their child has to supply DNA evidence. So why should we be any different? Boy was I glad that Nuala was on our side. She was a thoroughly nice woman yet tough too from years of dealing with the courts system.

While Nuala proceeded with the case, the rest of us lived on adrenaline. Each morning I would get up, feed the dogs and go to work, trying to treat it like any other day. Sometimes the case seemed to grind to a standstill like the traffic in Dublin. In fact, the traffic became more chaotic as the Queen's visit continued; at one point it had taken me four hours to travel what would normally have been a five-minute journey. Anywhere near the legal quarter was guaranteed to have tailbacks galore. With a packed itinerary, the Queen and Prince Philip attended various functions across the city, whether at the Garden of Remembrance, the Guinness Storehouse, Government Buildings, Croke Park or Dublin Castle, and all to rapturous welcomes. It felt like heads of state were making historic visits to Ireland every week. Another one was in the offing; President Obama was flying in for a quick trip the following week. Security around the capital was tight for weeks and every manhole and sewer in the city had been searched and sealed and Gardaí were everywhere. If only Ava could make some exciting history of her own . . .

Our greatest fear was that the case would be referred to a higher court. If that happened, we were gone. There was just no way we could afford a quarter of a million euro to bring the case before the High Court; that in effect would be a test case.

Over in Anand, Caroline would ring home frantically each day for news.

'What's happening? What's happening?' she asked, nervously awaiting the outcome.

'There's no more I can tell you yet,' I would say after giving her the news in brief, reluctant to paint too bad a picture.

During the court proceedings I tried to remain as calm as possible, at least outwardly. Happily, we had a successful outcome, which meant we could get a passport for Ava. Needless to say, I was overjoyed at the result. Having relayed the news to Caroline and our families, they were all ecstatic. Before long even the neighbours were celebrating our good fortune in Caroline's parents' house in Palmerstown. By then my ears and jaws were sore from grinning.

'Niall, get out to Caroline quick,' her father urged, when we got the chance to talk.

I knew he wanted to be on the plane as much as I did. Although I knew too that I couldn't book a flight anywhere until I held Ava's brand new passport in my hands.

We were eventually told that we could collect the passport from the Department of Foreign Affairs on St Stephen's Green. It was a Saturday morning towards the end of May before the passport was finally issued to us at Iveagh House. That wine-coloured passport was worth its weight in gold. It was better than clutching a winning Lotto ticket any day. At last, I could book a flight for India. I spent the rest of the day trying to do just that, and of course arrange with Caroline's parents to look after the dogs. Those lassies had nearly been forgotten in all the chaos of the past few weeks. It would be interesting to see how they would take to the arrival of Ava.

Chapter 19

Reunion in India

In Anand I counted down the seconds and minutes before I would see Niall again. The events of the past few days had left me exhausted, living on a daily diet of adrenaline and anxiety. The day before the court case had been particularly memorable, and makes me laugh when I think of it now. On that Thursday, Vimla was preparing to go to an evening wedding. She had looked for the time off, hoping I would be okay on my own. I was only too happy to oblige, relishing some time to myself and feeling much more confident looking after Ava. By now Vimla was as much immersed in the tale of the passport as I was. She shared my tears and joys and even prayed to Hindu gods for us.

A new sari for the wedding was the order of the day for Vimla. With so many exquisite saris on sale in Anand and quite cheaply too, it was not hard to pick one up. Before long she returned with a vibrant orange and gold patterned sari with green trim that suited her perfectly. Laying her finery on the bed, she was excited and asked could she borrow my nail varnish. So we set up an impromptu nail bar and I painted her nails a muted pink that matched one of the flowers in her sari. The only thing she had overlooked to buy was a little bottle of perfumed talcum powder, popular as a drying agent in the Indian heat.

'We'll go to the shops and take Ava,' I suggested. 'I'll buy some for you.'

'It's very hot out,' she replied, a little concerned.

'We'll just go to the chemist down the road and come straight back.'

It was a distraction too from thinking about the passport all the time. So we all set off for the chemist in a tuk-tuk and picked up the powder. On the way back, I spotted a shop that sold Cadbury's chocolate and of course had to stop off there. In the little supermarket the chocolate was locked up in a special type of glass display case for expensive items like imported toiletries. It was definitely manna from heaven. Seeing as it was so hot, I also bought a box of Diet Coke, which the guy in the tuk-tuk helped me carry. Once re-installed at the hotel with the cokes cooling in the fridge, I turned to Vimla, waving the huge bar of Cadbury's chocolate.

'We're going to eat this!' I declared with a grin.

'No, no, no, I'm not eating that,' she laughed.

'We're going to eat this and drink some coke,' I told her, not taking no for an answer.

She squealed with laughter, shaking her head. The cans of coke were the skinny versions but with the heat I consumed two or three in quick succession to quench my thirst. Meanwhile Vimla politely took one square of chocolate.

'I can't believe you are going to eat all this,' she said, 'a whole bar of chocolate!'

Gosh, I thought, she must think us western women are complete gluttons. But I hadn't eaten real chocolate for weeks and with all the passport business I needed a quick fix. Not surprisingly, I soon felt sick from devouring so much chocolate and coke. We were as giddy as two schoolgirls, and more so by the time Vimla had to dress for the wedding. I watched in fascination as she showed me how to wrap the sari and where she could discreetly place her tissue in the side fold. Then she finished off the outfit with diamanté earrings and a sparkling necklace, and of course, tons of bangles and bracelets to match her sari.

'You look so beautiful,' I said, noticing how everything was perfectly co-ordinated.

'Take a picture of me and Ava and show everyone in your world how beautiful I am with her,' she said, flashing a mischievous smile at me.

We roared with laughter and I treasure those photographs to this day. As she was about to leave the room, she looked around for something to put her money in.

'Hold on,' I said, dashing over to the closet, from where I retrieved a small gold-coloured evening bag.

'This will go perfectly with your sari.'

'It's beautiful,' she said, admiring the material and colour.

'You keep it,' I said.

'But you left money in it,' she said, noticing some coins I had deposited there.

'In Ireland it is tradition if I give you a purse, to put something in it for good luck,' I explained.

'No, I couldn't take the money,' she replied, shaking her head.

'But you're going to the wedding,' I insisted. 'Enjoy it!'

It was a small sum, just a little something to enjoy the wedding that evening. Finally, she relented and Ava and I accompanied her downstairs in the lift. Passing the statue of Ganesh in his alcove, Vimla touched him, as she did every day.

'We'll pray for the passport,' she whispered.

And then she took the coins I had left in the bag and placed them as an offering before Ganesh.

'I'm leaving it here. It's for the gods for the passport.'

I smiled, overwhelmed by her thoughtfulness. I was the recipient of so many random acts of kindness and generosity from Vimla that it astounded me sometimes. With just Ava for company I spent a restless night and didn't get much sleep, owing to her three-hourly feeds as well. The next morning, Friday, I was tense as I waited for a suitable time to call Niall given the time difference. By midday it was early morning back in Dublin so I could ring and wish him good luck. It was now or never. We had had so many false dawns before that I was sick with anticipation.

As midday moved to afternoon, I sat in front of my mobile phone and laptop in the hotel room, phoning, texting and emailing Niall and his sister and my father, anyone who could give me updates. I had heard from Niall's sister and my mother that he had gone into court at that stage. By now Vimla had returned from the wedding and joined me in the waiting game. The sheer tension made me break down in tears at times and Vimla was nearly as bad as me.

'I can't take it,' she uttered at one stage.

Around that time, she was having some family issues and hence the reason for her tears.

'Today you cry and tomorrow I cry,' she said, throwing up her hands in despair.

We used to behave like that all the time; we were a right pair. Soon the news filtered out to the others in the hotel and those at Dr Patel's clinic. Everybody knew that Niall was in court dealing with the passport issue. That Friday was a significant one in many respects. It coincided with Payal's last day in Anand. Since our first meeting at Dr Patel's clinic the previous August we had come a long way and she was almost like a sister to me. That day she was frantically packing up and preparing to leave with her husband and newborn baby. I was pleased their surrogacy had all come to a happy conclusion, but desperate too, thinking how was I going to face it when she was gone. My greatest fear was that I would slide into a massive depression. She was leaving and I wasn't going anywhere fast! Not wishing to dampen her spirits, however, I insisted on hosting a little get-together with pizzas on Saturday in my room, as it was a little bigger. The surrogate mother and her husband and children were due to come along as well. I just hoped and prayed I would have the strength to host it, if things didn't go our way at the courts.

It was late afternoon when the long-awaited news finally arrived. I could hardly believe Niall at first, thinking there must be a 'but' or a 'maybe' at the end of his words, but no it was true.

'We got the passport!' I shrieked at Vimla.

Within seconds Vimla and I were hugging each other and crying tears of joy for a change. Running from the room, the first person to tell was Auntie, Sharmila's mum next door, who was overjoyed for us. After that Payal and

Meenakshi heard the news as literally did everybody in the hotel – the relief plainly etched on their faces, showing their solidarity. It was like doing a lap of honour at the Olympics after that. Next I darted over to Hitesh's office.

'Guess what? We got the passport!'

Hitesh was thrilled for us, practically ecstatic. It was as good as India winning the Cricket World Cup. By coincidence Dr Patel herself came into the office in search of something just in time to hear the news. Taking a seat, she turned to me and said.

'You just didn't give up, you were fighting and fighting. I knew it would work out.'

I wish I could have had her confidence back in the days when despair and anxiety seemed to stalk us at every turn.

'I'm exhausted,' I admitted, 'it's been such a long haul.'

'You are making history for Ireland,' she said, her big brown eyes widening eagerly. Whether it was history or not, it was definitely time for celebration. However, we heard later that evening that it would be Saturday before the Passport Office would issue the passport to Niall. This would delay his arrival in Anand but it was only a minor setback. Though disappointed, at least we had won a victory. The following day, Saturday, was a wonderful day because we could all celebrate our prospective homecomings in style at the Rama Hotel. We ordered in the pizzas and had a ball.

'I'm going too!' I rejoiced. 'I don't know when but I'm going!'

Later that day, I heard that the Department of Foreign Affairs had finally issued Niall the passport. With all the shenanigans it was Wednesday before Niall eventually set foot in Anand. It was in the early evening just before sunset and exactly a month after Ava's birth.

***

Flying alone all those thousands of miles to India gave me plenty of time to absorb the news and reflect on it. While other passengers dozed comfortably on the plane, I could not. My mind was in a flux. To be honest, I never thought I would have a family. Now I could put all the turmoil behind me and concentrate on seeing Caroline and Ava. The relief to hold Ava's wine-coloured passport in my hand was still beyond description. Within hours I would get to see her for real. She really was our miracle baby. Though surrogacy was not the usual means of pregnancy in our society, you could not deny a child had been created, a beautiful baby girl, and we were now a family.

It still irked me to think about the very antiquated viewpoints that some Irish organisations and adoption agencies and even individuals held of surrogacy, seeing it as human trafficking. It was regarded as an underground, almost criminal activity. It was seen as something to be condemned because it was associated with women selling or renting their bodies. Wombs as commodities, you could say. However, if surrogacy were conducted properly by medical professionals, there was no difference between it and the likes of organ transplants, whether livers, hearts, kidneys or stem cells. These organs were all commodities too, whether the donor was living or deceased. On the flight, I was reminded of my own uncle who had received a kidney transplant in the recent past, donated by a nephew on his in-laws' side. Transplants could save lives, or from years of dialysis in my uncle's case. However, surely those pious organisations should have moral objections to transplants as well. It's just swapping body parts, you could say, which could be considerd equally as bad, if not worse. What religion would actually allow that? I had heard some groups do have certain objections to organ donation and transplants, like the Amish, Roma Gypsies and Shinto, or else leave it as a matter of individual conscience, like Jehovah's Witnesses. It's not stated in the Bible that you can or cannot do it. In fact, the official Catholic view is that organ and tissue donation is an act of charity and love. I would argue the same for surrogacy.

During my research on the internet I found some negative comments in relation to surrogacy, a lot springing from religious beliefs. In today's society, I don't agree that religion should have any bearing on surrogacy, despite surrogacy dating back to biblical times. If people believe that surrogacy is morally wrong, would they have the same view on IVF or perhaps cosmetic surgery? Is it okay to alter the body you were born with? What about the child abuse

controversy that came to light in recent years within the Catholic Church –
do the people that view surrogacy as immoral believe those priests were
immoral and do they still attend weekly mass? Ask a vegan is it immoral
to drink a glass of cow's milk and eat a beef burger? Do you think
that's immoral?

One thing for sure, many people in Ireland know nothing about surrogacy
or rather the exact meaning of the term. Whenever I would tell someone
about Ava being born through surrogacy, the reaction was predictable.

'That's great!'

And then in the next breath.

'What is that exactly?'

I'm sure most of them thought I had sex with the surrogate mother, or
were too afraid to ask! Other people would look at me in horror. Their
impression of surrogacy was not far off that depicted in the 2009 science-
fiction film *Surrogates*, starring Bruce Willis. I remember seeing the trailer at
the cinema and it stuck in my head for a long time afterwards. In the futuristic
world of the film, all the humans lived in the isolated comfort of their own
homes, while their surrogate robots interacted in society on their behalf.
Maybe it's a lack of education that makes people think surrogacy is all very
alien and robotic. If people want to take a moral stance when it comes to
children, there are plenty of other more pressing issues than surrogacy, neglect
and child abuse by their natural parents for starters.

However, whenever I explained the process people would appear to
understand it and act positively towards it. I honestly believe the negativity
comes from lack of knowledge; people are not fully aware of what's involved.

***

Being back in India felt good, all the more so because the passport dilemma
was finally resolved. I loved India, even with its heat and humidity. As the taxi
shot along the expressway towards Anand I took in the familiar sights,
bustling traffic and the dry arid countryside becoming more industrialised by
the second. This was my perception of India, not that I knew exactly what to

expect on my first visit, but seeing it for the second time, I was impressed. To me it was no longer a Third World country, although admittedly poverty was still a huge concern in places. India was a rapidly developing economy with massive wealth on a scale to rival Brazil, Russia and China. Yet most people back home would still probably see it as a backwater and Anand as literally the dog end of nowhere. I suppose that's how many developed nations like America saw Ireland decades ago.

However, the poverty in India was poles apart from that in the so-called western world. Even in Anand you could still go from one extreme to the other. As we approached the outskirts of Anand, my eyes red and gritty from lack of sleep, the fantastic infrastructure of the expressway contrasted sharply with the archaic railway system. Overcrowded carriages were the norm; people were crammed in the aisles like sardines, hanging out of windows and doors, perched atop the roof, sky riding to their heart's content. It was just crazy to witness.

Along the railway tracks scores of people, young and old, waited for trains to come by and stop. Bunches of kids rested and played there as if sitting on a kerb. There were no warnings to indicate the train was arriving, at least none that I heard, although they did hoot their siren for wayward cows. I presumed the people just saw the trains coming in the distance. Vegetable vendors and other vendors were also setting up shop along the tracks to hawk their wares. The railway station was one of the greatest reference points in Anand. Everybody took their bearings from it. There were no level crossings to speak of; you literally had a road where you stopped, looked left and right, closed your eyes and took your chances. The open country was so vast you could see for miles and miles around. Yes, it was good to be back.

***

As Wednesday dragged on, everyone at Dr Patel's clinic and at the hotel, from manager to receptionist, knew that Niall was coming. I was jubilant and it was impossible to hide it. By now Payal had left, but with Niall's arrival imminent, I was buoyed up no end.

'He's a big guy,' I had informed the guy in reception, 'you won't miss him!'

It was late in the evening, after sunset, by the time Niall stepped inside the hotel. Meanwhile in my room, I was waiting, not so very patiently, attiring Ava in a pretty little pink dress with white love hearts, bought locally, and with little white bootees to make her look nice for her dad. Instantly, I recognised his footfalls on the corridor, the tiniest of sounds on the polished floor tiles reverberating throughout the building. I darted to the door and threw it open to greet him. Having spotted Ava lying on the bed, he swiftly dropped his travel bag and inched closer.

'Oh, give her here to me!'

Gosh, he was so overjoyed. I hadn't seen him like that in years. All he could do was cradle Ava in his arms and stare at her, completely captivated.

'Aaahhhh, look at her,' he exclaimed. 'She's like a doll.'

I smiled, thinking it was the start of a classic father-daughter relationship. It was only then that I spotted the size of his travel bag – barely big enough to hold a toothbrush and pyjamas.

'Niall, where's your clothes?'

In all the commotion with the passport, he had forgotten to pack half his clothes. One t-shirt summed up his entire clean wardrobe for the next day. However, the one thing he hadn't forgotten was a toy for Ava. A big black and white Dalmatian pup was duly presented to his little princess, but still he would not leave Ava go. Every hair on her head and pore on her skin was scrutinised like she was a priceless treasure. She truly was!

By now Vimla had returned home to her family and so Niall and I could enjoy the privacy of being a family together. The next day was a helter skelter of activity. Originally, I had hoped that we could stay on for several days after Niall arrived and he could finally meet all those people who had showed such marvellous hospitality and kindness to me. But the passport business had seriously delayed things so it was not financially possible to extend our time in Anand. Niall too had work commitments that couldn't be postponed. I felt bad for Niall because he would have loved to hang around and soak up the culture and climate even more. My friends were always saying that they never saw a couple who took to a country as much as Niall and I did. But for now, we would have to settle for a return trip sometime in the future.

Our return journey was booked for the early-morning Thursday flight out of Ahmedabad. At first it was intended that Niall would stay a second night with us at the Rama, but that would involve a 2AM rise to leave for the airport on time. At Uday's suggestion we decided to spend the night at a hotel near Ahmadabad airport instead, for the sake of the baby. That meant all the organising was concertinaed into a much shorter space of time. In the flurry of activity, I didn't know whether I was coming or going. Seeing that I could not book a flight for Ava online, it meant a trip to the local travel agent in Anand to show her passport in person. Without Uday's help that day I don't think we could have managed it. There was also one final legal document required before we could fly home. This was the exit visa for Ava. Now that we had her passport this was just a formality, although we had to put together a list of paperwork first for the superintendent of police at Uday's instruction. It included our tickets showing our departure date, our passports and visas, Ava's birth certificate and passport, two passport-sized photos of Ava, the surrogacy contract, and a letter from Dr Patel's clinic confirming the surrogacy and that everything had been concluded to the satisfaction of the clinic and surrogate mother.

Uday, being such a trooper, made sure we had all the documents in tow when he drove us to the local police station to catch a meeting with the superintendent of police. In comparison to Ireland, we got the exit visa in double-quick time. The superintendent of police, dressed in a pristine khaki uniform and Sam Browne belt with police insignia on his peak cap, looked quite officious at first as we all sat before him. He was a stocky guy, with a thick but tidy moustache, but thankfully didn't obstruct us in any way. More than likely he was quite accustomed to signing exit visas for surrogacy babies. At the back of a courtroom, he just looked over the paperwork, checking everything was in order, never once asking a question. The exit visa form was duly signed and stamped, and after paying roughly the equivalent of €100 we promptly left the building. At least that was one hurdle easily surmounted.

Wednesday was just a frantic series of phone calls, picking up documents, packing, shopping and endless goodbyes. Saying our farewells was particularly emotional for me. I was talking to this girl and that girl, rushing hither, thither and yon. In the chaos, there were lots of hugs and kisses from everybody: Dr Patel, Hitesh, Hansha and the other nurses, Meenakshi, Sharmila and Auntie and others staying at the Rama Hotel. Everybody wanted to meet Niall. He had been this mystery husband for so long that everyone was curious about him. *Where is the father? Where is the father?* Now at last I could say, yes he does exist, he wasn't just some figment of my imagination, some guy I conjured up to get a passport.

'Hang on! I can't believe I'm going now,' I found myself saying over and over again.

But the farewells being so rushed upset me. I needed a few days to take it all in, now that Niall was here, but it was not to be. There had been a great deal of stuff to sort out and get ready. It was like packing up a house. So much of the acquired stuff I couldn't bring home to Ireland. Things like extra baby clothes, sterilisers and bottles, a clotheshorse, special baby washing powders, rubber gloves, you name it. More than anything I wanted time to give it to people personally. I certainly wasn't going to throw out anything because that would have been unheard of and unthinkable. In the end, many of the baby clothes, bottles, sterilisers and a light car seat were given to one of the neonatal nurses who had given birth recently and whose circumstances were rather straitened at the time.

It was probably just as well that Niall had brought so few clothes because of all the stuff we had accumulated. Buying another suitcase was in order, which meant one final trip to the Big Bazaar. It was just like during our first trip to Anand. Kids were constantly following Niall around, especially in the supermarket, transfixed as ever. In his shorts, with his white freckled legs showing, he was such an oddity and source of great amusement. They would point at his legs, laughing and sniggering. I had got quite used to people staring at me, but the kids were mesmerised by Niall. Some of them thought he was an American footballer.

'You American?' they asked him.

Yes, people still thought we were Americans, although after the bin Laden affair, we were very quick to deny it. At the clinic, during our first visit, people had told us not to give money to the kids begging on the streets. We usually complied with this request, knowing if we didn't, we would have hordes of children following us like the Pied Piper of Hamelin. That Wednesday, a bright-eyed kid on a fruit stall, who wasn't begging, started to talk and joke with Niall about being a footballer. In a playful mood, Niall had given him a high five. The boy was so taken with having fun with Niall that as we left Niall instinctively put some money in his hand. The boy just couldn't believe his luck. I knew when I left Anand that I would miss all the street vendors and shop assistants who I had come to know. There was no end to their generosity; they were always willing to extend themselves to help a customer out. You just never knew what to expect – the streets were always full of colour and life. I remembered the day Vimla and I had spotted a gang of children hanging off the back of a truck all covered in pink powder laughing and shrieking. It was some festival or feast day. I suppose it was like us celebrating St Patrick's Day when everything is dyed green.

It was strange leaving the hotel in the afternoon, saying goodbye and tipping the hotel staff, especially the owner in reception for kindly photocopying so many documents for me in the previous month. And then before I knew it we were in Uday's car and bound for the hotel in Ahmedabad. I grew sad as the familiar sights fell away and we neared the expressway, the sense of leaving home growing stronger with each passing mile. Though Anand was gone from view I knew I would never forget the place, the scene of such bittersweet memories for me. Part of me felt there was unfinished business there, our farewells too rapid, but I suppose life intervened and you have to get on with things. We were going back to Dublin to start a new life with Ava; we were a family and soon she would get to meet her grandparents, uncles, aunts and cousins. And speaking of cousins, we needed to get presents for young Caelan and Ethan. That meant dragging poor Ava around in a taxi as we searched for suits for the young boys in Ahmedabad.

The return flights passed uneventfully and thankfully Ava was okay travelling. Luckily, she distracted me from my fear of flying and planes crashing and God knows what. At Heathrow airport on Friday afternoon we were met by Bina holding a big, beautiful pink blanket. She had earlier insisted, when we were booking our flights, that we stay with her and Philip in Hampshire before travelling on to Dublin.

'The boys will be devastated if you get on a plane and go to Ireland and not see them.'

For weeks the boys had been eating, drinking and sleeping news of the little baby that had been born in India. Now the thrill of finally seeing her was here and they could hardly wait. It had been Caelan's idea to buy the pink blanket, knowing how cold England and Ireland were in comparison to India. He insisted his mother bring it to the airport so Ava would be nice and warm. What a sweet boy!

Though exhausted, we were delighted to see a familiar face at the airport. Later back at the house, we were greeted by Bina's parents and brother Kartik, the paediatrician, who joined in the celebrations. Fortunately for us he examined Ava from head to toe and looked over her medical notes, checked what medications she had been on, which had been mainly vitamins, until he was satisfied that all was well. The weekend also gave us a chance to recover from serious jet lag. It was so bad I ended up walking into the bedroom wall in the middle of the night. Despite it, I still had to get up to feed a baby every three hours during the night. But I wasn't complaining! I would have that any day over living in limbo in India. By the time we left the family on Sunday, things were starting to come back to normal. I ached to return to Dublin so our parents could at last see our darling Ava.

Chapter 20

Returning to Ireland

Our longed-for arrival in Dublin airport was one I had dreamed about so many times before. The reality was far more thrilling and emotional than I could have imagined. My dad and Niall's mum came to greet us and more so to see their grandchild landing on Irish soil. But before they could lay eyes on her, I nipped into the baby-changing facilities and dressed her in clothes my mother had given to Niall to bring over – a soft pink dress along with delicate white tights – so she could look her best for the family, and then fed her. I felt so pleased and proud for them fussing over Ava, oohing and aahing.

'Isn't she gorgeous!'

'She's so small!'

'Look at the head of hair on her!'

I felt like I had been away for months on end, been through the wars but now Niall and I were returning as a family. Everything felt real and normal for the first time in a long while. In Niall's absence, my parents had moved into our house chiefly to mind the dogs. That was where my mother was now, preparing a homecoming party and readying the house for our arrival. I couldn't wait to see her, especially for three generations of women to be together. As the car pulled up outside the house, an hour or so later, I grew emotional at the small crowd that had gathered. My mother along with Niall's sister Alison and several of our neighbours cheered and waved as we arrived.

Everyone was just dying to see Ava. It was marvellous to see them all, despite our exhaustion. A big hug from my mother went a long way to undoing all the stress I had been through. She had gone to great lengths to mark the occasion. The conservatory was festooned with balloons and party decorations, and she had prepared cakes and sandwiches, while the house was immaculate. Aside from the jet lag, I couldn't have been happier.

As the days went on, I established a routine with Ava at home and threw myself into it. I relished every minute of it, especially settling her into her own cot in her own bedroom. Pretty soon, the room was filled with teddies, mobiles and squeaky toys to entertain and stimulate her. It was amazing how quickly our life changed when we came home, though. The dogs did not have as free rein in the house as before, though they adjusted pretty well to the strange new creature in their midst. All the while we grew more and more into family life. Ava's life stretched ahead of her and I even started to think of where she could go to playschool or school when the time arrived.

When the BBC World Service came to finish their documentary shortly after we came home, it felt strangely normal as they recorded the sound of me going about the business of the day, preparing feeds and sterilising bottles. It had all seemed so unreal the first time the crew had arrived at the house in early January, when Nita was pregnant. Now it was no longer something abstract; nothing now was as real as our darling Ava. When I looked at her and saw a perfectly healthy and gorgeous baby looking back at me, I thanked our lucky stars that she had come into our lives. I told the reporter that the whole journey had been worth every single bit of stress that we had to go through.

'We still can't believe that she's here after all this time. And we'll always, always be so grateful.'

Eventually hearing the programme, broadcast in July, gave rise to mixed emotions. It was very professionally made yet it annoyed me somewhat that it gave the impression that Nita had never seen Ava at all. That once Nita had delivered her that was the end. The truth was something entirely different. For all the misunderstandings about the breast milk and nannies, Nita had visited Ava and me several times at the Rama Hotel and we had parted on good terms. I stopped short of searching the internet to gauge the reaction to the broadcast, unlike Niall who was more curious. Some British commentators had adopted the high moral ground and condemned the practice of surrogacy from a religious point of view. Countless views of it were negative, ranging from the exploitation of vulnerable women to the damage done to the sanctity of marriage. But often their arguments were countered by those who had experienced the profound pain and loss of infertility and had little or no choice in the matter. It always seemed to be the same old arguments. Niall used to say the religious fanatics had absolutely no clue what they were talking about, when quoting various passages from the Bible. Ignorance was at the heart of their opinions, as indeed of many people we encountered ourselves.

Like Niall, I don't see surrogacy as being immoral provided all parties are doing it of their own free will and the welfare of the surrogate mother along with the unborn child is paramount. I don't believe that surrogacy is unethical. That said, to remove any opportunity for an individual or organisation to act unethically, it is important for both intended parents and surrogate mothers to avail of surrogacy through a reputable clinic. They should make sure that the clinic has provisions in place for the well-being of the surrogate mother, unborn child and the intended parents in all aspects of their health, including their mental health. So I feel strongly that counselling should be made available for all parties.

It was interesting to observe people's reactions to Ava and their preconceptions of surrogacy. In the main my friends and acquaintances were very positive about it, but occasionally you came across a remark that literally left you stunned. One day when Ava was several months old I was in a Marks and Spencer store in Dublin and got talking to the girl at the till, the day not being particularly busy. She was admiring Ava lying sound asleep in her buggy.

'Oh, I was a long time waiting for her,' I found myself saying.

'Really?'

At first I wasn't going to say anything but the girl was so pleasant and friendly that before I knew it the words had come out.

'I went to India and had her by surrogacy,' I admitted.

'Oh, like all the stars!'

Her words stung me. It was like saying that Ava had been born from a whim, a flippant decision; I was too posh to push or didn't want to be inconvenienced by nine months of pregnancy. It all felt so far from the truth.

'Actually no, not like all the stars,' I found myself retorting.

And so I walked away, wishing I had said nothing.

**

The weeks of living on my nerves and adrenaline and our quick departure from India came back to haunt me. All that physical and mental energy eventually took its toll. My body kind of went into shock. A few months after coming home, I found myself getting very down. At night I would wake up with severe sweats and get panic attacks for no particular reason. I just couldn't understand why I was upset; I kept saying to myself this was the happiest time of my life. By now Ava was three months old and everyone was saying it was postnatal depression. Yet I was not convinced.

'No, this is not me. I don't get down like this.'

It was just a horrible sickly feeling and I felt entirely in the dark. The euphoria I had felt just before Ava was born had alarmed one of the doctors at the practice where I worked. This was before I had ever set off for India.

'Caroline, you want to be very careful,' she had advised, knowing that I had been through years of waiting and trying for a child, 'because when it happens you will come down with a bang.'

And never a truer word was spoken in all my life. By God, I did come down with a bang. I went from talking about our predicament, morning, noon and night, for weeks on end to calm waters very rapidly when it was resolved. Living with the uncertainty, fear and distress had defined my days for so long. When it was all over, my body reacted. And so at my father's insistence, I went to my GP for help. There was nothing physically wrong;

it certainly was not postnatal depression, but a reaction to the emotional upheaval I had been through. As a result, I decided to air my thoughts to someone neutral, someone not involved in the whole process. As it turned out, the sessions proved extremely helpful. From her vast experience, the counsellor recognised the signs as the after-effects of a trauma.

'You have just been through a massive trauma.'

That was exactly it. In her estimation, I was the kind of person who thought they could get through any situation unscathed. But the whole experience had completely overwhelmed me. As I began to talk to her, it also emerged that something else was bothering me. It was then that I got upset, thinking I had left India too quickly. It was the crux of the matter. We were gone in a flash. In hindsight, I had needed about a week to get used to the idea. *Niall, are you sure you have the passport and this is not all a dream. Are we really going home?* I had wanted to go home but at the same time nearly didn't want to leave, as crazy as that sounds.

Today I still have this feeling that I have to go back. And one day I will. It's a promise to myself. It was the only way I could deal with the issue for the time being. The couples I had met in India and my friends were keenly aware of how I felt about my experience of surrogacy and time in Anand.

'You can't just go home and close the door and say that's it. I'll forget about it all now.'

Well, at least I could not. Granted, I did meet couples who just wanted to get the hell out of India once they picked up their babies, but that was never our case. I suppose that is why I kept in contact with everyone so much. I vowed to go back and all because I could not forget our experience. The memories of all those years of waiting for a child and Nita's pregnancy and the arrival of Ava, even the passport dilemma, could not be denied or dismissed. It was a choppy journey, admittedly, but luckily I weathered the storm.

One thing our experience has taught us is that there are many couples in Ireland looking for reliable and sound advice about surrogacy, yet it is not so easy to come by. There is no support group for surrogacy as such. Knowing only too well the strife people are in, Niall and I tried to pass on information in whatever way we could. Niall, more so than myself, has been eager, freely offering advice on Facebook and Rollercoaster.ie. In fact, we were no sooner back in the country when Niall posted a comment on Rollercoaster giving brief details of having received a passport for our baby. Within hours, he was bombarded with emails and right up to the present day we are constantly being contacted by couples through email and phone. By hearing our story, it gives so much hope to other couples, knowing there is a way through the minefield. Those couples, either interested in pursuing surrogacy or signed up for it, are desperate for information on surrogacy, solicitors, and wanting us to share our experiences. And the thing that always crops up is that we did not have to go the High Court to argue our case. Surrogacy has now become a hot topic in the media, especially seeing that many couples, originally thinking of adoption, might jump ship and go for surrogacy because of the cost and time element.

One source of support has come from the National Infertility Support and Information Group (NISIG). This is a voluntary organisation, established in Cork in 1996 by a group of people who experienced infertility and wanted to connect with others who understood their grief. They host meetings regularly, which we attended from time to time, especially after I got back on my feet. To his great surprise one evening, Niall met a couple that had been on the adoption course with us but were still childless. They couldn't believe that we now have a baby. In fact, couples in general were quite amazed when we told them our story, particularly how we managed to get a passport. Admittedly, other couples have not been so lucky. Right now, we know there are many parents living in limbo here in Ireland, without passports for their kids – babies that might have been born in India, Ukraine or Eastern European countries. No one knows for sure how many couples are affected. Hundreds say some, but I have no idea. I heard one solicitor say their firm had thirty such cases on their books. Anecdotally, I have heard of forty to fifty couples.

The absence of regulation of surrogacy is really a disservice to the people of Ireland. There is no legislative protection for children born through surrogacy, who in some cases might have up to five parents – as in the sperm and egg donors, the surrogate mother and two intended parents. The Department of Justice, in its guidelines published in February 2012, does not take account of all such scenarios. The guidelines centred on citizenship, parentage, guardianship and travel document issues in relation to children born as a result of surrogacy arrangements entered into outside the State. Basically, one of the intended parents has to be an Irish citizen and a donor for the State to recognise that the child is eligible for a passport. In practice, this often falls to the father.

Many couples share our views as do many lawyers and human rights activists. They point out how rigorous the procedures are for child adoption in contrast to the lack of regulation for assisted reproductive technologies. Ireland seems to be one of the only jurisdictions in the world that do not protect children's rights in these situations.

From what I can gather, no two Irish women have had the same experience of surrogacy in India. A lot depends on the legal advice they receive and the clinic they attend, whether in rural Anand or metropolitan Delhi. Many couples want to flee India as soon as their baby is born, unhappy with the sanitary conditions. I loved the place and enjoyed my experience, despite the mishaps that occurred. In fact, some people expressed complete surprise at my real affection for the country. In their experience, India was nothing but filth and poverty and they just wanted to get in and get out.

There is also great credit due to Dr Patel's clinic. Whether you agree with her practices or not, at least she does have certain ethical standards and is not a 'rogue clinic'. As she always says, 'we are lost when there are no laws'. That is true whether it's Ireland or India. The story of surrogacy is set to change in India, with the Artificial Reproductive Technology (Regulation) Bill working its way through parliament. It will tighten up the laws on surrogacy and remove unscrupulous practices where they exist. But at least India will still provide hope and opportunity to Irish couples. We, as just one couple, will be forever grateful that it brought our lovely Ava into being.